U N I O N

CHINA

Kunduz

H I N D U   K U S H

Salang
Pass

Panjshir
Valley

Barikot

Baghram

ghman

KABUL   *Kabul R.*

Jalalabad

handeh

Fatehabad

Landi
Kotal

Maidan
Shahr

Khogiani

Torkham

Safed Koh

Kolangar

*Tirah
Valley*

*Khyber
Pass*

Peshawar

Darra

Islamabad

Khost

Miram Shah

P A K I S T A N

N

0   50   100   150   200 Miles

0   100   200   300 Km

SOLDIERS *of* GOD

SOLDIERS
of GOD

With the Mujahidin

in Afghanistan

ROBERT D. KAPLAN

Houghton Mifflin Company
Boston 1990

For information about permission to reproduce selections from
this book, write to Permissions, Houghton Mifflin Company,
2 Park Street, Boston, Massachusetts 02108.

Library of Congress Cataloging-in-Publication Data

Kaplan, Robert D.
Soldiers of God : with the Mujahidin in Afghanistan / Robert D. Kaplan.
p.   cm.
Includes bibliographical references.
ISBN 0-395-52132-7
1. Afghanistan — History — Soviet occupation, 1979–1989 — Personal
narratives.   2. Kaplan, Robert D. — Journeys — Afghanistan.
3. Journalists — United States — Biography.   I. Title.
DS371.2.K366   1990   89-13101
958.104′5 — dc20   CIP

Printed in the United States of America

S 10 9 8 7 6 5 4 3 2 1

Endpaper map by Jacques Chazaud

For my mother
and
for my late father,
Philip A. Kaplan

I have seen much war in my lifetime and I hate it profoundly. But there are worse things than war; and all of them come with defeat.

—Ernest Hemingway, *Men at War*

Contents

PROLOGUE   *Walking Through a Minefield*   1

ONE   *Frontier Town*   23

TWO   *A World of Men*   49

THREE   *Going up Khyber*   79

FOUR   *Noble Savages*   106

FIVE   *The Growth of a Commander*   144

SIX   *Haji Baba and the Gucci Muj*   180

EPILOGUE   *Something I Only Imagined*   226

Acknowledgments   231

The Seven-Party Mujahidin Alliance   233

Chronology   235

Bibliography   238

Index   241

SOLDIERS *of* GOD

———➤

Walking Through a Minefield

AMPUTATIONS were the most common form of surgery in Afghanistan in the 1980s. A West German doctor, Frank Paulin, traveled around Nangarhar province in April 1985, cutting off the limbs of mine victims with a survival knife. "Sometimes I'd use a saw, basically anything I could get my hands on," he recollected. The only anesthetic that Paulin had available for his patients was ordinary barbiturates. Some of the patients died, but the ones who survived wouldn't have had a chance without him. Radio Moscow accused Paulin by name of being a "CIA spy." While being hunted by Soviet troops, he contracted cholera and had to be carried on the back of a mule over a fourteen-thousand-foot mountain pass to safety in Pakistan. Paulin had only one fear: that he too would step on a mine.

An Afghan who stepped on a mine frequently died of shock and loss of blood a few feet from the explosion. More often, he was carried by a relative or friend to a primitive medical outpost run by someone like Paulin. If the victim was really lucky, he made it to a Red Cross hospital in Quetta or Peshawar over the border in Pakistan — antiseptic sanctuaries of Western medicine where emergency surgery was conducted around the clock.

I remember a Scottish surgeon at one of these hospitals who had just come off a long shift and needed to talk and get a little drunk. In the bar at Peshawar's American Club, he sat at a table with me and two other journalists and recited from memory several stanzas of Rudyard Kipling's poem "The Ballad of East and West" in a deliberately loud and passionate voice, as if to demonstrate that he didn't give a damn what people thought of him:

> "Kamal is out with twenty men to raise the Border-side,
> And he has lifted the Colonel's mare that is the Colonel's pride.
> He has lifted her out of the stable-door between the dawn and the day,
> And turned the calkins upon her feet, and ridden her far away."

At the table there was an embarrassed silence. Then the surgeon talked about what was really on his mind. "The philosophy of war is truly sinister," he said in a hushed tone. "Now, you take the Russians. Most of the mines they've laid are designed to maim, not kill, because a dead body causes no inconvenience. It only removes the one dead person from the field. But somebody who is wounded and in pain requires the full-time assistance of several people all down the line who could otherwise be fighting. And if you want to depopulate an area, then you want many of the casualties to be small children. The most stubborn peasants will give up and flee when their children are mutilated."

These were old facts that left everyone at the table numb. In Peshawar the journalists and relief workers all knew these things. But the surgeon had discovered them on his own in the lonely, pulsing stillness of the operating theater, where he was in constant physical contact with the evidence. When he recited Kipling's poetry it showed all over his face.

"The future battlefield is to be liberally sown with mines," wrote the British military historian John Keegan in his prophetic work *The Face of Battle*. Never before in history have mines played such an important role in a war as in Afghanistan. Nobody knows precisely how many were sown by Soviet troops and airmen in the ten years between their invasion and their withdrawal. The figures offered are biblical. The British Broadcasting Corporation, on June 8, 1988, simply stated "millions." The Afghan resistance claimed five million. The U.S. government's first estimate was three million. Later, on August 15, 1988, State Department spokesman Charles Redmon said the figure was more likely "between 10 and 30 million." That would be 2 mines for every Afghan who survived the war; between 40 and 120 mines per square mile of Afghan territory. Tens of thousands of civilians, if not more — many of them small children — have already been disabled by mine detonations in Afghanistan. Even though the Russian phase of the war has ended, mines threaten to kill and maim thousands more, some of whom haven't been born yet.

"The widespread sowing of millions of land mines has added an ominous new dimension to the rehabilitation effort," Undersecretary of State Michael H. Armacost told the Senate Foreign Relations Committee on June 23, 1988. According to both American and United Nations officials, mines will cripple Afghanistan's economic life for years to come, inhibiting the tilling of fields, access to pasture areas, and collection of firewood.

No group of people knew as much about mines in Afghanistan as news photographers and television cameramen. Getting close-ups of the war meant traveling with the mujahidin, the "holy warriors of Islam." And the muj — as journalists called them — walked through minefields. "It's like walking a tightrope," said Tony O'Brien, a free-lance photographer who would later be captured and then released by Afghan regime forces. "You're in a group, yet you're totally alone. Still, there's this absolutely incredible bond with the person ahead of you and behind you. You forget the heat, the thirst, the diarrhea. Then you're out of the minefield and instantaneously you're hot and thirsty again. The minute I start thinking about it I start worrying and I get totally freaked."

For several days I rode in a Toyota Land Cruiser through the mine-strewn desert outside the southern Afghan city of Kandahar. The trails were marked with the rusted carcasses of trucks that told you it was almost better not to survive such an explosion. My driver kept safely to previous tread marks. But when another vehicle approached from the opposite direction we had to make room for each other, and I became so afraid that I held my breath just to keep from whimpering. At night, or in the frequent dust storms when we lost the track, the fear went on for hours at a stretch, leaving me physically sick.

Joe Gaal, a Canadian photographer for the Associated Press, had been around so many minefields and had collected enough fragments of different mines that he had developed a sapper's tactile intuition about them, which was apparent in the movements of his hands and fingers whenever we discussed the matter. An intense, gutsy fellow, Gaal had an encyclopedic knowledge of Soviet mines. His terror had turned into an obsession.

The mine that could really put him in a cold sweat was what the mujahidin called a "jumping" mine, a Russian version of the "Bouncing Betty," used by the Americans in Vietnam. It is activated by a trip wire that causes a projectile to shoot up from underground a few feet ahead. The mine is designed to go off several seconds later and explode at waist level, just as you pass over it. "It blows off your genitals and peppers your guts with shrapnel," Gaal explained.

The Bouncing Betty was one of several different antipersonnel mines the Soviets employed, mines that had to be dug into the ground by special units and were meant to kill or maim anyone within a radius of twenty feet. But the vast majority of mines in Afghanistan were dropped from the air. The most common of these was the "butterfly" mine. The butterfly was *the* mine of Afghanistan, so much so that it had become part of the country's landscape, like the white flags above the graves of martyred mujahidin. Soviet helicopter gunships would fly in at one or two thousand feet and litter the ground with mines. The butterfly's winged shape caused it to go into a spin, slowing its descent. The detonator pin was set on impact with the ground. Green was the most common color, but the Soviets had a light brown version for desert areas and a gray one for riverbeds. Some mujahidin, not knowing this, thought the mines actually changed color.

Only eight inches long and blending in with the ground, the butterfly mine was hard to spot, especially if you were fatigued from hours of walking, which was most of the time. Except for the light aluminum detonator it was all plastic, so it was difficult to detect with mine-sweeping equipment. The mine was often mistaken for a toy by Afghan children, who paid with the loss of a limb or an eye. Its explosive power was about equal to that of the smallest hand grenade: sufficient to maim, not to kill. Contrary to Soviet claims, the mine has no self-destruct mechanism, and will be mutilating Afghans for a long time to come.

Butterfly mines, along with aerial bombardment, were the centerpiece of Moscow's strategy of depopulation. Depopulation had come after pacification had failed and before the Communist-inspired bombing campaign in Pakistani cities. During the heyday of depopulation, in the early and mid-1980s, the Soviets dropped plastic mines disguised as wrist-watches and ball-point pens over Afghan villages in the heavily populated Panjshir Valley northeast of Kabul.

There were even reports of mines disguised as dolls. The New York–based Afghanistan Relief Committee ran an advertisement in a number of American magazines featuring a photograph of a doll with its left arm blown off and a caption that read, "The toy that's making a lasting impression on thousands of Afghan children." The larger version of these ads contained a line in small type advising the reader that the doll in the photograph was not a real Soviet bomb, but a replica constructed on the basis of refugee accounts. In fact, no photographs of such dolls exist, even though one would have been worth thousands of dollars to a news photographer. Peter Jouvenal, a British television cameraman who made over forty trips inside Afghanistan with the mujahidin and saw every other kind of Soviet mine, suspected that the story of the dolls was apocryphal. "The Soviets were guilty of so much in Afghanistan. Why exaggerate?" he remarked.

Right up to the time of their withdrawal, the Soviets kept introducing new kinds of mines. When journalists entered the garrison town of Barikot, in Kunar province near the Pakistan border, after the Soviets had evacuated it in April 1988, they discovered mines stuck on stakes in the bushes. They dubbed them Noriega mines, on account of their pineapple texture. These were sonic mines, fitted with diaphragms that picked up the lightest footstep and sprayed shrapnel thirty feet in all directions.

In Barikot, the Soviets also booby-trapped grain bags in some of the places they evacuated, using a grenade with its detonator pin pulled, hooked up to a trip wire concealed in the sack. Several mujahidin and a dozen refugees were wounded when they opened the bags.

The overwhelming majority of hospital patients in Peshawar and Quetta were mine victims. After Red Cross doctors operated on them, the wounded were dispatched to clinics run by the various mujahidin political parties to recover. These clinics lived on donations from the refugees themselves and usually received little or no aid from either international relief organizations or the Pakistani government. Pakistani landlords owned the clinics and charged as much rent as they could. In the heat of summer, when temperatures rarely dipped below ninety degrees in daytime, there were no fans or air conditioners for the patients, who were accustomed to the bracing mountain climate of Afghanistan. The clinics were short of nearly everything, including food.

Of the twenty patients I saw at a clinic in Quetta one day in July 1988, sixteen were missing at least one limb. Many of the mine accidents had occurred only two or three weeks earlier. But there were no signs of illness or general physical weakness on the victims' faces, even though most of them not only had lost large quantities of blood and eaten little in the intervening period, but also had to endure days of travel on a mule or in a lolloping four-wheel-drive vehicle before getting to a proper medical facility.

Many people have the idea that once a limb is amputated the pain stops. That's not true. Pain from damaged nerve tissue lasts for months, usually longer if a clean amputation is not done soon after the accident, which was always the case in Afghanistan, where painkillers were not always available. Add this to weeks of drugged discomfort, for patients were all but drowned in antibiotics in order to prevent tetanus and other infections caused by mine fragments.

Yet, despite the pain and a missing arm or foot, the patients in these wards looked healthy and normal. There was a vibrancy in their faces, a trace of humor even, and a total absence of embarrassment. "I have given my foot to Allah," said a twenty-seven-year-old man who also had only one eye and a burned, deformed hand. "Now I will continue my *jihad* [holy war] in another way." This man had a wife and three children. At first, I dismissed what he said as bravado meant to impress a foreigner. I found it impossible to believe that he really felt this emotion, that he truly accepted what had happened to him. His eyes, however, evinced neither the rage of a fanatic, which would have accounted for his defiance, nor the shocked and sorrowful look of someone who was really depressed. If anything registered on his face when I spoke to him, it was bewilderment. He didn't seem to understand why I thought he should be unhappy. He had lost an eye, a foot, and part of a hand — and that was that.

The Afghan mujahidin came equipped with psychological armor that was not easy to pierce or fathom. They had the courage and strength of zealots, but their eyes were a mystery. Their eyes were not the bottomless black wells of hatred and cunning that a visitor grows accustomed to seeing in Iran and elsewhere in the Moslem world. There was a reassuring clarity about them. Sometimes, while I was talking and sipping cups of green tea with the mujahidin, their eyes would appear so instantly recognizable to me that I thought they could have been those of my childhood friends. How could people with such familiar, nonthreatening eyes walk so readily through minefields?

Western journalists and relief workers were not so brave. We were afraid of going "inside" — crossing into Afghanistan from Pakistan. And the more often you went "inside," the more terrified you became. Only a handful of photographers and cameramen went repeatedly, for after a few trips over the border, a print reporter could understand the story from Pakistan. This was why so many of us didn't venture far from Peshawar, the capital of Pakistan's Northwest Frontier province, which functioned as the rear base of the Afghan resistance. The relief workers who went "inside" were doctors trained in emergency surgery and vetted for mental and physical toughness. "The longest, most searching interview I ever had for a job was with Aide Médicale Internationale prior to being sent to Afghanistan," said Simon Mardel, a London surgeon and an accomplished mountain climber who had also worked in a state hospital in India.

In addition to Afghanistan's mines, a reporter had to contend with boredom, disease, and exhaustion. The food, when there was more than plain rice and onions to eat, was abominable. The meat was often filled with maggots. You could be felled by bad water. Dysentery was prevalent, along with hepatitis; getting a mild case of vivax malaria was definitely preferable. And all this was what a journalist went through merely to get to the fighting.

Every war, particularly in the Third World, involves risks of disease and danger. But no other war in recent times required journalists to walk up and down mountains as much as fourteen hours a day. Vietnam had helicopters. Every country in Africa has small planes and jeeps. Beirut offered luxury hotels with first-class cuisine next door to the fighting. Afghanistan, though, had only mules for carrying your backpack. In the south, near Kandahar, where vehicles were available, it was too dangerous to travel until the last phase of the Soviet war because the flat terrain was good not only for four-wheel-drive trucks but for helicopter gunships on the lookout for moving mujahidin units. Charles Thornton, a reporter for the *Arizona Republic,* tried traveling by truck. He was killed in an ambush in September 1985 as soon as he crossed the border.

In "The Man Who Would Be King," Kipling's story about two Englishmen who depart the Northwest Frontier to seek their fortune in Afghanistan, one returns to Peshawar a "rag-wrapped, whining cripple." As for the other, only his "dried, withered head" remained. Nothing like that happened to any journalist I knew, but some came pretty close. Richard Mackenzie, an Australian writer for the *Washington Times*'s publication *Insight,* lost forty-five pounds from dysentery during his three and a half months in northeastern Afghanistan in late 1987. Very early in his journey, he was abandoned by his guide and horseman, and later on, while very ill, he was taken prisoner by an extremist mujahidin faction. When Mackenzie showed up in Peshawar, his friends described his physical appearance as "frightening." Hugo Eriksen, a Norwegian journalist, arrived at a friend's doorstep in Peshawar in June 1988, after a two-week trip "inside," with a peptic ulcer and malaria. The rugged, six-foot-plus army veteran collapsed in a chair and whimpered, "I couldn't take the food, I just couldn't." A week later, Eriksen went back inside.

Kipling's Afghanistan was described by Louis L. Cornell as

"a place of extremes," where "circumstances corrode and destroy false appearances." In the 1980s that was still true. There was no journalist covering the war who didn't become fearfully ill at least once. If only about a dozen reporters were killed or imprisoned during the ten years of Soviet occupation, it was only because relatively few ventured over the border in the first place.

Many were intimated by Soviet threats. The Soviet ambassador to Pakistan, Vitaly Smirnov, told Agence France Presse on October 5, 1984, that journalists traveling with the mujahidin "will be killed. And our units in Afghanistan will help the Afghan forces to do it." This statement drew almost no response or criticism from the media establishment in America, but every newsman assigned to the war heard about it.

This was the only war in which having large amounts of money to spend on coverage did absolutely no good. Elsewhere in the world, American television networks leased vehicles and planes to get to remote areas. In Afghanistan there were none to lease, but mules were cheap enough that the poorest freelancer could afford them.

By mule, the fighting in Afghanistan was at least several days of hard traveling from a television satellite transmission station, sometimes as far as several weeks. Had the Soviets invaded Afghanistan in the 1950s, before the satellite age, the war might have seemed less remote and certainly would have garnered more attention than it did in the 1980s.

CBS News based a full-time cameraman, Kurt Lohbeck, in Peshawar. He was one of the handful of journalists who repeatedly risked their lives for several years running in order to cover the war from inside. Lohbeck used to say that part of his "soul was up in those mountains, and you have to go back there and check on yourself from time to time." But none of the American TV networks had a bureau for a war in which — according to a study by the University of Geneva in Switzerland and the Gallup organization in Pakistan — a superpower killed 1.3 million people. That is more deaths than in the Iraq-Iran war and ten times more than the number killed in Lebanon in all the years of civil conflict there since 1975. The Israelis would have to repeat their 1982 invasion of Lebanon seventy-five times over before equaling the Kremlin's Afghan carnage.

Five and a half million Afghans were made refugees in Pakistan and Iran, a third of the prewar population of the country. In the 1980s, one out of two refugees in the world was an Afghan. Considering that another two million Afghans were forced by the war to migrate within the country, no conflict since the end of World War II created more homeless people save for the 1971 Bangladesh war.

The bloodiest year in Afghanistan was 1985, the first year of Mikhail Gorbachev's rule in the Soviet Union. In that year, according to a survey conducted by Swedish relief experts, well over half of all the farmers who remained in Afghanistan had their fields bombed, and over a quarter had their irrigation systems destroyed and their livestock shot by Soviet or Afghan Communist troops.

Lars Grahnstrom, a shy, relaxed Swedish nurse with piercing blue eyes, arrived in Afghanistan a few weeks after Gorbachev came to power. Grahnstrom spent six months with four other male nurses and doctors in a cave near the Soviet-held city of Mazar-i-Sharif. They treated over a hundred patients a day, the majority of whom had war-related injuries. This was in the extreme north of Afghanistan, where the fighting was heaviest. "In the little part of Afghanistan where I lived, there were more people killed while I was there than in South Africa or Lebanon the whole year," Grahnstrom said. "Every day I listened to the news on my short-wave radio. It was always South Africa, Lebanon, Sri Lanka — two people killed here, three killed there . . . I was always hoping to hear something about Afghanistan. But there was nothing."

In his book *Under a Sickle Moon,* the British travel writer
Peregrine Hodson recalled his three months in Afghanistan:
"Every evening we tuned in to the [BBC] World Service but
there was no mention of any new offensive in the Panjshir
Valley. It was disturbingly unreal to be caught in the middle of
a forgotten war. At times it was like being in the grip of a
massive hallucination: living on nuts and berries in a cave,
being bombed by Soviet jets."

The Soviet bombing had little effect on the mujahidin. By
1987, it seemed that the Soviets' last, best hope was to destabi-
lize the guerrillas' rear base, over the border in Pakistan. The
State Department reported 127 terrorist incidents in Pakistani
cities that year, resulting in 234 deaths — more than in any
Middle Eastern country. Pakistan suffered one third of all the
fatalities and one half of all the wounded in terrorist attacks
worldwide in 1987.

The terrorists whom the Pakistani police managed to capture testified to working for the Afghan Communist Bureau
of State Security, Khedamat-e Aetelaat-e Dawlati, known as
KhAD. Neither the State Department nor any Western diplomat in Pakistan had any doubt that this was true. KhAD (which
has been called the WAD Ministry of State Security since 1988)
had been built up by the KGB into a force of 25,000 agents
soon after the Soviet invasion, and about 1,500 Soviets were
thought to be working at KhAD's Kabul headquarters. According to State Department officials, KhAD was the largest
known sponsor of terrorism in the world, next to which the
record of Abu Nidal and other Palestinian terrorists was —
until the December 1988 bombing of the Pan American jet-
liner — statistically insignificant.

In the same week in April 1988 that the Soviet Union signed
an agreement in Geneva to withdraw its troops, terrorists blew
up an ammunition depot outside the Pakistani capital of Islamabad, killing one hundred and injuring more than one thousand people. It was one of four terrorist incidents in Pakistan

over a forty-eight-hour period. The equipment destroyed at the depot was destined for the mujahidin. It included a large shipment of primacord, a rocket-fired cable that explodes two feet above the ground, used to clear a path through mine-fields.

This would have been the first mine-clearing equipment that the mujahidin received. Indeed, throughout the Soviet occupation the only such "equipment" that the guerrillas ever had was the winter hail, dubbed "Allah's mine sweeper" be-cause the crashing pellets of ice sometimes triggered the mines.

Hundreds of journalists covered the signing of the Geneva agreement. Close to a hundred more arrived in Kabul after-ward to watch the start of the Soviet withdrawal on May 15, 1988, when the press began to speculate about the return of the five and a half million refugees.

A month later, in Nangarhar province near the Pakistan border, I encountered a group of refugees ascending a moun-tain with nothing but the clothes on their backs. They asked me for water from my canteen, something Afghans rarely do unless they are ill. The refugees were not walking back to their homes in Afghanistan but leaving them. Soviet jets had bombed their village in the Kot Valley south of Jalalabad a few days earlier, killing thirty-four people. This was nothing un-usual; since the start of their withdrawal, the Soviets had been bombing civilian areas around major cities in order to create free-fire zones where minefields could be extended and invad-ing mujahidin units easily spotted. The Soviets were deter-mined not to leave Afghanistan "clinging to helicopters," like the Americans in Vietnam. Anyway, the idea of millions of refugees returning home while millions of mines littered the countryside was considered absurd by relief workers in Pe-shawar.

None of this mattered, however. As soon as the Red Army

withdrawal commenced, even as the Soviets were still dropping mines and bombing villages, the press shifted elsewhere
what limited attention it had bestowed on Afghanistan. (Only
at the conclusion of the Soviet withdrawal, in February 1989,
did the media tune in.) "Afghanistan is already being forgotten," lamented Zia Rizvi, a top UN official involved in the
refugee repatriation program. "The worst enemy of the Afghan refugees is the short memory of world public opinion."

Everybody in the West was at least aware of Afghanistan, and
regarding the role of the Soviets, most people probably assumed the worst. But even for these people, the war was an
opaque presence half a world away. It wasn't *felt* with the im-
mediacy of other news. Political conservatives in America believed the fault rested with the liberal media. There was certainly an element of truth in this, but less than was thought.
And it wasn't a revealing truth: liberals I knew cared deeply
about this war and occasionally risked their lives to report it.

Even from Peshawar, thirty-five miles from the Afghan border, the war was, in a visual sense, inaccessible. Television
cameramen trekked for weeks on little food, only to return ill
and half starved, with almost no footage that could compete
against the heartbreaking backdrops of black townships in
South Africa or the spectacle of a hijacked jumbo jet on the
tarmac at a Mediterranean airport — images that people in
the West could immediately relate to. Though a few journalists
managed to get close to the fighting, the war was never
brought close to the audience. Over a million were killed, but
there were no images of epic battles, as there were in the Middle East, or of mass death, as in Ethiopia.

There were major battles in Afghanistan, but the only way
to get to them on short notice was to fly, which was impossible,
since the only people with planes were the Communists. Instead, for nearly a decade, the public was shown the same
monotonous film clips of smoke billowing in the distance and

of bearded, turbaned guerrillas with old rifles sniping at convoys — images that only increased the war's unreality.

Afghanistan was too physically rough an assignment and offered too few rewards to draw the world's best television cameramen. And it is the cameramen — not the high-profile correspondents — who hold the key to a television story's impact. Had the very best cameramen traveled to the front lines, however, they would have been frustrated by the visual material they had to work with. The mujahidin were exotic all right, with their wide turbans, Lee-Enfield rifles, and great black beards. But the effect was static, flat. In Afghanistan, there was absolutely no clash between the strange and the familiar, which gave Vietnam and Lebanon their rock-video quality, with zonked-out GIs in headbands and rifle-wielding Shiite terrorists wearing Michael Jackson T-shirts.

Afghanistan existed without bridges to the twentieth century. The country was mired in medievalism; a "mass of mountains and peaks and glaciers," as Kipling noted; a place where terrible things always happened to people. The Soviets destroyed it — but didn't the Mongols too! In the January 20, 1980, issue of the *Village Voice,* the left-wing writer Alexander Cockburn employed such a rationale to justify the Soviet invasion of the month before:

> We all have to go one day, but pray God let it not be over Afghanistan. An unspeakable country filled with unspeakable people, sheepshaggers and smugglers. . . . I yield to none in my sympathy to those prostrate beneath the Russian jackboot, but if ever a country deserved rape it's Afghanistan.

Cockburn's tone was, of course, politically motivated. But given the West's tepid public response to the subsequent Soviet occupation, it appeared that many people, deep down inside, reacted to Afghanistan in similar terms.

The images coming out of Afghanistan were simply beyond the grasp of the Western television audience. The Soviets had taken American tactics in Vietnam several steps further and fought a twenty-first-century war, a war that was completely impersonal and therefore too dangerous for journalists to cover properly, in which the only strategy was repeated aerial carpet bombings, terrorism, and the laying of millions of mines. The Hind helicopter gunship, the workhorse of the Soviet military in Afghanistan, packed no less than 128 rockets and four missiles. It was able to incinerate an entire village in a few seconds. Against such measures, the very concept of battle had become nearly obsolete.

While the Soviets waged a twenty-first-century war, the Afghans fought a nineteenth-century one. The Afghans were able to survive and drive out the Soviets precisely, and only, because they were so primitive. High birth and infant mortality rates in an unforgiving mountain environment, where disease was rife and medical care absent, had seemed to accelerate the process of evolution in rural Afghanistan, making the inhabitants of the countryside — where most of the mujahidin came from — arguably the physically toughest people on earth. They could go long periods of time without food and water, and climb up and down mountains like goats. Keeping up with them on their treks and surviving on what they survived on reduced me and other Westerners to tears. They seemed an extension of an impossible landscape that had ground up one foreign invader after another.

The mujahidin borrowed little from other modern guerrilla struggles. They had a small number of vehicles and, until the later stages of the war, few walkie-talkies, leaving the enemy without communications to intercept. Like the ancient Greeks, the mujahidin used runners to carry messages between outposts. Some areas of the country were blessed with exceptionally talented guerrilla commanders. But for the most part, the resistance fighters had no strategy to speak of, and their command structure was often so informal as to be nonexistent. A KhAD or KGB agent in their midst would have been hopelessly confused: there was nothing to infiltrate, and no pattern — often no logic or planning — to guerrilla attacks. Predicting the mujahidin's actions was like forecasting the wind direction. In Peshawar, it was said that their very incompetence helped to defeat the Soviets (though after the Soviets departed, the complete disorganization of the resistance hindered its efforts to capture major Afghan cities still held by the Afghan Communists).

The mujahidin were a movement without rhetoric or ideology or a supreme leader — they had no Arafat or Savimbi or Mao. Their Moslem fundamentalism lacked political meaning because Afghanistan, unlike the Arab world and Iran, never had an invasion of Western culture and technology to revolt against. The guerrillas had no complexes, no chips on their shoulders regarding the modern world, since they had never clashed with it until the Soviets came. Religion for them was inseparable from the other certainties of a harsh and lonely mountain existence. In sum, the mujahidin had no politics; therefore, with few exceptions, they could not be extremists. Concepts like "the Third World" and "national liberation" had absolutely no meaning for them. After a trip to Paktia province in November 1987, William McGurn wrote in the European edition of the *Wall Street Journal* that the Afghan guerrillas were "simply ornery mountain folk who have not cottoned to a foreign power that has seized their land, killed their people and attacked their faith."

If the mujahidin resembled anyone, it was the early-nineteenth-century Greek *klephts,* who with foreign help liberated their country from Ottoman Turkish occupation. Like the Afghans, the Greeks then were an unruly hodgepodge of guerrilla bands driven by a fervid religious faith (in their case, Orthodox Christianity). They were at a stage of development similar to that of Afghan peasants today: they lived an austere life in the mountains, were riven by blood feuds, and never forgot an insult. Lord Byron and the other foreign eccentrics who flocked to Greece in the 1820s to assist the rebels might have felt at home among the relief workers and journalists in Afghanistan in the 1980s.

The Afghans were able to withstand a late-twentieth-century military onslaught by relying on nineteenth-century values and methods. In *The Face of Battle,* John Keegan observed: "Impersonality, coercion, deliberate cruelty, all deployed on a rising scale, makes the fitness of modern man to sustain the stress of battle increasingly doubtful." There is an awful lesson here: even conventional warfare is now so horrible that only the values of the past may make victory possible. And in Afghanistan, the lack of all-weather roads and a national press left the Afghans only the values of the past to fall back on, inward-oriented village codes that were undiluted by the rationalism that pervades not just the West but the more technologically developed parts of the Third World.

The Soviets killed a larger percentage of Afghans than the Nazis killed Soviets in World War II. Were Americans or Europeans to suffer the same level of mass violence today, it is questionable whether they would fight back as the Afghans have. More likely, they would seek some sort of compromise with their occupier.

The Afghan mujahidin, numbering over 100,000, were the first group of insurgents to drive out a Russian army since Czar Peter the Great began his empire's southward expansion three hundred years ago. The mujahidin were attacked with more firepower than any Moslem group in the Middle East could imagine, yet almost never did they resort to terrorism. Though the guerrillas were responsible for political assassinations, the brutal treatment of enemy soldiers, and rocket attacks in Kabul and other cities that killed civilians, to my knowledge or that of any journalist I know, groups of Soviet or Afghan civilians were never deliberately singled out as targets. Because the mujahidin were innocent of the modern trait of terrorism, they did not inspire the horror and fascination of the car bombers and airplane hijackers, with their black hoods and nihilistic beliefs. The mujahidin, despite their many accomplishments, were not traditionally good subject matter for the media: they were neither complicated nor fanatical. They were the most understated of resistance fighters, and so, after a decade of war, they still had no face.

What the television images did not translate was that despite their apparent primitiveness, as individuals the mujahidin were easy for a foreigner to talk to and befriend. There was none of the stiffness and forced probing that characterized relationships between Moslems and Westerners elsewhere. Because they had never been colonized, the Afghans didn't have the fears and prejudices toward the West with which other peoples in the Orient are burdened. "After the lowering fanaticism of Meshed [in Iran]," wrote Bruce Chatwin, crossing into the mountains of Afghanistan "was like coming up for air." In *The Road to Oxiana,* the 1937 classic considered the *Ulysses* of twentieth-century travel writing, Robert Byron, having just arrived from the Middle East, exclaimed about Afghanistan: "Here at last is Asia without an inferiority complex." The Afghans seemed wonderfully straightforward, and journalists and relief workers took to them because in them we saw a stronger, more heroic version of ourselves.

Sympathizing with guerrilla movements is an occupational hazard of foreign correspondents everywhere, but the Afghans were the first guerrillas whom journalists not only sympathized with but actually looked up to. As romantic and unprofessional as this was, we were not the first Westerners to fall under the spell. Generation after generation of British colonial officials who had fought the Afghans in defense of the Northwest Frontier of British India had learned to admire and identify with their foes. Mountstuart Elphinstone, who led a mission to the court of Afghan ruler Shah Shuja in 1809, noted that the Afghans "have not that indifference to truth, and that style of habitual and gratuitous falsehoods, which astonishes a European . . . in India and Persia." Sir Olaf Caroe, the last British governor of the Northwest Frontier, wrote, "For the stranger who had eyes to see and ears to hear, . . . here was a people who looked him in the face and made him feel he had come home."

The British invaded Afghanistan three times, and on each occasion they were driven out. Out of an invasion force of 4,500 that retreated from Kabul in January 1842, only one man was left alive. Never had the British met such a formidable adversary. This forced them to meet the Afghans on an equal plane without a trace of condescension.

Kipling paid the ultimate tribute to the Afghans in "The Ballad of East and West." Because of its simple truth and catchy rhythm, the poem's first line, "*Oh, East is East, and West is West, and never the twain shall meet,*" has become a cliché. But read in its entirety, the ninety-six-line epic tells the story of how a friendship is forged between the son of a British colonel and an Afghan brigand named Kamal, whom the colonel's son was sent to capture.

> They have looked each other between the eyes, and
>   there they found no fault.
> They have taken the Oath of the Brother-in-Blood
>   on leavened bread and salt:
> They have taken the Oath of the Brother-in-Blood
>   on fire and fresh-cut sod,
> On the hilt and half of the Khyber knife, and the
>   Wondrous Names of God.

Kipling, whose imperialism is often misunderstood by modern readers, ends the story with this uplifting truth:

> . . . *there is neither East nor West, Border, nor Breed, nor
>   Birth,*
> When two strong men stand face to face, though
>   they come from the ends of the earth!

The poem, which was published in 1889, captures the spirit of the naïve and idealized friendships that existed one hundred years later between mujahidin commanders and some extremely brave journalists and relief workers whom I knew in Peshawar.

Kamal, the hero of Kipling's poem, was more than just an Afghan. He was a Pathan (pronounced "pah-*tahn*"), as were most of the mujahidin and the Afghans whom the British encountered on the Northwest Frontier. The Pathans are the largest ethnic group in Afghanistan (one of every two Afghans is a Pathan) and the largest existent tribal society in the world. They live by a medieval code of honor called Pukhtunwali and have given the country all of its kings and political leaders. Until recent decades, in fact, "Pathan" and "Afghan" have been synonymous. The Pathans inhabit a huge arc of territory in the eastern, southern, and southwestern part of Afghanistan. They speak Pukhtu, an Aryan tongue that borrows much from Persian and Hindustani, and employs Arabic script. R. T. I. Ridgway, an officer in the British colonial service, described Pukhtu as "a strong virile language, capable of expressing ideas with neatness and accuracy." Actually, the Pathans prefer to call themselves Pukhtuns, or Pushtuns if they live in southern Afghanistan, where their accent is softer. But the name Pathan, first used by the Indians to describe the Afghans on the Northwest Frontier, has become commonly accepted.

The origins of the Pathans are shrouded in myth. By various accounts, they are descended from the ancient Hebrews, from an Aryan race called the White Huns, and from the Greek troops of Alexander the Great who passed through Afghanistan in the fourth century B.C. Pathan genealogies read like tracts from the Old Testament. According to one legend, the Pathans are descendants of Afghana, a grandson of the Israelite king Saul, whose ancestors were carried away from Palestine by Nebuchadnezzar, the Babylonian king, and planted as colonists in Persia, from where they migrated eastward to present-day Afghanistan. The name Afghana cannot be found in the Hebrew Bible, but many Pathans still believe the story. Even more believe themselves to be Aryans, but all will admit that they are not certain of their own ancestry.

Almost every one of Afghanistan's twenty-odd ethnic groups took part in the struggle against the Soviets, but it was the Pathans who gave the resistance its mythic, larger-than-life quality, its lack of political pretensions, and its chivalry — as well as its primitiveness, tribal disorder, and recklessness. Only Pathans could have invented a game that requires a man to pick up a butterfly mine and toss it in the air without losing a hand (not all succeeded). Only Pathans could make walking through a minefield a test of manhood.

The Pathans are a purer, crystallized version of everything that is good and bad in the Afghan character. More than any other single factor, it was their harsh and unforgiving tribal culture, free of subtleties and introspection and unaffected by the modern world, that defeated the mines and other weapons of the Soviet invaders. As the seventeenth-century Pathan poet Khushal Khan Khatak wrote:

> The very name Pukhtun spells honor and glory,
> Lacking that honor, what is the Afghan story?

1

Frontier Town

THE CEILING FAN rattled like an airplane propeller in the breathless, mud-baked heat of the room, blowing new, crisp 100-afghani notes all over the floor. The money changer in the Peshawar bazaar had handed me the notes in heaps of 10,000. The afghani was devaluing fast. For years already, in one of the CIA's most successful covert operations, millions of counterfeit afghanis had been printed in order to wreck the Kabul regime's economy and allow the mujahidin to buy weapons and ammunition on the open market on the Northwest Frontier. But the CIA program wasn't good enough for the KGB. Near the end of the war the Soviets, needing to handcuff the Afghan economy to their own in the wake of a troop withdrawal, started buying up vast amounts of U.S. dollars on the black market in Kabul, driving down the afghani further in order to make Western products prohibitively expensive for the Afghan population. So there I sat, sweating on a sagging jute bed with a draft at my back, stuffing stacks of possibly counterfeit money into my rucksack, just to pay for a mule in case I got sick.

My room was on the roof of a house that overlooked an expanse of rice fields, through which the same water buffalos plodded home every day at dusk, as in a silk screen or bas-relief. On my last evening in Peshawar, my eyes were drawn to a shimmer of fire-red in the distance: the gossamer *chador* (veil) of the young woman driving the herd along a mud embankment. To me, that lone flash of a primary color symbolized the rich and voluptuous civilization of the Indian subcontinent that ended, literally, beyond those fields, where the landscape lost its watery, terra cotta glow and was replaced by a mass of corrugated, pie-crust hills, whose scarred, cindery gradients warned of heat and cold and all other means of physical discomfort. That was where the war was, and to understand who the mujahidin really were, you had to go there.

On the bed I'd laid out the native costume I had just purchased for a total of 400 rupees ($25) from a Pathan merchant in the bazaar. It consisted of a *pakol,* a flat woolen hat from the Hindu Kush mountain region of Chitral, and the traditional *shalwar kameez* worn by the Pathans — a pair of baggy cotton pants held up by a string and a long, flowing shirt with a collar and deep side pocket. I tried the costume on, wearing no underwear as recommended, since among the guerrillas, the only opportunity to bathe would be in a stream with all my clothes on. Like Kim in Rudyard Kipling's novel, I "felt mechanically for the moustache" and beard that were just beginning to sprout on my face. Kim, too, had put on a native costume given him by a Pathan to espy the Northwest Frontier. And if I thought of Kim as I looked at the pathetic imposter in the mirror, it was not, I hoped, the effect of a romantic inclination but simply because, as in so many other instances, Kipling's writing offered the only sure guide to this war. (One of my colleagues, Jonathan Randal of the *Washington Post,* had told me, "Had the Russians read Kipling more carefully, they might never have invaded Afghanistan.")

In the side pocket of the *shalwar kameez* I placed my notebook, camera, and water purification tablets. My rucksack was small, since I might have to carry it everywhere. There was room inside only for the afghanis, a second *shalwar kameez,* a sleeping bag, towel, comb, toothbrush and toothpaste, flashlight, film, pocketknife, short-wave radio, toilet paper, flea powder, mosquito repellent, painkillers, antibiotics, and malaria pills. The canteen I would carry separately.

Reporters permanently covering the Afghan war were tied to a wheel of psychological torture that never stopped turning. First there was the boredom and insecurity of waiting in Peshawar for the trip inside to materialize, something that didn't always happen, and when it did it was often weeks later than the mujahidin had promised. Then there was the attack of fear and dread when you suddenly found out — usually the night before departure — where exactly you would be going and that it was too late to back out. Finally came the loneliness, physical torment, and pure wonder of the trip itself. I was now in the second phase of that cycle, surrounded by four walls and a glimpse of desolation from my room, about to travel alone with a group of mujahidin into Afghanistan and feeling more scared and lonely than I ever felt before.

The fact that I had a wife and son back in Greece only increased my sense of isolation. Among the journalists who regularly went inside, I knew of only one who had a family, and he had told me never to carry along pictures of loved ones in Afghanistan. "You should put your family out of your mind completely," he said. "Just do what you have to do, survive, and get out." Looking at the picture of my wife and son at the harbor on the Aegean island of Paros, I decided not to take his advice. I slid the color photograph into my pocket.

"May you never be tired, Pathan!" said the horse dealer Mahbub Ali to Kim when the boy departed. I hoped this benediction might apply to me too.

Peshawar, the capital of Pakistan's Northwest Frontier province, was always a city of colonial clichés where adventures, both real and imagined, began. Edward Behr, an Indian army veteran and for years a foreign correspondent for *Time* and *Newsweek,* once observed: "Though the British Raj was about to fall apart with terrifying suddenness, Peshawar . . . was still a bastion of tradition and Kiplingesque behavior." The Afghan war made this even more true in the 1980s than in the 1940s, the period Behr was writing about.

Peshawar (literally, Frontier Town) lies on a teeming panel of reddish-black earth at the foot of the Khyber Pass, the fabled gateway between the Indian subcontinent and the gaunt mountains and plateaus of central Asia, over which the sun sets in a blaze of garish pigments every night. Layered with mud and fine dust and smelling of baked brick, diesel exhaust, sickly sweet incense, and dung, Peshawar is a typical Dickensian town of the industrialized Third World.

Only in the old cantonment, built and formerly occupied by the British, is the city's soot-smudged tableau lightened somewhat by green lawns and stately red brick mansions, built in Anglo-Indian Gothic style. In the tidy parade grounds, if you use your imagination, Peshawar evokes a smoky nineteenth-century lithograph of British India. But everywhere outside the cantonment there is only noise, traffic, and a hot, dense bath of electrified air suffused with embers and metallic sparks. The warrened, cratered streets are cluttered with horse-drawn tongas, careening auto rickshaws, and gaudy Bedford trucks, which feature gruesome examples of popular art on their sideboards, such as a picture of an F-16 squadron zooming out of the lipstick-smeared mouth of an Asian diva. Despite such vulgar touches, the city still retains enough potted, old-fashioned romance to seduce a foreign correspondent in search of the exotic.

Peshawar has a bazaar, of course — where I had bought my costume and Afghan money — filled with all sorts of gongs, trinkets, and the best selection of reasonably priced oriental carpets in Asia. There's an eccentric hotel too: a run-down, rambling hostelry dating from the time of the Raj, called Dean's after a British colonial governor, staffed by zombielike waiters and known as a hangout for spies and other intriguers. And then there are the Pathans, who with their beards, turbans, bandoleers, and eyes darkened with kohl are like extras in a Hollywood movie. At the far end of town, just before the road begins its dramatic, winding ascent toward Afghanistan,

is an official Khyber Gate that is inscribed with several verses
from a Kipling poem, "Arithmetic on the Frontier":

> A scrimmage in a Border Station —
> A canter down some dark defile —
> Two thousand pounds of education
> Drops to a ten-rupee jezail —
> The Crammer's boast, the Squadron's pride,
> Shot like a rabbit in a ride!

Was there ever such rich terrain for romantic self-delusion?

At the end of the 1970s, Peshawar went from being a quaint
backwater to a geopolitical fault zone, and new, worse clichés
were piled on the Kiplingesque ones. The Islamic revolution
in Iran closed off an important route for international drug
smugglers. No longer could opium, extracted from locally
grown red poppies, be transported west from Pakistan. Instead, laboratories were set up in the barren, dun-brown hills
that loom on either side of the Khyber Pass. In small, concealed mud brick redoubts the opium was refined into billions
of dollars' worth of heroin before being brought by truck and
airplane to the port of Karachi and smuggled to Europe and
America. A year after the Iranian revolution, the Soviet Union
invaded Afghanistan and placed the Red Army at Peshawar's
doorstep. Refugees poured down the mountains into the plain
surrounding the city. Mujahidin political parties set up their
headquarters in the refugee camps. Peshawar's population
doubled, from 500,000 to a million. And journalists, relief
workers, drug enforcement agents, aspiring mercenaries,
both real and would-be spies, and a rabble of weirdos who
defied categorization filled Dean's and nearby Green's Hotel,
a gloom-ridden, poured-concrete sepulcher that was half the
price of Dean's.

But it was Dean's, more than Green's, that began to evoke a
setting for low-grade intrigue. It was said that every room was
bugged, and some even believed that the awful posters and oil

paintings on the walls were really huge microphones in disguise. But that didn't stop reporters from screaming at the top of their lungs. One night I listened to a Scandinavian writer rant and rave about why a certain mujahidin commander was secretly a Maoist. Another night, a drunken American journalist loudly accused a British colleague of being a Communist merely because she had dared to criticize the guerrillas.

The hotel staff couldn't cope with the onslaught, and the food at Dean's, never very good, suddenly got much worse. But the hotel drivers prospered, for the journalists and aid workers needed to be chauffeured from one sprawling refugee camp to another. The most popular driver was a fellow named Gujar, whose lugubrious manner, nervous twitch, and white beardlike stubble on his chocolate-brown head made him, along with the terrible food at Dean's, a Peshawar "in" joke that got mentioned in nearly every recent book and article about the place.

Because of Islamic law in Pakistan, alcohol could be served only at foreign "clubs" with special liquor licenses. Given the nature of the clientele, the Peshawar bar scene was rowdy. Proud locals compared the atmosphere at the Bamboo Garden to the scene in the movie *Star Wars* in which space cowboys, alien monsters, and robots collide at an intergalactic truck stop. In the summer of 1987, two strung-out West German hippies at the Bamboo Garden were badgering a young Swiss woman to take heroin. She tried to ignore them, but they injected the drug into her buttocks while she talked to a friend at the bar. It turned out to be an overdose. The woman was rushed back to Europe but died en route. The bar closed before the year was over.

After that, the only place left in town to drink was the bar at the air-conditioned American Club, which was soon being mentioned in international travel magazines as one of the "great journalist bars in the world" — on par even with the bar at the Commodore Hotel in Beirut. An American friend, who for years had been writing in obscurity about Afghanistan and the Northwest Frontier at a time when nobody cared, became so intoxicated by the sudden interest in Peshawar that he innocently exclaimed to me, "Peshawar in the 1980s is one of the great place-dates of the century, like Paris in the twenties!"

Peshawar became a place where men could act out their fantasies. Koshiro Tanaka, a struggling Japanese businessman in his late forties who had a sixth-degree black belt in karate, believed that "since World War II, there has not been an honorable way for a Japanese man to die in the true samurai spirit." So he exchanged his cubbyhole in a Tokyo trading office for a bare room and sagging jute bed in the $1.15-a-night Khyber Hotel. This was Tanaka's base for going out on Rambo-style combat missions with the mujahidin. He also trained hundreds of guerrillas in hand-to-hand combat. The only medical supplies he brought with him on his missions inside were three elastic tubes to use as tourniquets. "Three is enough," he explained to me. "If all four of my limbs are cut, then I am finished." Tanaka always carried at least two hand grenades, one for throwing at the enemy and the other for killing himself. "I can't be taken alive, because if I'm captured — big diplomatic problem for Japan." Tanaka's reputation was secured when Tass, the Soviet news agency, actually taking the threat he posed seriously, reported him killed in action in September 1986. "I was in Japan at the time, training," Tanaka said with a crazed, jack-o'-lantern grin. He was on his way back inside when I last saw him. Though he had killed quite a few Soviets with grenades and his AK-47 Kalashnikov rifle, he still had not attained his ultimate goal: killing a Russian with his bare hands.

I met an East German refugee in his late twenties who came to Pakistan "to even the score with the Russians." Imprisoned for two years in East Berlin for trying to scale the Berlin Wall, he was eventually allowed to immigrate to West Germany. He was happy there until the letters he wrote to his father and girlfriend in East Berlin started to be returned unopened. "The Communists wouldn't let me communicate with my family, so I decided to fight back." Afghanistan provided him with an opportunity. He converted to Islam, learned Pukhtu, and took the nom de guerre of Ahmedjan in order to protect his family in East Germany from Communist retribution. Ahmedjan made three trips as a mujahid into the Kandahar region, participating in several battles before handing in his assault rifle to take the job of project manager for the German Humanitarian Service in Afghanistan. But he swore that he wouldn't "withdraw from Afghanistan until the Russians do."

No one I knew fought for money; mercenaries quickly learned that they were unwelcome in Peshawar and stopped coming, because the mujahidin didn't understand the concept of paying someone to fight their war. Typical of the kind of person who occasionally passed through the frontier town's revolving door was a London window cleaner whose father had given him a one-way air ticket to Peshawar. The fellow casually mentioned to anybody who would listen that he had "always wanted to kill someone." Eventually, he went on a mission with an obscure guerrilla group, whose members let him pull the trigger of a rocket launcher aimed at a tent full of Afghan regime troops. After the explosion, in the distance he saw two bodies lying on the ground. The window cleaner then went home to London. This time his wife paid the airfare.

Fantasy, reality, and cliché came together at Darra, an hour's drive south of Peshawar. The dusty storefronts and jagged, biscuit-brown hills rising from behind the line of shops evoked a Disney re-creation of Dodge City, except that Darra was real, and the gunslingers were Pathans. Also, even Dodge City had some kind of law; there never was any law in Darra. The town is in a "tribal agency," a belt of land adjacent to the Afghan border that the Pakistanis, like the British before them, have never been able to control.

In the last century, having failed to subdue the border-area

Pathans, and discouraged over the number of rifles they were stealing, the British decided to help the tribesmen in a very unhelpful way. They taught the Pathans of Darra how to make their own guns and gave them the lathes to do it, knowing that the metal mined from the surrounding hills was of poor quality. This ensured that after a few hundred rounds, the barrels would expand and the guns would lose their accuracy. Today, making guns is Darra's one and only industry. The garishly painted shops along the main street sell locally made versions of AK-47 assault rifles, as well as M-16s, Stens, Uzi submachine guns, Makarov pistols, single-action Lee-Enfields, rocket-propelled grenades, recoilless rifles, antiaircraft guns and rockets of all sizes, and much more. You can even buy a pen gun that fires a .22 caliber bullet and costs under $6. But it dropped from popularity after nine foreigners were arrested at Pakistani airports when the x-ray machines spotted the weapons-grade metal.

In one shop, grinning Pathans feverishly work the lathes and smooth the gun barrels under a sign reading, "God helps those who help themselves." Mujahidin, blood-feuding Pathan tribesmen, and the occasional Sikh extremist from the Indian Punjab are among those who purchase Darra's wares. Prospective customers can fire as many rounds as they want right on the streets, provided they pay for the bullets.

Darra has two smells: cordite and hashish. A shop with a sheepskin or goat's tail hanging outside indicates a place where drugs are sold. There are plenty of those shops at the north end of town. A kilo of brown heroin sells for under $100 in Darra; the New York City street value would be around $1 million. The going price for a credit card–size brick of opium is $4 in Darra. At dusk, the shops are bolted shut because of the risk of brigands. I never met a relief worker or journalist who hadn't visited the town at least once. It's what the Northwest Frontier is all about.

*

On the map, the Northwest Frontier is just another province of Pakistan, along with Sind, Punjab, and Baluchistan. But for Westerners what made the Northwest Frontier *the Northwest Frontier* was not just its proximity to Afghanistan but the fact that culturally, topographically, and even, to a degree, politically — as far as the tribal areas were concerned — the province was part of Afghanistan, despite what the maps said.

For Afghan war freaks, a group that included locally based journalists, relief workers, and an odd assortment of barflies with questionable life stories, the Northwest Frontier's tenuous link to Pakistan was something to be ignored, and even irritated and embarrassed about. In their minds, the very word Pakistan suggested the Indian subcontinent: a noisy, overcrowded, polluted, and closed-in space seething with devious, money-hungry, and weak people who were morally and physically inferior to the heroic men who inhabited the pure open spaces of central Asia on the other side of the Khyber Pass, where adventure beckoned. An American from Wyoming or Montana might look upon New Yorkers in much the same way. This was, in fact, how the wild and woolly Afghans, particularly the Pathans, looked upon their Pakistani hosts. The same prejudices were transferred to many of the Afghans' foreign supporters.

On the Northwest Frontier, a Pakistani usually meant a Punjabi, someone originally from the adjacent province of Punjab, in the industrial and agricultural heartland of Pakistan. To an Afghan — and therefore to the war freaks — all Punjabis looked and acted the same. They were dark, beaky, and mustachioed, and oozed a false sophistication. They jabbered like birds in their piercing rattle of a language and banged into you on the street with their "Third World briefcases": cheap, pretentious-looking constructions of plastic and cardboard with cumbersome locks, which held nothing but a few slices of flat bread and soft-porn movie magazines. Punjabis were physically frail compared to Afghans and were either too skinny or too fat. Pathans ate meat; Punjabis ate *dal,* a lentil-based gruel. Punjabis were thought to be spineless and without principles; regardless of their commitments, they were poised to sell you out once the price became high enough. In *The Way of the Pathans,* James W. Spain, a U.S. diplomat in the region, relates how his Pathan guide looked down on his Punjabi tonga driver: "I know that fat Punjabi," the guide told him. "He is a snake."

In the Pathan mind, Punjabis acted like women. And women, according to a Pathan, are physically weak, shifty, and tempestuous. The war freaks went a step or two further, declaring Punjabis "brain dead," unable to follow even simple orders or to think for themselves. On the Northwest Frontier, the only thing worse than a Punjabi was a Hindu. At least Punjabis on the Pakistan side of the India-Pakistan border were Moslems, and that connoted a fierce, fanatical, and therefore martial (read *manly*) culture — even if, as everyone on the Frontier supposed, Punjabis had "religion on their lips and money in their hearts." Hindus practiced a religion that was subtle and introverted, which meant it was feminine. Hindus were concerned only with their personal salvation and not with the duty of a man to his tribal kinsmen. Their religion attracted hippies, mystics, and homosexuals. Hindus lacked all honor: the official policy of their country, India, was to support the Soviet occupation of Afghanistan. Pakistan at least backed up the mujahidin and was caring and providing a home for three and a half million fellow Moslems from Afghanistan, though not even this fact would get the war freaks to change their minds about the Punjabis.

That's because they all knew that it wasn't the "filthy Punjabis" who were providing a home for the refugees but Pakistan's president, General Mohammed Zia ul-Haq, backed up by hundreds of millions of American taxpayers' dollars. Without Zia, the refugees might have been turned back at

the border and massacred or starved to death in their own
country.

Zia's most prominent opponent was Benazir Bhutto, the
daughter of former Premier Zulfikar Ali Bhutto, who was executed by Zia in April 1979. The Bhutto family was Sindhi,
but in the lexicon of the Northwest Frontier, Benazir, as she
was always called, might as well have been a Punjabi because
she thought like one. Throughout the 1980s, her Pakistan
People's Party was on record as opposing the very presence of
the Afghan refugees on Pakistani soil. Benazir was attractive
and telegenic, but she was also willing to consign millions of
refugees to a horrible fate. Only when it became clear that
Zia's gamble had paid off and the Soviets were going to withdraw from Afghanistan did she begin to shift her position
regarding the refugees.

Benazir, the thinly disguised "Virgin Ironpants" of *Shame,*
Salman Rushdie's novel about Pakistan, fooled no one on the
Frontier with her Oxbridge English and her calls for "free
elections." Free elections were the war freaks' nightmare: *Why
should those millions of treacherous Punjabis be allowed to decide the
fate of the refugees and mujahidin? No, never.* "Not for another
twenty years should there be free elections in Pakistan," said
one Western relief worker. Many stories circulated about the
things Punjabis said about the Afghans: "They're making so
much trouble for us." "Why don't they just go back home?"
(Never mind that there was a war on, millions of land mines,
and no food.) "It's those refugees who are planting all the
bombs in our cities." (Never mind that the evidence indicated
that it was the Communist authorities in Kabul, through their
Soviet-backed intelligence service, KhAD, who were responsible for the terrorist bombs.)

Zia, with his slicked-back hair, deep-set hypnotic eyes, and
trimmed black mustache, looked like the quintessential Punjabi — touched by the devil. But he was also a tough Islamic
disciplinarian who armed the mujahidin to the teeth. Benazir

would never have come to power had Zia not been killed in an air crash in August 1988, for which KhAD and the KGB likely bear responsibility. As far as the war freaks and the Afghans were concerned, Zia was less a Punjabi than an honorary Pathan.

After just a few weeks on the Northwest Frontier, a Westerner's thinking along such sharp racist lines became natural. The Pathans really were waging a noble struggle. And many Pakistanis really were willing to cave in to Communist terrorism and run for cover behind flowery rationalizations. But as in other places in the Third World where journalists and relief workers inevitably found themselves on one side of a conflict, the border between "clientitis" and outright prejudice against the clients' enemies was crossed too easily.

The journalists who covered the Afghan war regularly were different from any journalists I encountered before. Because traveling in the country was so dangerous, so physically punishing, and because the war rarely made the headlines, those who made going inside a full-time occupation were of necessity either deeply committed to the mujahidin cause or were war freaks who weren't satisfied unless they were in danger and physical distress. Almost all were stringers on special contract or earning a living on a story-by-story basis. Most were weapons enthusiasts; *Soldier of Fortune* was among the most widely read magazines in Peshawar. If you had a story in *S.O.F.,* every journalist in town soon knew about it — and nobody snickered, either.

Journalism in Peshawar was a self-consciously macho activity. Locally based newsmen made a point of smoking a lot and drinking hard. There was a distinct hostility toward the elite establishment media and the new brand of 1980s foreign correspondents who stocked their fridges with Perrier water and talked incessantly about their computer modems — the kind of journalists who came out to Peshawar for short visits, stayed at the deluxe Pearl Continental Hotel rather than at Dean's, directed "hostile" questions at the mujahidin, and never went inside. The objectivity and priggish yuppie values of the establishment media had no place on the Northwest Frontier — a Wild West, sepia-toned outpost of masculinity where it was still possible to escape from the modern world.

Objectivity didn't help you much in Peshawar, and there was a reason for this. Arranging a trip over the border was not always easy, and getting inside on short notice, if an editor in America or Europe requested it, was often exceedingly difficult. Not all of the seven main resistance parties were actively engaged in the fighting, and the most important groups were selective about whom they took in. The mujahidin sized you up. A big expense account and a business card from a world-class newspaper meant nothing to them. They had only two criteria: your physical and mental ability to cope in a war zone and your degree of sympathy for their cause. You had to be trusted. Getting inside all the time, whenever you wanted — which was what the resident stringers were paid to be able to do — required a close personal relationship with a leading figure in a guerrilla group. Since each group was suspicious of every other group, and since everyone in Peshawar knew everyone else, having a close relationship with one resistance organization often precluded a relationship with the others. The result was that most every resident journalist was identified with a particular faction, and the enmities dividing the guerrilla movement were mirrored in the foreign press corps. The situation in the aid community was similar, as relief projects in Afghanistan or the refugee camps in Pakistan depended on cooperation from one or another mujahidin organization. The seating arrangements around the bar at the American Club often told a visitor who was aligned with whom.

Generally, most of the journalists and aid workers in Peshawar were split into two principal factions, with allegiance to the two most militarily powerful guerrilla groups, which in turn reflected the major ethnic division within Afghanistan: that between Pathans and Tajiks. Never mind that because both Pathans and Tajiks were religious Sunni Moslems and operated in different areas of Afghanistan — each isolated from the other — they were rarely in serious conflict during the Soviet phase of the war. Never mind that the leading Pathan commanders tried not to criticize their Tajik allies in the presence of outsiders and that Tajik commanders avoided criticizing Pathans. Each group's foreign supporters observed no such truce. In the dining room or bar at the American Club, where everyone intimately familiar with the war talked in code — using first names and abstruse abbreviations for mujahidin commanders and their parties — a person was quickly identified with one ethnic faction or the other. Subtle hints alone were required, though sometimes they weren't so subtle. One night at dinner, an aid worker said, "Don't ever trust a greasy Tajik. I just hate Tajiks."

No Pathan would ever say a thing like that. Afghanistan was a forgotten war, but among the foreigners risking their lives for the sake of the mujahidin, the conflicts were more noticeable than the camaraderie. In the oppressive, glass-house atmosphere of the frontier town's foreign community, where heat, filth, disease, loneliness, and the constant tedium of dealing with the "brain-dead Punjabis" made tempers flare, supporting the mujahidin cause wasn't enough for many people. You were trusted only if you supported the same faction as your colleague did.

The Tajiks and the Pathans were very different from one another, and so were the foreigners who supported them. The Pathans were by far the more numerous and important group, around which much of the Afghan drama — and my own experiences in particular — revolved. But the Tajiks played a role far out of proportion to their numbers, and many a Western writer was absolutely committed to their superiority over the Pathans as fighters.

The Tajiks, who accounted for roughly a quarter of Afghanistan's prewar population, are the largest minority in the Pathan-dominated country. They are concentrated in northeast Afghanistan and speak Dari, a provincial form of Farsi spoken in the old Persian court. The Tajiks are a typical upwardly mobile minority, who flocked to Kabul in order to become educated and to fill administrative jobs in government and business. Louis Dupree, the foremost specialist on Afghanistan, compares the Tajiks to the Jews and Armenians in their desire for self-improvement. Though twice as many people in Afghanistan speak Pukhtu, the influence of Tajiks in the capital has helped make Dari the lingua franca of the country. In addition to education, the Tajiks have one other advantage over the Pathans: they are not riven by tribalism, but instead are identified with the particular valley in which they live. Of all these valleys, the most important is the Panjshir, a word that in Dari means "five lions."

The Panjshir is a seventy-mile-long strategic corridor in the heart of the Hindu Kush mountains, which every army that has ever invaded Afghanistan from the north has had to cross. The only main entrance to the Panjshir is at its southern end, about sixty-five miles north of Kabul. But there are numerous side valleys, cutting between mountains that soar up to nineteen thousand feet, into which guerrillas can easily escape an invading force. The Panjshir is excellent guerrilla country, and it produced a charismatic mujahidin leader, Ahmad Shah Massoud.

Massoud, who was born around 1950, studied engineering in France and speaks fluent French. The absence of tribalism among Tajiks and their penchant for Western-style organization allowed him, early in the war, to mobilize 3,000 mujahidin regulars along with pools of several thousand part-time partisans. By the end of the 1980s, that combined force would reach an estimated 50,000, the largest single guerrilla army in Afghanistan.

Massoud set up military cadet schools, mujahidin courts, and a tax collection system. The Soviets threw everything they could against him: mines, tanks, and heavy artillery. Carpet bombing and hideous reprisals against civilians were all too frequent; on one occasion, the Soviets lined up six hundred people and crushed them to death with tanks. Each time, however, Massoud and his men, and as many civilians as they could alert in advance, disappeared into the side valleys, sniped at Soviet troops, and eventually drove them back out. This happened seven times in the first half of the 1980s. It was an impressive show, and every journalist and relief worker who was able to penetrate the Panjshir came back to Peshawar singing the praises of Massoud, whom they dubbed "the Lion of the Panjshir."

The guerrilla leader first became known to the outside world through Dr. Laurence Laumonier, a strapping French woman with sparkling blue eyes and a steely resolve, who in July 1980 was the first relief worker to visit the Panjshir after the Soviet invasion the previous winter. Dr. Laumonier alerted French journalists to what was happening, and they filed into the valley to write stories about Massoud, who was able to communicate with them in their own language. Other journalists followed, almost all of them European.

Massoud had a hawk nose, sharp features, and a wiry physique. The adjectives most often applied to him were "wily" and "scrappy." Journalists compared him to Che Guevara and Marshal Tito, and his mujahidin to Castro's Cuban guerrillas. The fact that he represented an ethnic minority and was getting some military aid from the Chinese further increased his allure. Massoud's peculiar characteristics made it easy for left-wing European journalists to support him against the Soviet Union. Because Massoud's Tajik spokesmen in Peshawar were thoroughly Westernized — they spoke foreign languages and

actually arrived on time for appointments — the European
relief agencies, particularly the French and Swedish ones, carried out most of their humanitarian assistance projects in territory controlled by him. Massoud became Europe's favorite
Afghan; spurring his fame was Ken Follett's best seller *Lie
Down with Lions,* the hero of which he based on the Tajik commander.

The Europeans (especially the French) who visited Massoud
had to be tough, or at least a little crazy. The trek into the
Panjshir took up to three weeks on foot. It involved climbing
several Himalayan-style passes and negotiating some of the
most dangerous mine-strewn terrain Afghanistan had to offer. Few Americans — for whatever reason — made the journey, and because Massoud never emerged from inside, few
Americans met him, so they were suspicious of him. As one
Peshawar-based American reporter argued: "Every interview
with Massoud is conducted by a journalist who has just completed a difficult journey to the Panjshir and practically owes
his life to the Tajik commander, and the result is that all the
articles about Massoud have been written in a tone of fawning
adulation."

Massoud's arms relationship with the Chinese added to
American suspicions. Calumnies surfaced about him. For example, one rumor had it that he was rarely in the Panjshir at
all, but was secretly spending much of his time in a luxurious
and secluded Peshawar villa. In the outside world, Massoud
was a hero; in Peshawar, the center of the guerrilla war effort,
he was controversial.

The biggest stone that Massoud's enemies had to throw at
him was his short-lived 1983 cease-fire with the Soviets. He
used the respite to build new supply trails into Pakistan, to
initiate personal contacts with other resistance leaders in the
far north, to train new recruits, and to clean out areas infested
with an extremely radical mujahidin faction that was causing
him and other guerrilla groups trouble. It was time well spent,

and he built his later successes on that period of consolidation. But Massoud's enemies had a point too, if a mean-spirited one: the cease-fire was "a very Tajik thing to do." In other words, it was, in a sense, selfish, since it allowed the Soviets to put more military pressure on the Pathans, who were fighting everywhere else in the country. More important, the cease-fire was a very rational — and worse, a very Western — way of dealing with a superior Soviet force that was razing Afghanistan with the same abandon as the thirteenth-century Mongol hordes.

Tactically speaking, the cease-fire was smart, but it certainly wasn't the way the mujahidin were going to drive the Soviets out. The Pathans would never have considered something so logical and prudent as a temporary truce. It would have been an affront both to their manhood and to Pukhtunwali, their code of honor, whose supreme precept is *badal* — revenge.

So Massoud was the exception to the general reason the Soviets were losing the war: because of the wild, quixotic, completely unreasonable mentality of the Pathans, to whom the whole notion of tactics was anathema because it implied distinctions, and Pathans at war thought only in black and white.

Like the Tajiks, the Pathans also had a great commander. To Abdul Haq's supporters in Peshawar, he, not Ahmad Shah Massoud, was — in the words of a glossy poster with Haq's picture on it — "the Afghan lion." Actually, Abdul Haq wasn't a lion at all. He was a big, friendly bear of a man with black hair, a beard, and an impish smile who had a much more difficult task to accomplish than Massoud.

While Massoud's lair was a valley perfectly laid out for a guerrilla struggle, Abdul Haq stalked the Afghan capital of Kabul and its environs, the center of the Soviet and Afghan Communist power structure, which was packed with government ministries, division-size military bases, KhAD agents, barbed wire fences, checkpoints, and minefields. Haq had to fight an urban war of sabotage, as well as a guerrilla war in the adjacent mountains and villages. This called for even greater organization than Massoud required in the Panjshir Valley. And Haq had to do this with Pathans, who, because of their tribal rivalries, were more difficult to organize than Tajiks.

Yet, compared to Massoud, Abdul Haq had little written about him until the last years of the Soviet occupation. Few knew him well, and those who did were not print journalists. In the early and mid-1980s, Haq moved swiftly and constantly around the Kabul region, stopping briefly in Peshawar every few months in order to straighten out matters of manpower, logistics, and financing. He had family concerns to attend to as well, and those were far more important than his military problems. Haq's family was a highly unusual one, and the Pathan war effort was inextricably tied up with the complicated relationships among its members.

Born in April 1958, Abdul Haq had two older brothers, Abdul Qadir, who was about five years older than Haq, and Din Mohammed, who was ten years older. (Pathans don't use family names, and noms de guerre further complicate matters.) Abdul Qadir was the mujahidin commander of Shinwar, an Afghan district just over the border from the Khyber Pass, on the main route linking Kabul with Pakistan. Din Mohammed was the chief political and administrative operative for Yunus Khalis's Hizb-i-Islami (Party of Islam), one of the two most militarily powerful Afghan resistance organizations. (The other was Jamiat-i-Islami — Islamic Society — which Ahmad Shah Massoud was affiliated with.)

While Jamiat was a Tajik-dominated party, Hizb-i-Islami was the ultimate Pathan party: it presented a facade of Moslem fundamentalism, but in reality it was tribal. Yunus Khalis, a respected Moslem cleric and former schoolteacher, played the role of figurehead and spiritual guide; Din Mohammed ran the party's daily operations. This party, which constituted the strongest mujahidin force in the major cities of Kabul, Jalalabad, and Ghazni, appeared to the uninitiated outsider as one big, disorganized mess.

Hizb-i-Islami had few foreign-language speakers. Its spokesmen rarely kept appointments. Its leaders seemed unable to keep track of one another. Trips inside for journalists, postponed for weeks, often fell through at the last moment. Nor was the party especially interested in help or attention from the Western relief community. The only aid worker whom Hizb-i-Islami appeared to have any regular dealings with was Anne Hurd, an American from Mobile, Alabama, who worked for the Washington-based Mercy Fund. Hurd's friendly Southern accent concealed a tough, militarylike personality that was neither intimated nor discouraged by the party's diffident, fundamentalist exterior. Hurd always took care to "dress up" as if she had a "business appointment in Washington, D.C.," she said. "Even though I'm a woman, the Afghans treat me as an equal because I try to be perceived as being totally outside their culture and range of control." Still, it took her years of daily effort to establish a working relationship with Hizb-i-Islami officials.

To judge by its power, Hizb-i-Islami obviously *worked*. How it did so was a mystery, and because of the difficulties in dealing with its leaders, few foreigners bothered to find out. While the smooth-talking Tajiks at Jamiat headquarters had telephones in working order, clear, positive answers to most requests, and ice-cold Coca-Cola and Fanta on hand, the Pathans at the Hizb-i-Islami office offered only Afghan green tea and words riddled with ambiguity.

Abdul Haq himself was the only exception to the confusion. He spoke English, albeit with a lot of profanities mixed in (courtesy of a Dutch journalist who taught him in the early 1980s). He kept appointments and had a reputation as one of the few mujahidin leaders who had really interesting things to say. It was thought that the forceful impression Haq made on President Ronald Reagan and Prime Minister Margaret Thatcher was pivotal in the subsequent American decision to supply the mujahidin with Stinger missiles in 1986. "I told Mrs. Thatcher," Haq said, "that my great-grandfather and his

father before him fought the British, who invaded Afghanistan to keep the Russians out. So I asked her: Now that the
Russians have finally come, as the British once feared, why are
you so quiet? Why did you send everything a hundred years
ago and yet now you send nothing?"

The Tajiks at Jamiat headquarters spoke in catchy sound-
bite phrases ("In six years we've gone from stones to Stingers"
and "We ask for mine-clearing equipment and our allies give
us coin detectors"); Haq offered substance. Jamiat's people in
Peshawar were just spokesmen; Haq was a commander with a
self-deprecating sense of humor, a good analytical mind, and
a sense of rebellion against his own family and party, all of
whose members seemed very different from him. But Haq
was not usually in Peshawar in the mid-1980s, and he rarely
took journalists inside with him.

It was only because of a terrible injury that I got to know
Abdul Haq and Hizb-i-Islami. It was the kind of accident that
occurred all the time in Afghanistan. Months later, after I
knew him better, Haq told me how it had happened.

It was in early October 1987. At eight thousand feet in the
mountains overlooking Kabul, winter had already come. The
plan was to attack six Soviet targets: the Kabul airfield and
radar station and several military bases north and west of the
capital. On October 11, Haq's particular destination was
Qarga, a lake region that was the site of a golf course used by
foreign diplomats and a major Soviet base. Qarga had once
before been lucky for him: fourteen months earlier, in August
1986, he launched a spectacular raid that destroyed the base's
ammunition dump.

At about 7:15 in the evening, Haq and a forward guerrilla
unit were advancing on Qarga from the west. The Soviets,
perhaps anticipating an attack, had flown over the region several hours before, peppering the bare, eroded mountainside
with butterfly mines. To avoid the mines, the mujahidin took

a detour. It was dark, with strong winds and heavy rain mixed with snow. The mud might have been as deep as two feet in some spots.

"There was a mud trench, about six or seven meters long, which we had to cross to get to the road," Haq told me. "Four or five mujahidin were walking in front of me. There was some shooting and firing nearby, which you know there always is in Afghanistan. Each of us placed our foot into the hole made by the one ahead. Though we took the long way around, we still had to be careful of mines.

"You have to remember how dark and muddy it was. Anyway, because of the mud I did a stupid thing. I slid a few centimeters off the path, something I never did before. Then I saw my boot fly up in the air in front of me. It was like I was dreaming. I was wounded fourteen times before, but this time I really felt nothing at first. I tried to take a few more steps, but then the rocks crushed against the exposed bone and nerves of my right foot and suddenly I got dizzy and fell. I told the major behind me that I needed a tourniquet. When he saw the blood pouring out on the snow he started screaming and all the others came. You see, they were all afraid to touch me because I was their commander. We had no doctor or medical supplies. We Afghans are so stupid sometimes.

"So what did we do? We started arguing. I argued against going back. I said I must write a letter explaining how the operation is to continue without me. But it was difficult to write because it was so dark and cold. I must have been completely delirious."

The men made tourniquets out of a turban and tied them above and below his knee. Haq, who weighed over two hundred pounds, was carried piggyback for almost a mile until someone found a horse. Even with help he had trouble putting his good left foot in the stirrup. "By now there was so much blood and it was snowing harder," Haq said. "All I could think of was how cold I was. On the horse I started vomiting so I had to get off and be carried again." Strangely, he recalled, the pain was less vivid than the cold and the nausea.

Four hours later, Haq was lying on a jute bed in the house of another mujahidin commander in the town of Maidan Shahr (twenty-five miles southwest of Kabul), and the pain was "everywhere." The guerrillas found a local doctor with some sort of knife, but he had no anesthetic and liquor is prohibited under Islamic law. A piece of bone hanging from what remained of his right foot had to be cut. "When the knife hit the bone, that was a bit difficult for me. Mujahidin rubbed my palms to take my mind off the pain. It didn't help much." Haq laughed when he told me this.

Someone took a snapshot of the commander five days later, after he had been transferred to a medical compound in Wardak province run by Médecin du Monde, a Paris-based relief group. Part of his foot had just been amputated by a French-trained Hungarian doctor, a refugee of the 1956 revolution against the Soviets. (This time an anesthetic was available.) In the photograph, Haq is pointing his exposed stump toward the camera and smiling. "Because I knew I lost part of my foot for a logical reason, I felt less depressed," he said to me. "I pity such people who lose limbs in car accidents and other stupid things." Haq was lucky. The mine that wounded him was a pressure-pad mine, a powerful antipersonnel weapon that would have blown off his whole leg or killed him if he had stepped on it directly rather than slid down on it at an angle.

His pain seemed to grow day by day. I rarely saw Haq when he wasn't in some physical discomfort. Always, he would be taking off his Reebok running shoe, fitted with a special plastic shin support, to massage the ball of his foot. I met him for the first time a week after the snapshot was taken. He was drawing deep, wheezing breaths against the pain and sweating in streams. He had just been jammed into the back seat of a car, without any drugs, for a three-hour trip to Islamabad in order to meet with the U.S. ambassador to Pakistan, Arnold Raphel, before being flown to a hospital in Pittsburgh at the U.S. government's expense. There he was to have a second amputation, to remove more bone fragments and damaged nerves. When he got to Pittsburgh he was given painkillers for the first time since his accident.

I sat in the front seat of the car and asked him how he felt. He was told only a few minutes earlier that I was a journalist who wanted to ask him some questions. He had a huge round head covered with short black hair, graying sideburns, and a close, scruffy beard, which partially concealed a mild case of acne. Though he was personally responsible for the deaths of hundreds of Soviet soldiers, his eyes didn't reflect this. Haq's small, dark eyes registered considerable pain, but they weren't jaded, nor were they lifeless or cynical looking. He could have been a Jewish actor hired to play the role of a Third World guerrilla leader.

Speaking was hard for him. Between breaths, he explained that the only thing he wanted to do was return to Afghanistan to fight. It was what every Afghan said when wounded, so the words had little effect on me. He was a burly man but his voice was not deep at all. There was almost nothing about him that was menacing. He thanked me profusely for my concern and I left the car. I was with him for less than five minutes. When I saw him next, three months later, he remembered me instantly and apologized for not having been able to say more.

I had met Palestinian leaders in Syria and Jordan, Polisario leaders in Algeria, Kurdish guerrillas in Iraq and Iran, and Eritrean and Tigrean guerrillas in northern Ethiopia. Most had eyes that appeared to undress you and peer into your innermost secrets. All of them were burdened by an emotional austerity bordering on asceticism which saw individual people only in the abstract, as mere symbols that could be wiped off a board without remorse. The Eritreans were less like this, but they had a sadness and a cynicism that was beyond belief. You couldn't really get to know any of those leaders; it seemed as if there were an invisible, high-voltage field between you and them. You could observe them, and write about them, but you couldn't get to know them.

Abdul Haq emitted no intimidating emotional charge. He threw up no barriers when he spoke. Because he wasn't paranoid, you weren't. With him, at least, you had the feeling that you were innocent until proved guilty.

2

A World of Men

WOMEN ARE OPPRESSED in all Moslem societies. But among the rural Pathans, women simply don't exist. "They're not even in the background. They're just not there," said a Pathan woman who left the Northwest Frontier to live in New Jersey. Here are three Pathan proverbs:

Women have no noses. They will eat shit.
One's own mother and sister are disgusting.
Women belong in the house or in the grave.

You rarely see women on the Northwest Frontier or in Afghanistan; you do see moving tents with narrow holes for the eyes. Photographers who walked through minefields and sneaked into Soviet bases were afraid to take close-ups of Pathan women unless they were at least a hundred yards away and had a lens the size of a mortar — and provided not a single mujahid was looking. A close-up of a Pathan woman was more prized and difficult to get than a photograph of the undercarriage of an MI-24 helicopter gunship.

The only Pathan females I was ever allowed to see were all five years old and younger. Some of those girls were beautiful, with long, dark hair, sharp cheekbones, and doe eyes. What Pathan women look like when they are older is a secret that only Pathan men know.

A desert Arab, after he gets to know you, may invite you to

his home, where you may steal a brief glance at his wife while she serves the food. A Pathan may also invite you to his home, but either he or another man will carry in the food that has been prepared in the women's quarters. The food, in turn, is often the traveler's only clue to the presence of a woman nearby. If the dish is relatively clean and the meal appetizing, it means there is a woman in the adjoining room who cooked it; if the food is inedible, a Pathan man did the deed.

A Pathan won't even tell you the names of his wife and mother. To ask him is an insult. It would be like asking him to undress in front of a crowd. "Women are as private to a Pathan as his private parts," a Pathan lawyer remarked to me. "Women are the holy of holies in a culture where the men act as the barricades." The first time I interviewed Abdul Haq I made the mistake of asking him the names of the men and women in his family. The names of the men he told me. Concerning the women, he blushed and turned away. "I wish you wouldn't ask such personal questions," he said. I felt ridiculous for days afterward and worried whether he would agree to see me again.

The very existence of women in a Pathan's life is an intimate secret, sacred to him but also a source of shame. Women threaten the façade of splendid male isolation that is central to a Pathan's sense of self. A Pathan knows women are needed for procreation, but that is an unfortunate and embarrassing fact to him, and if he could change it, he would. In the Arab world and even in Iran, pregnant women are a common sight. Among the Pathans, one never sees them, for as soon as a woman's womb begins to expand, she is locked away in the house.

After enough time on the Northwest Frontier you forgot about Pathan women altogether. They became invisible. You forgot that the mujahidin had wives and mothers, because you never saw them and the men encouraged you to forget. Only rarely did that other, hidden world break through to the surface, as when a colleague of mine asked Abdul Haq why he always kept his hair short. "Because my mother would slap my face if I grew my hair long," he said, turning his head away, embarrassed.

In Kabul and the other cities of Afghanistan, many women were educated, held proper jobs, and didn't hide themselves in black sheets. That was more because of Westernization than Communist influence. The mujahidin were, for the most part, backwoodsmen, and they suffered no threats or complexities in any of their personal relationships. They inhabited a self-contained world of men, a world of sharp cutouts, where women were held in contempt and the only sure touchstones of masculinity were bravery, the ability to endure physical pain, prowess with a rifle, and the length and thickness of one's beard.

Men without beards were distrusted by the mujahidin. After all, women didn't have beards — and neither, thought the mujahidin, did homosexuals. Nor did the Soviets and their Afghan Communist allies. Nor, for that matter, did the more modern, secular mujahidin within the seven-party resistance — the ones who drank Coca-Cola with journalists at the Pearl Continental Hotel and who were thought to do little of the fighting. In Peshawar, a beard meant credibility. It was striking how many Western journalists and relief workers who had contact with the guerrillas had beards. You would grow one before you arrived in Pakistan and shave it off as soon as you went back home. Once, when I shaved off my beard before leaving Peshawar, a mujahid friend laughed at me and said, "You look like a woman — no, like a Christian!"

The Pathans had no patience with the fine lines or ambiguities of other cultures. Either you were a man or you weren't. It was a barren, stunted vision of life that made sense only under impossible conditions — which was why it flourished in the 1980s. In such a harsh and sterile social environment, male friendships took on an archetypal character, based on the

bread and salt of absolute trust and the respect that could be
earned only by bravery and the willingness to endure terrible
physical hardships. It took a rare kind of individual to be able
to pass through the crucible of Pathan friendship, especially if
the friendship was with someone like Abdul Haq.

In a decade of war, a few foreign journalists managed to
become close friends of Haq. They were the only people he
trusted outside his family and guerrilla organization. Haq
would often agree to meet a journalist only if he was recommended by one of Haq's friends — getting close to the commander meant first getting close to the commander's friends.
By ordinary, conventional standards, none of the journalists
whom Haq considered his friends were well-established pro-
fessionals, and they lacked the clout of other media person-
ages to whom he wouldn't give the time of day. But Haq had
his own ideas about what constituted a good newsman. To
him, a good journalist was a strong, brave man who would
regularly risk his life just as any fighter would. And when it
came to spotting brave men, Abdul Haq was an expert and an
uncanny judge of character.

John Wellesley Gunston did not have a beard, and he was the
only journalist in Peshawar who wore a suit and tie to some
appointments. Of average height and weight, Gunston had a
smiling, cherubic countenance and the pale English complexion that seemed the epitome of youthful innocence and vul-
nerability. No matter whom he was with, his light brown eyes
always sparkled with friendliness and enthusiasm. Gunston
was one man in Peshawar who was not trying to prove himself:
he possessed the absolute self-confidence that came from
being born into a wealthy British colonial family and having
served in the commonwealth's best army units. Unlike other
Westerners in Peshawar, who preferred hiking boots, khaki
pants, and sleeveless military jackets from Banana Republic,
Gunston was a real soldier and was therefore content to dress

as a civilian. In the cowboy environment of the American Club bar, he always wore pressed slacks, a pin-striped shirt, and well-shined loafers.

Gunston was born in July 1962 in Nyasaland (later Malawi), where his father was the local British commissioner in the town of Blantyre. Gunston gave his address on business cards as the Cavalry & Guards Club, one of London's few remaining gentlemen's clubs, where officers, both serving and retired, of Her Majesty's Footguards and the Cavalry can dine together in an atmosphere reminiscent of glories past. Gunston would use such exclusive surroundings to entertain visitors before showing them his personal library of over two thousand books on travel, photography, military history and tactics, and opera. He owned eighty books on Afghanistan alone. Having never finished secondary school, he considered himself self-taught. His room at Dean's Hotel was always littered with good books, lying all over the tables, beds, even the floor. He had a particular affinity for Lord Byron and could recite sections of *Don Juan* and *Childe Harold's Pilgrimage* by heart. Gunston was only twenty-five when I met him, yet he exuded an air of seasoned maturity of the sort that members of the British upper class display like a coat of arms. His passion for Byron may have been his only youthful affectation, but given everything else I knew about him, I never dismissed it as ridiculous.

You couldn't help but like Gunston; for one thing, he genuinely liked everybody else. He could talk for hours on the most banal subjects with embassy mechanics and security officers who probably didn't know who Byron was. If he harbored a trace of condescension toward anyone, I never noticed it. Perhaps it was just good breeding, but he never spoke badly of others behind their backs, even the few people in Peshawar who he knew disliked him. Gunston was like a relic from a bygone era, without the doubts and complexes of most people.

Gunston had lived in Blantyre, Cape Town, Johannesburg, and London before being enrolled, when he was fifteen, at

Harrow, where Byron himself was educated. (Byron wrote poetry atop a grave in St. Mary's churchyard, near the dormitory Gunston would live in.) Harrow was also a family tradition. Gunston's was the fourteenth-oldest Harrovian family, going back to the 1700s.

Gunston lasted a year at the school. "I got bored of studying," he once told me. "I thought it necessary to join up and fight communism in Rhodesia. I was running the British branch of the Save Rhodesia Campaign from Harrow. Politically naïve, I now readily admit, but I was only sixteen. I had a terrible row with my family about it."

Lying about his age, and making use of his father's colonial service connections, Gunston returned to Africa and joined the Police Anti-Terrorist Unit of the British–South African Police, which was founded by Cecil Rhodes. Gunston was one of nine whites and ninety blacks who patrolled an area in the Zambezi escarpment the size of Wales, at the point where Rhodesia, Zambia, and Mozambique met. The man he replaced in the unit had been killed a few days before Gunston joined. In April 1980, after he served in the unit for eighteen months, Rhodesia became the independent state of Zimbabwe. Gunston was given forty-eight hours to leave the country.

He returned to England and a few months later enrolled at the Royal Military Academy at Sandhurst, where, after a six-month course, he was given a short service commission. It was a stormy period. Gunston kept getting into trouble with his weapons instructors. "Their way of teaching was pedantic," he said. "They hadn't seen action, I had."

The next step was a place in the Queen's Household Troops, better known as the Irish Guards, a branch of Her Majesty's Footguards who patrol and troop the colors outside Buckingham Palace. "It was the sort of regiment where you were never asked how much money your father made but how many acres he owned." Gunston's career at the palace came to an abrupt end after two years as a lieutenant when a car he was driving hit a brick wall, resulting in broken ribs, arm, and leg.

Having recovered, at age twenty-one he was offered jobs at a merchant bank and the stock exchange, traditional careers of Irish Guardsmen. Instead, in August 1983, Gunston decided to win his spurs as a war photojournalist. "I was always good at drawing and composition, and it seemed to be one of the few professions where I could make use of my experience as a soldier, get paid, and be on the fringes of history at the same time." Afghanistan in particular had caught his eye for personal reasons. Gunston's step-grandfather, a Colonel Bertie Walker, had commanded a cavalry unit on the Northwest Frontier after the third British-Afghan war of 1919 and was decorated twice. Moreover, Afghanistan seemed like the kind of place where Byron might have turned up. And, like so many Brits, Gunston was enamored of Kipling. In addition to quoting *Don Juan*, he could recite "Arithmetic on the Frontier" by heart.

First Gunston did a little research on Afghanistan at the Institute of Strategic Studies in London, where he learned about a maverick mujahidin leader called Gulbuddin Hekmatyar, who it seemed should be avoided at all costs. Hekmatyar ran Hizb-i-Islami (Party of Islam), an extremist, anti-Western resistance faction that, though it went by the same name as Yunus Khalis's party, shared few of its values. Traveling with Hekmatyar's men, Gunston learned, was not considered wise. They had a reputation for stealing journalists' gear, leaving them stranded in the war zone, and occasionally killing them.

"But, as it happened, two days before I left London on my first trip to the Northwest Frontier, I met a charming old Pakistani major at the Cavalry & Guards Club who gave me a personal introduction to General Fazle Haq, the governor of the Northwest Frontier at the time, who arranged for Hekmatyar to take me inside. I decided to let fate take its course."

The foray had a mad, magical quality to it. Gunston and a

group of Hekmatyar's fighters made it into the center of Kabul in the middle of the night undetected. But the guerrillas couldn't decide whether to aim their mortar and recoilless rifle at the Afghan Defense Ministry or the headquarters of the Soviet High Command, some four hundred yards apart. They asked Gunston what they should do. "I held no strong views either way," he said. Eventually, they picked the Defense Ministry. Then the mujahidin realized that they had neglected to bring a shovel to dig in the mortar and rifle. So they knocked on house doors, waking people up, until they found someone who would lend them a shovel. The mujahidin made a lot of noise digging up the street only twenty yards from the mud wall surrounding the Ministry building. Finally, after shouts of *"Allahu akbar"* (God is great), they opened fire with five bursts of the rifle and a half-dozen mortar shells. A section of the Defense Ministry erupted in flames. With no ammunition left, the guerrillas and Gunston ran away as every Communist position in the area haphazardly opened fire. "It wasn't such a bad trip," Gunston said, and he recalled a stirring snippet from *Childe Harold's Pilgrimage:*

> Perils he sought not, but ne'er shrank to meet:
> The scene was savage, but the scene was new;
> This made the ceaseless toil of travel sweet . . .

The following year, he went back with Hekmatyar's forces. In Laghman province, north of the Kabul–Jalalabad road, Gunston and his escort from Hekmatyar's Hizb-i-Islami were caught in an ambush mounted by Tajiks from Jamiat. In the fracas, Gunston was bayoneted in the leg with the needle-point blade of a Chinese assault rifle by a fourteen-year-old who Gunston claims was "high on dope." Next, his horse was killed by a direct hit from a rocket-propelled grenade. Hekmatyar reported Gunston dead, a fact that the British Foreign Office relayed to his family in England. As it turned out, Gunston was taken prisoner by Jamiat forces and sent to the Panjshir Valley, where he met up with the Lion of the Panjshir, Ahmad Shah Massoud.

"I arrived the unwanted guest of Massoud in June 1984," Gunston recalled. "He was as displeased with my appearance as I was to be there. Those mountains in the Hindu Kush are damned high, and it took ten days of tramping about to find him. I hate mountains! I followed Massoud for a week. He was terribly charismatic, with the same military professionalism I recognized from my army days. He would start after dawn, listening to commanders' problems before leaving for another location four or five hours and another bloody mountain away. Then he would listen to sitreps [situation reports] and give orders, working through the night. All the while there was heavy, high-altitude carpet bombing by Tu-16s. I never established a rapport with Massoud — my French is as bad as my Farsi — though I did manage an interview, printed on the back page of *Newsweek*." It appeared in the magazine on October 8, 1984.

Another positive outcome of his detour in the Panjshir Valley was a photograph that is still Gunston's most famous: of a Soviet MiG pilot who lies dead, parachute collapsed, still in his ejection seat in an open field. The pilot's empty hand is cocked to his head, through which there is a hole, with a heap of brain tissue beside it. Rob Schultheis, in the February 15, 1987, issue of *The Washington Post Magazine,* wrote that "you could see the whole harsh story": the pilot's leg had broken off as his ejection seat cleared the cockpit. In terrible pain, he then shot himself after he landed to avoid falling into the hands of the mujahidin. A guerrilla came along later and stole the pistol from the dead man's hand.

It was an eight-hour trek to the crash site, seven hours of which were uphill, and he had to walk through a field of butterfly mines. "There was still a whiff of aviation fuel in the air, I remember," Gunston told me. "The pilot had been there for several weeks and had turned black in the sun, though the snow had kept his body from decaying. Maggots were eating a hole in his face. I found his radio sigs and MiG-21 instruction book. But damn, the muj wouldn't let me keep it."

Gunston parted company with Massoud and arrived at Hekmatyar's headquarters in Laghman over two months late, sick with hepatitis, and was put under the protection of a Commander Niazi. The next morning, the guerrillas and Gunston were caught in a rocket attack. Niazi was killed. "The program Niazi had arranged for me was now in grave doubt."

To fill the time while new plans were made, the mujahidin took Gunston to photograph the largest Soviet air base in Afghanistan, at Baghram, about thirty-five miles north of Kabul and west of Hekmatyar's base. Gunston took refuge in a deserted house near the main gate. When a squad of Soviet soldiers came out for a run in the direction of the house, Gunston took cover under a mulberry tree in a field close to the runway just as an Antonov-12 troop transport plane came thundering overhead. He began clicking away with his camera. Two Su-17 fighter jets followed close behind. "I started to get clobbered by a shower of stones from gibbering muj anxious to leave. But I was having too much fun," Gunston said and grinned at me, blushing like a little boy, something he did often.

The shots taken at Baghram, along with the one of the dead pilot in the Panjshir, were published as an exclusive in the October 12–18, 1984, issue of the French news weekly *L'Express*. They were the first of what Gunston would later call his "pickies," described by Rob Schultheis, in *The Washington Post Magazine,* as "close-ups of high-tech Soviet bloc equipment, unsuspecting Soviet officers and other ultra-sensitive subjects that must have caused the ulcers to burn at the Kremlin when they appeared in the world press."

Gunston had expected to spend four weeks traveling with Hekmatyar's men. But when he arrived back in Peshawar in

September 1984, he had been inside Afghanistan for five months. The experience only whetted his appetite for more.

It was around this time that Gunston first met Abdul Haq. The two were introduced to each other in the lobby at Green's Hotel. Haq listened silently as Gunston related his experiences, giving names, dates, and descriptions of various weapons and battle formations in the clipped, technical style of an army officer. He talked about how the Soviets used transport aircraft to provide battlefield illumination during night engagements. He went on to describe the actual configurations of the flares. Unlike the other journalists, Gunston was able to judge the fighting ability of the mujahidin as a military professional and was quite direct in his criticisms. "You have a very good memory," Haq told him somewhat cryptically. "Get in touch with me if you want to make more trips inside."

Gunston gave Haq color enlargements of all the pictures he had taken of the Soviet planes at Baghram. Every photograph that Haq put up in his war room was taken by Gunston. Like Gunston's step-grandfather, Haq also had relatives who fought in the third British-Afghan war, in 1919 — but on the other side. The two ribbed each other with tales of their forebears. It was a natural friendship: both men were soldiers. And Gunston was a bit mad, free of Western hang-ups and complexes, and convinced of his own soldierly virtues — just like all Pathans.

Gunston was equally impressed with Haq. "The first time I was able to observe him inside was in May 1985, right after Ramadan had started. It was hot and dusty, and we were traveling constantly. But Haq kept the fast. He never ate or drank during the daylight hours, not even when walking, fighting, or meeting deputations of other commanders. The muj loathed him for this, because it meant that they had to keep the fast as well. But I suppose they respected him too, or at least feared him. Keeping the fast while on the move was something that not even Massoud did."

In February 1988, Haq offered Gunston the ultimate trip inside. No Western journalist had been in Kabul with the mujahidin since 1985. In the mid-1980s, Gunston and several others had been able to penetrate the capital's single security perimeter. Then the Soviets built two more security belts; there were now three checkpoints to pass through, each with barbed wire and minefields. Haq told Gunston not only that he could get him into Kabul but that he could also arrange meetings for him there with the regime's army officers and KhAD agents who were secretly working for the mujahidin. "I know you won't crack up and tell everything if you're caught," Haq told him. Gunston swore it was the first time in his life that he was humbled. "Anyway," Haq added, "if you are caught, you can scream a lot, then you'll be too busy to talk."

It wasn't until late April that Gunston got the go-ahead from Abdul Haq to cross the border. Haq gave Gunston a thirty-eight-year-old former Afghan army major, Syed Hamid, as an escort. In 1984, Hamid had defected from an army transport division in the southern city of Kandahar and joined Yunus Khalis's Hizb-i-Islami, which is how Haq had met him. For the Khalis organization, Hamid was a rare kind of mujahid. He was a dandy who doused himself with Estelle perfume (not knowing it was for women), preferred a trimmed, Pakistani-style mustache to a beard, and was always dressed in a clean, tailor-fit *shalwar kameez* (the traditional Afghan trousers and shirt were loose and baggy). An educated Tajik from around Kabul, Hamid was also a bit of a wheeler-dealer. In a few short years since defecting from the Afghan army he had managed to procure himself a new Honda car and a partial ownership in an Islamabad video rental shop. He had the same qualities that help make a good intelligence agent, and that was why Haq recruited him. Later, Hamid merged his own network of Kabul friends into Haq's much larger underground labyrinth in the capital.

Haq was the only commander in the whole Afghan resistance who was fighting an urban, Beirut-style war, and this required not only the backwoods mujahidin but city slickers like Hamid too. The fact that Hamid was a Tajik meant little to Haq. "I don't give a shit," Haq told me. "I'll take a hardworking Tajik or Turkoman any day over a lazy, stupid Pathan." Haq's chief accountant, who handled all the money for the Kabul underground, was also a Tajik.

Hamid and Gunston crossed the border at Terri-Mangal, a smuggler's town one hundred miles west of the Khyber Pass that was perched at the edge of a salient of Pakistani territory, which brought the pair directly into Logar province, only a three-day trek from the Gardez–Kabul highway. Hamid bought himself a horse for 80,000 afghanis ($400). Gunston walked the whole way.

They reached the vicinity of the highway, patrolled by Soviet paratroopers, at the town of Kolangar, thirty-five miles south of Kabul, where Hamid's Tajik friends from Jamiat gave him and Gunston a place to stay. Here they waited for Haq's vehicle that was supposed to sneak them into Kabul. It was scheduled to arrive within a few days, but more than two weeks went by without any sign of it. They dispatched runners with messages for Haq. Meanwhile Hamid was up to three packs of cigarettes a day, and pushing four, trying to work out alternative schemes. One such scheme involved hiding inside the tank of an empty hijacked gasoline truck with Hamid's cross-eyed brother at the wheel. "I had accompanied a few hare-brained muj missions in the past, but this promised to surpass them all," Gunston later remarked to me. At the time Gunston pleaded with Hamid: "Don't you realize that the fumes would kill us both if we sit inside the petrol tank? And anyway, you can't even stop smoking!" According to Gunston, it was the last taunt, about his smoking habit, that decided Hamid against the idea.

Hamid eventually left for Kabul on his own, using his brother's identity card, to find out what was causing Haq's delay.

Hamid promised to send for Gunston when he arrived. Though the wait was nerve-racking, it was without physical hardships. "Hamid insisted on living well," said Gunston. "When we first got to Kolangar, the food was okay, but Hamid always sent it back, shouting and complaining. Then the food got exceptionally good — for Afghanistan, I mean. The man was nothing if not resourceful. He could stretch the law of hospitality quite far."

Gunston spent three weeks in Kolangar, but Hamid was as good as his word. A civilian sedan finally arrived, driven by an Afghan army major who secretly worked for Abdul Haq. Gunston was stuffed into a specially built secret compartment in the trunk with an air hole and view outside. "The muj kissed a copy of the Koran as we left," Gunston said. "I rather self-consciously crossed myself." Hamid put on a pair of Christian Dior sunglasses and sprayed himself liberally with perfume. He intended to run the gauntlet into Kabul disguised as a rich trader.

On the road to Kabul, the car fell in behind a Soviet convoy of tanks, trucks, artillery, and airborne troops in armored personnel carriers who were firing long bursts of cannon into the surrounding farm area, trying to provide cover for a retreating group of comrades on their way back to the Soviet Union.

After passing through two checkpoints, the car was abruptly flagged down by three Soviet paratroopers led by a junior sergeant with a Lenin badge on his khaki shirt, the kind awarded for meritorious service to the Party. The three, who were on their way out of Afghanistan, offered to sell Gunston's driver a toolbox for 150 afghanis (under $1). Rather than arousing suspicion by giving them the brush-off or buying the toolbox for the asking price, the driver haggled noisily with the paratroopers until he got the price down to 100 afghanis — while Gunston crouched in the secret compartment. "I was shaking with fear," Gunston told me. "I wanted to shout, 'Take it for 150 afghanis, man. Just get us out of here!'" But his fear didn't stop him from snapping away with his camera through the view hole.

At the last checkpoint, Afghan Communist troops were looking under the seats and even unscrewing the door panels of the other cars. But as it turned out, Gunston's driver knew one of the guards, a cousin of a friend, and the vehicle passed into the city without a search.

"At a bus station, an Afghan army major in full uniform greeted us with embraces. We ducked into his waiting Volga staff car — courtesy of the Afghan Ministry of Defense, where the major worked — and drove to the safe house. We were saluted at all the checkpoints. Wearing civilian clothes, I was taken for just another Russian out for a drive with his Afghan comrade."

Hamid, meanwhile, put on a three-piece suit with flared trousers and platform shoes for his clandestine meeting.

One of the safe houses where Gunston was hidden in the capital was right near the Soviet embassy. It was there that he interviewed an Afghan army general and a KhAD captain, both members of Haq's underground. The general gave Gunston a bottle of Russian vodka to take back to Pakistan with him.

The reason the vehicle that was to take Gunston into Kabul had not arrived in Kolangar on time had to do with Abdul Haq's temperamental aide-de-camp, Khairullah. The youngest son of a wealthy Jalalabad trading family, Khairullah had literally been given to Haq as one of the family's many contributions to the *jihad* against the Soviets — in sort of the same way that sons are still given to the church to become monks in Orthodox Christian countries. Khairullah was a tall, elegant, urbanized guerrilla much like Hamid, with wavy, light brown hair and a mustache instead of a beard. Hamid and Khairullah had business dealings together in Pakistan, and they had had a falling out over money prior to Gunston's departure over

the border. Khairullah threw a temper tantrum and deliberately did not send Haq's message to Kabul ordering the car
and driver. With his bear paw of a hand slapping back and
forth across Khairullah's face, Haq later beat the whole tale
out of him in front of an office full of mujahidin. Khairullah
left in tears, utterly humiliated. Beating subordinates in front
of others was something that the big, soft-spoken commander
did frequently.

This episode spoke volumes about the problems Abdul Haq
was encountering, more and more, since the mine injury had
forced him to remain in Peshawar. Unable to communicate
face to face with his Kabul-area network, he was losing his grip
on it. Haq tried to compensate through increased efficiency.
He kept more detailed files on dozens of subcommanders. He
dispatched more messages to the field, using hand-carried
messages and a cipher machine with a complicated number
code he had thought up himself. He had his Tajik accountant
monitor more closely the flow of money that kept the Kabul
front going. Lumbering around his office like an injured foot-
ball linebacker with a nervous, fatigued look on his face, Haq
became compulsive about every facet of organization. He
would send me a written note just to change the time of our
next meeting by fifteen minutes. Such fastidiousness was not
all that common in my own culture, and in the midst of the
chaos of the Pathan world it seemed utterly bizarre.

Haq was not a happy man when I first got to know him. He
confided much more to Gunston than he would to me. Still,
Gunston was close to Haq only as one brave soldier could be to
another.

It hadn't taken Abdul Haq more than a few seconds to see
beyond Gunston's spiffy, boyish exterior to the sterner stuff
beneath. In 1983, after meeting with Savik Shuster, a Lithuanian Jew and former Soviet citizen, Haq, an extremely devout
Moslem at war with the Soviet Union, trusted him enough to
arrange a series of trips inside for him.

"At first, I didn't tell Abdul Haq that I was Jewish," Shuster told me. "I wasn't sure how he would react. When I did tell him, I quickly mentioned that I was an agnostic, that I didn't really believe in God. This second admission made him suddenly angry. 'Now you sound like a Soviet,' he said. So I told him, as kind of an apology, that I questioned everything in life, but that I was prepared to accept the existence of God. Eventually, Abdul Haq learned to live with my disbelief."

Shuster took risks inside that not even Gunston would take. If Gunston had been caught, the Afghan government would have accused him of spying and sent him to Kabul's infamous Pul-i-Charki prison, where he would have experienced several months of terror until the British government struck a behind-the-scenes bargain for his release. Shuster, who had lived in the Soviet Union until he was twenty, would simply have been shot.

"I was scared out of my mind by the things I did, sure." Shuster, who was thirty-five, always talked with the wry, self-questioning grin of an Eastern European intellectual. Growing up in the Soviet Republic of Lithuania had provided him with wisdom and pessimism in abundant amounts. Shuster seemed much older than his years. His eyes had a warm, intimate glow common to exiled Eastern Europeans, whose outer lives have been so restricted that their inner ones have taken on an ornate texture and symbolism that few in the West could approximate. He had dark curly hair, a dark complexion, and thin aviator glasses. Sometimes, because of the way his eyes lit up like sparks whenever he talked, he reminded me of Einstein.

Shuster claimed he did what he did in Afghanistan "out of historical memory." He considered himself a "Lithuanian nationalist." He could draw many parallels between the Soviet rape of his land and the rape of Afghanistan. He recited for me the whole sordid history of how Lithuania was grabbed by Stalin after the 1939 pact with Hitler, then grabbed by Hitler after the Nazis invaded the Soviet Union in 1941, and taken

back by Stalin near the end of the war. Anti-Semitism in Lithuania didn't bother him. Shuster believed that "the true partisans and resistance fighters against the Soviets were not anti-
Semites."

But I knew that Shuster, like most everybody else in Peshawar, had a stated reason for taking risks inside and a real
reason. The stated reason was "Lithuania"; the real reason I
could only guess at.

In the fifteen years since Shuster left the Soviet Union, he
had gone to medical school, worked as a doctor and journalist,
and taught himself French, English, and Italian. He wrote in
English for *Newsweek* and in Russian for his current employer,
Radio Liberty/Radio Free Europe. He had reported from Lebanon, Chad, Nicaragua, and numerous other places. He had
an Italian wife and newborn baby and was studying German.
He was writing two books simultaneously. Like his friend Abdul Haq, he never seemed to sleep, and the two often spent
half the night talking. When Shuster would finally return to
his room at Dean's, Haq would phone him about something
they had forgotten to discuss, or Shuster would phone Haq.
After he went back to Munich, the headquarters for Radio
Liberty, Shuster phoned Haq often.

Shuster took life so seriously that he could only live it in
overdrive. There was an intensity and self-awareness about
him that reminded me of the characters in a Milan Kundera
novel. Like many Eastern Europeans, only with alcohol did
Shuster unwind; his personality then became like that of an
ordinary person when sober.

When Shuster came to Peshawar for two weeks in late May
1988, he produced over a dozen long radio reports, went inside near Kandahar for two days, drank every other night at
the American Club, and helped negotiate a three-way deal
between Abdul Haq, Haq's oldest brother, Din Mohammed,
and the office of Secretary-General Javier Pérez de Cuéllar for
Haq to visit the United Nations. Shuster finished these nego-

tiations at 1:00 on the morning of his departure and dashed out at 1:30 on a three-wheel auto rickshaw to pick up a friend's tape of traditional Afghan music, which he needed for one of his radio shows.

UN officials had told Shuster that they were willing to welcome Haq in New York as a representative of the mujahidin commanders. Haq was willing to go, but only under certain conditions, conditions that were still unacceptable to perhaps the one person on earth whose respect Haq himself psychologically required: that of his oldest brother, the de facto head of Yunus Khalis's Hizb-i-Islami. Din Mohammed was not in favor of Haq's "exposing himself as a politician." Until now, Din Mohammed thought, his younger brother was seen by other Afghans as purely a soldier. It was in that context — or such was the perception in Afghanistan and Peshawar — that Haq had met with President Reagan at the White House in 1985 and with Prime Minister Thatcher in London the following year. At any rate, for all the press coverage these meetings brought, they stirred no controversy among the various mujahidin political factions in Peshawar. Reagan and Thatcher were so friendly to the mujahidin that meetings with them aroused no suspicions. But the United Nations, influenced as it was by the Soviets and their allies, was considered an enemy camp. Meetings with UN officials did arouse suspicions in Peshawar and were the responsibility of politicians, not soldiers. If he now came to be thought of as a politician, Haq could be in danger. Though the commanders and leaders of other resistance parties besides Hizb-i-Islami wanted Haq to represent them, he could never go to New York without his brother's approval. Shuster's challenge was to mediate between the two brothers and convince Din Mohammed that Haq should go to the United Nations.

Abdul Haq's father died when he was still a small boy, making Din Mohammed the family's father figure. He even looked the part. Although Haq, on account of his hefty size, appeared older than his twenty-nine years, Din Mohammed, with a bald head and long gray beard, looked like an old man at forty. And while Din Mohammed, Haq, and the middle brother, Abdul Qadir, had all gone on the *haj,* the pilgrimage to Mecca, only Din Mohammed was always referred to as Haji — Haji Din Mohammed, he was called. It was a title that seemed to suit the crusty graybeard better than it did the other two brothers.

In the 1970s, Din Mohammed had experienced the same trauma as his younger brothers: he watched as his house west of Jalalabad was burned down, his cattle were shot, and the village *mullah* and headmen were taken away to prison for summary execution by Afghan Communists. The soldiers even defecated on the ritually cleansed dishes, the most sacred items in a Moslem household. Unlike Abdul Haq, Din Mohammed seemed truly transformed and hardened by this experience. Whereas Haq, in his role as a field commander, had killed Soviets, he didn't seem to hate with the same fanatical intensity as his brother. "Din Mohammed is a bitter, inflexible man" was a remark I frequently heard from Afghans outside the fundamentalist fold.

I was one of the only reporters ever to talk with Din Mohammed at length, and the experience was disconcerting. For several hours he suffered me. He certainly did not feel comfortable with non-Moslem foreigners, although he would spend long stretches with Shuster, chatting and drinking tea.

Shuster, himself a product of totalitarianism, seemed to think in the same cynical, conspiratorial framework as Din Mohammed. He badgered Din Mohammed with a harsh reality designed to force the Haji's hand, in order to allow Haq to go to the United Nations.

President Zia of Pakistan was conspiring, in early and mid-1988, to make the anti-Western Afghan extremist Gulbuddin Hekmatyar the permanent chairman of the seven-party mujahidin alliance. Hekmatyar, whose three-month term of office as temporary chairman was set to expire, was loathed by all the other party leaders, fundamentalist and moderate alike. He was young, charismatic, highly educated, and power hungry, but his organization lacked fighting ability and squandered much of its resources attacking other guerrilla factions. Hekmatyar wanted personal power first, a mujahidin victory second. He was a Pathan from the northern Afghan province of Badakshan, but his eyes were not those of a Pathan. They resembled an Arab's or Persian's: pellets of hard black ice that never stopped moving unless they were looking down and away from you. A spellbinding demagogue before a crowd, in private he was eerily soft-spoken; his mouth flowed with honey that denied all bad intentions. Hekmatyar was forever calling press conferences, accusing the other parties of selling out to the Soviets while claiming credit for military operations that the other parties had carried out. It was a Peshawar truism that the split in the "hopelessly divided mujahidin" — as the media phrased it — was basically six against one. At times it seemed that the only issue all the factions of Westerners at the American Club could agree on was a hatred of Hekmatyar for "giving the mujahidin a bad name" in the outside world.

Yet Zia favored the thirty-nine-year-old leader. In addition to being a militant fundamentalist like Zia himself, Hekmatyar was a talented politician backed up by almost no grassroots support and no military base inside. He was therefore wholly dependent on Zia's protection and financial largess (courtesy of American taxpayers) for his party's existence. Hekmatyar, a former student leader at Kabul University, was the classic artificial creation of an outside power. But the mujahidin could not openly oppose Zia's choice, because it was Zia's personal support that allowed the guerrillas to operate from Pakistani territory over the opposition of most of his countrymen, who would have gladly cut a deal with the Kabul Communists in return for getting the 3.5 million refugees off their soil. And the price for Zia's protection was a mujahidin leader who was completely subservient to him.

Shuster pleaded his case to Din Mohammed: Abdul Haq and the other alliance leaders were the way around Zia's machinations. By accepting the invitation from Pérez de Cuéllar's office, which Shuster was asked to help relay, Haq could become, overnight, a unifying figure in the mujahidin alliance, overshadowing Hekmatyar and thus blunting the force of Zia's gambit without openly crossing him. Also, at that very moment in mid-1988, Ahmad Shah Massoud was forming a grand alliance of Tajik, Turkoman, and Uzbek commanders all over northern Afghanistan. With the Soviets starting to pull out of the country, it was critical that a Pathan commander get a quick dose of diplomatic legitimacy. It was time, Shuster dared to say to the graybeard Haji, for the Pathans "to stop looking backward to their own suffering and to start showing political ability." And whether Din Mohammed liked it or not, Abdul Haq was already being thought of in Peshawar as a politician, a role for which he had greater talent than several of the seven party leaders.

Even so, Shuster pointed out, whatever took place in New York between Haq and UN officials would probably turn out to be of little relevance, since the United Nations served only Soviet interests. The most important thing was how Abdul Haq's visit would be perceived in Peshawar by the refugees and party leaders. Shuster, ever the realist, was less optimistic about toppling the Kabul regime than anyone else I knew on the Frontier. He desperately wanted Haq to take over the mujahidin alliance because he knew that if Hekmatyar and the Pakistanis continued to run the war, the guerrillas would falter once the Soviet troop withdrawal was completed — which is exactly what happened.

After the final, four-hour session with Shuster, in broken English, Din Mohammed relented. Shuster had merely played back to him the Haji's own private thoughts in a more concise, pointed form. Abdul Haq departed for New York five days after Shuster left Peshawar. Haq's visit to the United Nations helped force Hekmatyar out of the chairman's post in mid-June 1988. This proved, however, to be only a temporary setback for Hekmatyar.

During his last days in Peshawar, Shuster would wait in his hotel room or in the dim, gloomy dining hall at Dean's Hotel for Abdul Haq's driver to fetch him. Haq would be reclining in the back seat of the well-upholstered Toyota Corolla with darkened windows like some mafia don, massaging his injured right foot and moving over to make room for his friend beside him. In the car, Shuster would begin patiently making his case about every nuance of the military and diplomatic struggle facing the mujahidin. Shuster could handle Haq, who occasionally fell into bad moods and acted like a spoiled child — as when he refused to answer calls from the State Department while recovering from his mine injury in the Pittsburgh hospital. (Actually, Haq was convinced that the Americans were trying to kill him. The reason? Since the U.S. government was paying his medical expenses, Washington regulations stipulated that he fly on an American carrier on the last leg of his journey to the United States. In horrible pain, Haq was forced to wait hours at a London airport for a connecting flight.)

Faced with Shuster's arguments, Haq would ease into a smile. He'd make a joke about getting diarrhea from the food at Dean's and ask about the latest gossip in the foreign community. Shuster would in turn loosen up. As though they were on stage, they would look deep into each other's eyes when they talked. There was something a bit pretentious about the way they acted in each other's presence. It was a self-conscious dialogue. Each was aware that the other came from the *other* side, and that was perhaps why, although they argued, they never really fought. What kept the relationship from being a cliché was the fact that they had been together under life-threatening conditions.

In the early years of the war, whenever Abdul Haq was in Peshawar he went everywhere on his motorcycle and ate many of his meals in local Afghan restaurants with a large group of friends. Assassinations by KhAD had later forced him out of public places and into a protected car. His world had narrowed, and consequently Shuster's role in it loomed larger. While John Gunston was the brash, soldierly comrade — the good mate who was forever slapping you on the back — Shuster was a sounding board for ideas with whom Haq could have late-night heart-to-hearts and do what was impossible to do with another Pathan: talk about his fears and vulnerabilities.

Haq felt himself to be a man alone. Even to his older brothers he wouldn't talk about many aspects of his Kabul operation, which he saw as something he created on his own without their help. He spent little time with his wife. Unlike other Pathans, he was satisfied with only two children and didn't want any more — something she couldn't understand. Like other mujahidin commanders I've met, he appeared to view sex as an undisciplined act of self-indulgence — something that Westerners needed, not toughened Pathans like himself. Sometimes he didn't tell his wife when he was leaving Peshawar to go to war inside Afghanistan. At home he smoldered. His wife and other family members feared his temper, which could turn violent. This fear was mixed with awe after his mine injury, when even deliberate pampering by the women in the family failed to soften his disposition. When his sister pleaded with him to talk, he once responded, "What do you know? You're only a woman." The one woman he felt truly at ease with was his mother. He always told her when he was going on *jihad*.

Charles Lindholm, a Columbia University anthropologist who lived for two years in a Pathan village, observed that the Pathans "live within a system which obliges men to present themselves as completely self-reliant. . . . Suspicion, defensiveness, bravery, vengefulness, pride, envy," and "a Hobbesian vision" characterize their world view and interpersonal relationships — meaning, the Pathan can trust no one but an outsider "to fill the role of friend." This was the basis of friendships between British colonial administrators and tribal Pathans in the last century.

At first I dismissed Lindholm's analysis as mere anthropological twaddle. But there was clearly something to it. Haq's men were known to resent their commander's emotional dependence on foreigners, but Haq required these friendships. There was a side of his personality that could find release only with outsiders. He needed contact with values that were vastly different from his own. And this need increased when he was sidelined in Peshawar, recovering from the mine injury, at a time when the Soviets were starting their withdrawal and the war was entering a complex military and diplomatic phase that forced him to think in ways that he was not used to.

By journalistic definition, Haq was a Moslem fundamentalist. He prayed five times a day. He kept the Ramadan fast. He didn't smoke or drink. When traveling, he refused to wear Western clothes or eat Western food: in London to meet Prime Minister Thatcher, he wouldn't eat in a Moslem Lebanese restaurant until the cook assured him that the food was *hallal.* The idea of a free Afghanistan not ruled by Islamic law was anathema to him. The media, and especially American think-tank specialists, sometimes lumped Haq and Hekmatyar together in the same category as "Iranian-style fundamentalists." But with us Haq laughed, made jokes, and liked to gossip. And he was not driven by ideology. He was the only man in all the fundamentalist parties whom the nonfundamentalist Afghans, especially the intellectuals, liked and respected. I kept asking myself whether, in the final analysis, Haq was, in effect, just a military tool of others in the alliance — and in his own family, in particular — who were fundamentalists.

Great as Abdul Haq's need for outside friendships was, he was still a Pathan, and a Kabul-area commander at that. Shus-

ter's closeness to Haq and Din Mohammed was ultimately a
measure of what Shuster had accomplished inside Afghanistan and of the physical risks he had taken. Haq and his
brother never confided anything to Shuster until after he had
made several cross-border forays.

Everything in Peshawar always went back to time spent inside. Whatever other factors influenced a journalist's access to
a mujahidin commander — his personality, his knowledge of
Pukhtu or Dari, his years covering the story, his commitment
to the cause — the reporters closest to the commanders were
those who had performed best under fire. There were no
exceptions. From anywhere in town you could see the brown
Khyber hills. Up there was where it was all taking place. As
long as you didn't go up there, the hills were a constant re-
minder of your fear, your guilt over remaining in Peshawar,
and your burning curiosity about what was happening over
the border. And once you returned from inside, the hills reminded you of how lucky you were to be back in Peshawar. I
really knew nothing about Haq or Gunston or Shuster or
much else about the war that was important until I went into
Afghanistan. Only then did I begin to understand about the
people I was interviewing, and why inside was all that mattered
in a journalist's relationship with a guerrilla commander.

Shuster went over the border with Abdul Haq for the first time
in October 1984. The trip lasted four weeks. The Soviets were
in the midst of an offensive, spearheaded by airborne troops,
to regain swaths of territory in the area south and east of
Kabul. This was around the time a French television reporter
was captured by Communist regime soldiers, when the mujahidin group he had been traveling with fell into an ambush.
Haq's force of three hundred was snaking fast through the
same territory as the Soviets, who were equipped with troop-
carrying helicopters and fighter jet support. Haq and Shuster
were bombed several times by the jets. Because Haq, as the

commander, had to be the last to run for cover, Shuster was forced to crouch beside him in the open, his bowels loosening from fear and bad food. The hardest thing to do was run *toward* a falling projectile, not away from it. Haq had taught Shuster that a bomb always drops at an angle; only by running toward its source are you safe from being hit.

Shuster admitted that he was perpetually frightened of either being killed or being caught. But he could never even start to explain why he persisted in going inside. I didn't buy his Lithuanian nationalism argument, even though he was an intellectual who clearly lacked the macho mentality of other journalists. Shuster seemed determined to earn Haq's respect, as if he knew that he and Haq were destined to be friends and he had no choice in the matter. Once Shuster tried to describe to me how he and Haq had stripped down to their waists and gone swimming in a deserted reservoir east of Kabul with all of Haq's men looking on. "You don't know what it is to be with Abdul Haq at such a moment! . . ." Words deserted him. Perhaps, like the Japanese karate master and the London window cleaner, Shuster was merely acting out a fantasy — another foreign male in the war zone who saw himself as a character in a movie.

But as so often happened on the Northwest Frontier, a great, irrational act of will had made the movie real. Shuster's first trip to Kabul, arranged by Haq in the fall of 1983, was such an act, during which his bravery and ingenuity endeared him forever to Haq, Din Mohammed, and the rest of Yunus Khalis's Hizb-i-Islami.

He and his escort of Haq's mujahidin (Haq himself didn't make the trip) had just climbed to the top of a mountain from where one descends into Kabul from the south. Soviet helicopter activity forced them to wait for four days at the summit, hiding in rock crevices from the snooping gunships constantly patrolling the environs of the capital. After the group finally started to descend into the city at 4:30 P.M. on a mid-October evening, two gunships, flying back from a raid near the Kabul airport, sprayed the ground with their remaining bullets. A few minutes later, Shuster's group was attacked by artillery. Evidently, the helicopter pilots had radioed to government ground posts in the area about the mujahidin presence. "There were explosions all around," Shuster recalled. "The muj lying next to me, an old man, threw a *patou* over both of us, as if the blanket could protect us from the artillery shells. Then he started to pray loudly. I didn't know how to pray, so I just trembled. After the shelling ended, we began walking again.

"Suddenly we heard footsteps in the dark. The mujahidin yelled '*Dresht,*' which means stop. But the sound of someone walking continued. Gun barrels clicked all over the place. There is nothing so frightening as being in a war zone and hearing bullets being slipped into breeches in complete darkness. '*Dresht,*' the muj shouted again. It turned out to be only an old man who didn't hear so well. One of the muj slapped him hard across the face for not identifying himself. Then we continued walking toward Kabul."

A little boy, a member of Abdul Haq's underground, led Shuster into downtown Kabul. Haq had provided his friend with mujahidin bodyguards after Shuster had explained to Haq what he planned on doing once inside the Soviet-occupied capital.

At eleven at night the boy brought Shuster to the house of a guerrilla in the central bazaar, where he had some tea. Shuster said he needed water in order to mix the glue he had brought with him, to paste anti-Communist newspapers on the walls of Mirwas Maidan, a square in the heart of town. He was told not to worry; when he got there, someone would have water for him. Then several mujahidin, armed with Kalashnikov assault rifles and grenades, arrived to accompany him to Mirwas Maidan, with two guerrillas falling out at each street corner to cover the retreat. Shuster and another mujahid were the only ones who weren't armed: they carried plastic bags filled with copies of the newspaper.

"We came to a lighted paved road where we could see groups of government soldiers about a hundred fifty feet away on either side. I asked the muj about the water. They handed me a glass. Can you believe it? One glass of water! I needed several barrels to dissolve the glue." As was the case with Gunston, the men started knocking on doors, waking people up. And again, after making a lot of noise, which the government soldiers ignored — it was they who were the more frightened — the mujahidin found someone who started bringing out kettles of water. Shuster himself glued sixteen copies of the newspaper to the walls around the square, then let the guerrillas do the rest after he was escorted out of the city. All he could say about the experience was that "it was unreal."

The newspapers were forged copies of the four-page Soviet Ministry of Defense daily, *Red Star,* produced in Italy by Shuster in cooperation with several European periodical publishers, including the Italian youth monthly *Frigidaire* (literally, *Freezed News*). The cover design was Shuster's idea. It depicted a Soviet soldier in Afghanistan breaking his Kalashnikov over his knee, exclaiming in Russian, "Stop the war, let's go home" — the same phrase Lenin had used during World War I to get Russian soldiers to desert the czar's army. Inside was a lengthy satire by Vladimir Voinovich, an exiled Russian writer living in Munich, about how a dynasty of cooks had taken over the Red Army and had convinced all the soldiers to withdraw from Afghanistan. That morning, Abdul Haq's subcommander, Abdul Wakhil, had six hundred copies of the newspaper distributed throughout the downtown area, including the lobby of the Intercontinental Hotel.

A few hours later, Soviet troops surrounded the neighborhood of the square, searching all the houses for copies of the paper. Two Afghan regime officers were reportedly shot on account of the incident. The Soviet publication *Literaturnaya*

Gazeta, in an article entitled "Forgers of Newspapers," said the prank was the work of the CIA. The West German weekly *Stern* also wrote a story about the affair in a 1984 issue. "Now you are a real journalist," Abdul Haq told Shuster when he returned to Peshawar. From then on it wasn't a problem for Shuster to see Din Mohammed whenever he wanted.

When I first met Shuster and Gunston, I was having difficulty getting access to Haq. I had originally been recommended to him by another journalist who knew him well, and this was enough for Haq to grant me an interview about once every seven or ten days, which I was not satisfied with. But Shuster and Gunston opened more doors for me, and soon I was with the commander several times a week.

Then one night Haq told me suddenly, "Be ready in the morning. You're going inside."

3

Going up Khyber

IT HAPPENED within the space of a few seconds. Three mujahidin arrived at the door at seven the next morning. Without
speaking, one of them took my rucksack and hid it, along with
the canteen, inside a filthy *patou* (Pathan blanket), which he
tied into a bundle and slung over his shoulder. I gave another
my watch and gold wedding band to hold until we crossed the
last Pakistani checkpoint. "Bob," said the one who would be
my interpreter, "from now on, your name will be Babar Khan."
I nodded. Then the four of us, all dressed the same, left.
Abrupt as that.

We jammed into a horse-drawn tonga. Bumping along in
the back seat as the road unrolled below me, I felt the sudden
exhilaration of total freedom and total loss. I was vulnerable
in a way I had never been before. But I also felt the security
that rests in anonymity, the sensation familiar to army recruits
of being welded to something sturdier than the self you are
giving up.

This was a false and temporary notion. It took no time at all
to find out how different I was from the young men I was with.

The mujahidin paid the tonga driver 5 rupees (30 cents) as
we jumped off the creaking carriage and onto a slow-moving
bus, painted in garish psychedelic designs and rebuilt from
the battered carcass of a Bedford truck. Inside, the bus was a
scarred shell of sharp, twisted metal and plastic seat cushions
running with sweat. I stumbled to the rear, where my handlers

packed me among a crowd of refugees and their squawking chickens. With my dark complexion and new beard, I caught only a few sideward glances. I felt almost invisible.

The bus rambled straight ahead on a flat table of increasingly dry earth that bred nothing, it seemed, except a rash of cinder block and mud brick shanties inhabited by refugees. The throngs of people and roadside stalls gradually thinned as the wall of mountains came closer. At the edge of the plain, just past the stone gate with the inscription from Kipling's "Arithmetic on the Frontier," stood the tan battlements of Jamrud Fort, built by the Sikh governor of Peshawar, Hari Singh, in 1836 to defend the entrance to the Pass. It was like a stage set for *Gunga Din*.

Then, quickly, the earth heaved upward, and what had minutes before seemed like a solitary sandstone wall disintegrated into a labyrinth of scooped-out riverbeds and folds reflecting the dull soldierly hues of gunmetal gray and plankton green. I had the sensation of being trapped in a tunnel. Topping each rise was a slash of red or ocher as the sun caught a higher, steeper slope at a different angle. Lifts of cooler air penetrated the bus, momentarily drying my sweat — my first fresh taste of the mountains after the gauzy heat film of Peshawar. The machine-gun rhythm of Pakistani popular music filled my ears as the winding bed of a Kabul River tributary led to a series of long, slowly rising switchbacks that constituted the heart of the twenty-five-mile-long Khyber Pass.

Disguised as a Pathan in this metal crate hurtling upward toward Afghanistan, I thought it was hard not to be a little impressed with myself. But I had just showered and eaten a hearty breakfast. I doubted that I would feel the same after two weeks of bad food and little sleep.

By themselves, the dimensions of the Khyber Pass are not impressive. The highest peak in the area is under seven thousand feet, and the rise is never steep. What makes the Pass spectacular is sheer scenery, historical association, and a present-day reality every bit as gripping and dangerous as in former epochs. Perhaps nowhere else on the planet are the cultural, climatic, and topographic changes quite so swift and theatrical. In a world of arbitrary boundaries, here is one border region that lives up to the definition.

In the space of forty minutes you are transported through a confined, volcanic nether world of crags and winding canyons, from the lush, tropical floor of India to the cool, tonsured wastes of middle Asia; from a world of black soil, bold fabrics, and rich, spicy cuisine to one of sand, coarse wool, and goat meat. And some would add: from a land of subtle, slippery justifications to one of hard, upright decision.

Alexander the Great, accompanied by his teenage Bactrian bride, Roxanne, must have experienced this very sensation as he came down into India (Hindustan) near the Malakand Pass, sixty miles north of here, in the early winter of 327 B.C. Some of Alexander's troops, under the command of his most trusted general, Hephaestion, trekked through these same Khyber defiles. So did Babur, the sixteenth-century Mongol king and descendant of Tamurlane, who had lost his father's central Asian kingdom as a young man, but before his death had conquered Kabul and Delhi and founded the great Moghul dynasty. Babur was a poet, whose fantastically detailed memoirs, the *Babur-nama*, exude a sensitive, lyric intensity that captures the awe and pain of travel in this part of the world. (On finding a cave in the middle of a blizzard in the first days of January 1507, he wrote: "People brought out their rations, cold meat, parched grain, whatever they had. From such cold and tumult to a place so warm, cozy and quiet!")

Though he conquered India, Babur preferred Afghanistan; his conquest of Kabul in 1504 had marked the turning point in his fortunes. And it was to Kabul, his favorite city, that his body was taken. He lies now under a garden of mulberry trees on the outskirts of the Afghan capital, in a marble mon-

ument built in the following century by Shah Jahan, the Moghul emperor responsible for the Taj Mahal. For the handful
of journalists and relief workers in Peshawar enamored of
such stuff, Babur's marble tomb loomed as the longed-for
summit of their Frontier odysseys, where, under the shade of
that mulberry arbor, they would one day rest their dirty, fatigued bodies and read Babur's poetry after having witnessed
— they hoped — the mujahidin conquest of Kabul: "*O Babur!
dream of your luck when your Feast is the meeting, your New-year the
face; For better than that could not be with a hundred New-years and
Bairams.*" Like Babur, some of us measured happiness by how
close we were to going up Khyber for the last time.

The British first marched up the Khyber Pass in 1839, on
their way to the first Afghan war, which was to end in disaster
three years later with the massacre of every soldier save one, a
Dr. William Brydon, who lived to tell the story. The British
came back up the Pass in 1878 and again were forced by the
Afghans to withdraw. The graves of British soldiers killed in
the second Afghan war lie near the Masjid Mosque by the top
of the Pass. Each time, the British lost hundreds of men just
fighting their way through the Khyber territory, controlled by
the Afridis, a tribal branch of the Pathans who since antiquity
have served the function of "guardians of the Pass."

In 1897, the British had to dispatch forty thousand troops
to this area just to quell an Afridi uprising and regain control
of the Pass. Alexander and Babur also fought pitched battles
with the Afridis. It is these tribesmen, numbering over
300,000 in their mud brick redoubts that dot the hills of the
Khyber Tribal Agency, who have given the Khyber Pass its
allure of danger and epic drama throughout history — and
never more so than in the 1980s.

In *The Pathans* by Sir Olaf Caroe, the definitive work on the
subject, the author provides evidence that the Aparutai, mentioned by the fifth century B.C. Greek historian Herodotus, are
the ancestors of the Afridis of today. (As Caroe writes, the

names sound similar when one recognizes that the Afridis, like other Pathans, "habitually change *f* into *p*.") The Afridis are also generally thought to have more ancient Greek blood than other Pathans who intermixed with Alexander's soldiers, evinced by their sharp features and fairer complexions. They dress differently too: you can always spot an Afridi by his turban, wrapped tightly with an ostentatious bow around a bulbous red hat, called a *kullah*.

But these are all minutiae.

What really sets the Afridis apart from other Pathans is their deliciously devious, amoral character — a legacy of the physical landscape of the Northwest Frontier and the Khyber Pass in particular. Unlike other regions of the Frontier and eastern Afghanistan, the Khyber area has no arable land. Through these poor, barren defiles, conquerors from time immemorial have come to steal the wealth of the subcontinent. So the Afridis learned to play the only card they had: their power to murder, ambush, and in general make life hell for any invading army. What they have essentially said to everyone was: Rather than kill you, all we ask is that you share a certain portion of your wealth with us. And to their fellow Pathans in the Afghan resistance the Afridis' attitude was: You fight the Russians, so they go after you but kill us too. So you must give us something in return. There had been frequent, violent clashes between the mujahidin and the Afridis. The Afridis were bristling with arms. They controlled the weapons trade at Darra, and in addition were supplied with guns by KhAD as a reward for fighting the guerrillas. So it had become more dangerous than ever to trek through Afridi territory on the way into Afghanistan, as I planned to do.

Smuggling, as well as bribes and thievery, was a source of income for the Afridis. A quarter of a century ago the Afridis in the Khyber Agency were among the poorest tribes in Pakistan. They had little to eat and were forced to weave shoes from grass. Their situation improved when they got involved in running Russian consumer appliances from Soviet-occupied Afghanistan into Pakistan. (A smuggled Russian air conditioner cost $300 in Peshawar; an Italian or Japanese one was four to five times the price.) But real fortunes were made with heroin, which, following the Islamic revolution in Iran, became the Khyber Agency's main business. The Afridis set up laboratories in hillside caves, where they organized smuggling caravans to bring the heroin to Pakistani ports. They often bribed police at the various Khyber Pass checkpoints. Unlike other Pathans, the Afridis have managed to keep their fundamentalist beliefs and their livelihood in two separate, airtight mental compartments. A Pakistani government official explained: "To them, nothing is immoral when you are making money." Often an Afridi will interrupt a drug sale if it is prayer time. Afridi merchants always close drug deals with the words "May God be with you."

The long, buff walls of the British-built Shagai Fort, now manned by the Khyber Rifles, came into view as our bus mounted the first of a series of plateaus. I was not impressed. These Pakistani troops, despite their drums, sashes, and breast-beating tradition earned during the time of the Raj, were not able to hold more than twenty yards on either side of the highway. Beyond that, permission was needed from the heavily armed Afridi tribesmen in order to pass. The real power here lay within the even higher, longer walls of the fortresses that appeared farther up the road: the homes of the wealthiest Afridi *khans* (large landowners), not a few of whom were implicated in the international drug trade.

Every few miles I saw a military checkpoint, where a Pakistani soldier would mount the bus, cast a quick glance at anyone or anything that looked suspicious, and then wave the bus on. I instinctively looked down and away: Never ever establish eye contact with a border guard. It was one of a reporter's more mundane nightmares out here that he would be pulled off a bus before even entering Afghanistan and be humiliated in the eyes of his colleagues and editors. This happened periodically to journalists in the course of the war, because the attitude of the Pakistani authorities was much more ambivalent than President Zia's open support of the mujahidin suggested. Many in the lower reaches of the Pakistani security services did not share Zia's enthusiasm for the resistance. Even Zia, though he was willing to help the mujahidin, did not want to be seen in the eyes of the Soviets as allowing Western journalists to cross an international border illegally in order to cover the war from the guerrilla side.

We got off the bus at Landi Kotal. We were still a few miles from the last Pakistani checkpoint and the thinly manned Afghan border post at Torcham. But that was not where we were planning to cross the border, and whatever the diplomats might believe, Landi Kotal was no longer in Pakistan. The air was cleaner and colder, and, as in Darra, I heard the constant sound of rifles going off. The streets were packed with mujahidin and Afridi cutthroats, who, in contrast to what I saw in Peshawar, were now armed. In the reeling jumble of fire-trap market stalls hashish and heroin could be purchased openly. Just behind the main road began a maze of high mud brick walls with imposing iron gates, which concealed warehouses full of guns, dope, electric appliances, and liquor, all destined for Zia's booze-free Islamic republic. This was a lawless smuggler's town and, more than any other spot on the Northwest Frontier, the nerve center of the most ambitious CIA arms program since the Vietnam war. But distinct from other Third World arms and drug bazaars where intelligence agencies operate and square off — Beirut and the Honduran border towns, for example — Landi Kotal gave no quarter to the demented affectations of the video age. There were no ghetto blasters, squealing tires of expensive cars, evil posters of rock stars and Ayatollah Khomeini, or gangs of teenage youths in tight-fitting khaki fatigues and gold chains around their necks.

Landi Kotal may have been bad, but it wasn't deranged. The town's Kiplingesque charm just couldn't be ignored; there was something almost wholesome about it.

Before the mujahidin hustled me off the main street and toward their local headquarters, I caught a brief glimpse of a railhead, where the Khyber Pass local used to start its run through no less than thirty-four tunnels down to Peshawar, until 1986 when the train was bombed by KhAD and the Pakistanis decided to stop the service. Paul Theroux devoted a chapter in *The Great Railway Bazaar* to this now-defunct train, which he described as a "pleasure" and an "engineering marvel." He wondered about the danger faced by Pakistan from a Soviet-backed Afghan government — this was written four years before the appearance of a Communist regime in Kabul and six years before the war.

The iron door of a warehouse creaked open slightly, revealing a pair of suspicious eyes. We exchanged some words with the watchman and were quickly ushered in without the gate opening more than a few inches. As it was being bolted behind us, I saw we were in a courtyard about the size of a baseball diamond enclosed by high mud brick walls and smelling of dried mud, dung, urine, and gun oil. For a second it reminded me of an Ottoman caravansary out of a nineteenth-century Edward Lear watercolor of the Holy Land. American-supplied, Soviet-made Kalashnikov assault rifles were stacked in the far corner along with new bayonets, banana-clip magazines for 7.62 mm bullets, and crates of ammunition. An old man in a *shalwar kameez* and turban sat on a rush mat beside the weaponry, making notes in a ledger. He jumped up and embraced each of us with the greeting *"Salaam aleikum"* (Peace be upon you). We removed our shoes before entering a dark, mud-walled room with a wooden table in the corner, crowded with neat piles of stationery, and sat around a carpet on the floor.

This was the Landi Kotal headquarters of Yunus Khalis's

Hizb-i-Islami. A blurry photo of Khalis appeared on a calendar hanging above me, and for the first time I found myself focusing on him as the mujahidin around me mumbled "Maulvi Khalis" this and "Maulvi Khalis" that (*maulvi*, in Pukhtu, means an Islamic scholar, a high-ranking *imam*). Though in reality a figurehead for a party that was run and controlled by Abdul Haq's family, Khalis was the most respected of the seven Afghan resistance party leaders in Peshawar, the only one of an otherwise pathetic, squabbling bunch who was not thought of as a politician but as a mujahid. And though a fundamentalist, Khalis, unlike Gulbuddin Hekmatyar, was truly respected by the moderate factions of the resistance. Everyone knew that he was the only resistance leader who spent much of his time — sometimes weeks on end — inside, living in the same awful and dangerous conditions as his troops. The other party leaders, especially Hekmatyar, went inside for "photo ops" and were out again within twenty-four hours.

Khalis, in his late sixties, was a lively character with a sense of humor, a trait that prevented him from being perceived as an Afghan version of Ayatollah Khomeini. Abdul Haq once told me a story about Khalis. In the first year of the war, when the mujahidin were fighting without any American aid and were so poor that they couldn't even afford mules, Khalis, then sixty, was trekking with Haq in the deep snow and had to be helped down a hill on a makeshift sled. At the bottom, his face covered with snow, Khalis laughed and said, "My watch is broken. It cost me two thousand rupees. This *jihad* is getting expensive."

Khalis was loved by every guerrilla, from Abdul Haq and Din Mohammed on down. Khalis was a figurehead only because of his age and lack of interest in details, not because he had been jostled aside in a power struggle. For the young mujahidin accompanying me, the personal example set by "Maulvi Khalis" carried great significance in their lives.

Khalis had given the Hizb-i-Islami its Spartan, no-frills, country-bumpkin personality. The party in Peshawar was so unsophisticated that it practically didn't exist as a political organization at all, but rather as a political front for a purely military organization — which is why it was powerful and well positioned inside while being underestimated by diplomats and journalists in Pakistan. Among reporters, it was not a particularly well-recommended group to travel with. Though the "Khalis muj" were respected as experienced, trustworthy fighters who were not likely to blunder into an ambush or minefield, they rarely provided interpreters and disdained the occasional tin of beef or powdered soup — the kinds of items that kept your spirits up on the march and prevented you from becoming sick, and which other factions stocked in their military camps for visiting journalists and relief workers. A Jamiat commander in eastern Afghanistan, for example, not only stocked coffee, soft drinks, and canned food but had a video-cassette player as well. Khalis's men wouldn't know what a videotape was, and even in Peshawar never offered you anything to drink except tea and water, and the water was sometimes foul.

At least I had an interpreter, specially assigned to me by Abdul Haq's middle brother, Abdul Qadir. Qadir was the chief commander in Shinwar, a district in Nangarhar province that was just over the border from Landi Kotal. The warehouse to which I had been brought and the mujahidin that had been accompanying me were under his command.

My interpreter, Wakhil Abdul Bedar, a twenty-five-year-old refugee from the village of Adah near Jalalabad, had graduated from an Islamic academy. He considered himself a *mullah*, and instead of a turban or *pakol* (a traditional flat woolen cap) he wore a knitted white prayer cap. Wakhil was the most laid-back *mullah* you could imagine. He smiled, laughed, and made jokes all the time. He was short for an Afghan, and not particularly rugged looking. Measured alongside the other mujahidin, Wakhil certainly seemed vulnerable. His brown spaniel eyes betrayed an underlying sadness and preoccupation at odds with his good humor. He was a tender soul, and it wasn't until we were back in Peshawar that I was able to coax his story from him.

Wakhil had been a student at a *madrassa* (religious school) near Jalalabad. He left Afghanistan in 1979, prior to the Soviet invasion, after having served a short term in prison for refusing, along with other *madrassa* students, to sing in honor of the Marxist ruler of Afghanistan at the time, Nur Mohammed Taraki. But Wakhil had more recently suffered a tragedy worse than imprisonment that had also helped propel him to Pakistan: his father had deserted his family to work in a restaurant in Iran, leaving Wakhil alone with his mother and younger brothers. I can only guess how deeply this affected Wakhil. Pathan men look upon their dependents — particularly their wives — as possessions so private that few others may even know their names. To desert them and leave them exposed to shame and suffering is nearly unheard of. Though Afghanistan at the end of the 1970s was becoming increasingly repressive, especially for a former political prisoner, Wakhil equally needed to escape the humiliation of what his father had done to him.

Wakhil came alone to Peshawar, where he stayed at an uncle's house. After finding temporary work painting cars, he sent for his mother and younger brothers. Eventually, he went looking for the Hizb-i-Islami office — an obvious decision, since Yunus Khalis had been a well-known figure in Jalalabad religious circles when Wakhil was a student there.

"It's right over there in our house. Come, I'll take you," said a broad, imposing fellow who towered over Wakhil and introduced himself as Abdul Haq. Haq, twenty-two at the time, had already established a reputation as a leading guerrilla commander and was an instinctive judge of character, aware that everyone, even a "little guy" like Wakhil, had a value to the resistance. Haq took the eighteen-year-old under his wing and got him a job as an aide to Khalis in the offices of the seven-party alliance. Wakhil also had an opportunity to attend the *madrassa* in Peshawar and take courses in English. He saw Haq infrequently after that, but like many people considered himself close to the commander, whom he clearly idolized. When I met Wakhil in 1987, he was working for Abdul Qadir and married with three children. He supported them, in addition to his mother and younger brothers, on a salary of 800 rupees ($45) a month, plus a cost of living subsidy, from Hizb-i-Islami. It was the same salary the party paid all its members, from field commanders to night watchmen in Peshawar.

Wakhil sat with the other men and negotiated the price of a mule while we ate a meal of grilled goat kebab, flat bread, and curd washed down with green tea and a gooey Afghani sweet called *nakal*. The meat was nearly hidden in a pool of grease and for all I knew could have been putrefying for hours in the hot sun with flies dancing on it. But it was doubtless the tastiest and cleanest food I was going to get for some time. I ate heartily, sopping up the grease with my bread.

One mujahid gave a letter to Wakhil, laboriously handwritten in Pukhtu on Hizb-i-Islami stationery, stating who I was and where I was to be taken. My two bodyguards signed for their rifles and ammunition in a ledger. Either Wakhil wasn't a skilled negotiator or at that moment there truly were no mules to spare for so trivial a task as transporting a soft, spoiled journalist and his fashionable new rucksack into Afghanistan. (Wakhil, like all other Afghans, brought nothing with him except a *patou* and the clothes on his back.) ·

Jihan-zeb and Lurang, my bodyguards, were in their mid-twenties, like Wakhil, and had wives and children living in Pakistani refugee camps. Jihan-zeb had some missing teeth and only one eye; the other he had lost in 1984 in a mine explosion. But he had a ready smile and seemed desperate to communicate with me. Lurang, in contrast, had a handsome face with dark, perfectly sculpted features and good teeth — another Hollywood actor playing the part of a Third World guerrilla. But Lurang was sullen, not happy at all about this situation. He sized me up for what I was: another burdensome foreigner who was going to get sick, slow down the pace, and end up doing nothing of provable importance to the war effort. Whatever it was I did, he didn't understand and he didn't care to. After all, I didn't have a gun and I wasn't supplying guns. I was without a proper camera with those wondrously large lenses that other, obviously more impressive foreigners carried.

After a few minutes of walking we left the last telephone pole behind us and descended into a bald, windswept tableland scorched the color of zinc that reminded me of the Judean wilderness. The earth cambered as my sweat-rinsed eyes worked to adjust to the dazzling white sunlight. There wasn't a tree or a water source in view. I was careful to offer my canteen to the others before I drank, but they refused it with such a contemptuous flick of the wrist that I never offered again, and neither did they ask. They watched me drink with gaping, dumfounded eyes, as though I were a creature from another planet whose physiological composition was strange and incomprehensible to them.

I asked how far it was to the Afghan border.

"A few hours," said Jihan-zeb to Wakhil, who translated.

It would turn out to be a very foolish question.

We marched quickly for over an hour before the plateau collapsed into a nest of canyons whose floors were carpeted with sharp rocks and pebbles that threatened to turn your ankle at every step. Suddenly a sprained ankle became the most terrifying of the many pathetic little nightmares that flashed through my mind as I stumbled beside the soaring walls of the canyon we were following.

Journalists had dubbed this and other tracks leading into

Afghanistan "the *jihad* trail." Soon we began to meet small groups of mujahidin coming out of the war zone in the other direction. As they passed us on the road, the men embraced one another with a studied passion I had never seen before. All over the Moslem world, strangers greet each other with calls of *Salaam aleikum* and a partial, perfunctory grip of the hands on the other man's shoulders. But here the squeezes were tight, and followed by a deep, longing look in the eyes. The sufferings of war, coupled with the bonds of male friendship among the Pathans, had broken down the psychological barriers that normally existed between strangers. They were transmitting real emotion dozens of times a day. And though my new beard, new clothes, rucksack, and lack of a gun instantly betrayed me as a foreigner to these men, just the fact that I was with them on this trail earned me an embrace, which I was expected to return with equal force. Now I saw myself as even more of an imposter. I was not worthy of the trust that such a display of feeling bestowed. No matter what I chose to tell myself or others, deep within me I knew I was there solely out of professional ambition. Without my realizing it, the mujahidin had made me contemptuous of myself.

I hugged the shade cast by the silvery black granite walls and leaped across the patches of painful sunlight as though they were rushing streams. My canteen was empty, but out of shame I dared not ask where I could fill it. After another forty-five minutes of marching, Jihan-zeb casually walked over to a hollow in the rocks, cupped his hands, and withdrew a mouthful of water, which he slurped while observing me with an impish smile. It was barely a trickle, and it took a full two minutes to fill up the plastic canteen, but it was clear and clean and ice cold — the best I had ever tasted, it seemed to me then. Jihan-zeb and Wakhil laughed as I drank up the contents of the canteen before filling it a second time. Each of them had taken only a single mouthful. Lurang gave me a disapproving stare: he hadn't drunk at all.

It was only a short walk before we reached another, more plentiful spring at the foot of a mountain bearded with thorns and lichen. "Rest and drink all you can," advised Wakhil. "It will be the last good water for a while."

It was about three in the afternoon when we started up the mountain. At first the climb was easy, but by the time we neared the seven-thousand-foot summit I was sweating and out of breath. The view from the top, like many scenes I was to see, was one of both beauty and horror. Ahead, unfurled below us, was a dust-wrapped, sulfurous plain marked by landslides and vibrating with intense heat. It billowed on for miles before finally rising into a wave of cathedrallike mountains that towered above the mere hill I had, with some difficulty, just scaled.

"There's water down there?" I asked Wakhil, already losing my discipline.

"Yes, but we must walk for some hours first."

"And where does Afghanistan begin?" I asked.

"After some hours will be Afghanistan, *inshallah* [God willing]," Wakhil said, hesitating. He probably never thought about the border in such terms.

"How many more hours?"

"Oh, I don't know that question." Wakhil smiled and turned up his palms, as though I had asked him to explain the meaning of a difficult Koranic parable.

We descended into the plain known as the Valley of Tirah Bazaar, the sanctum sanctorum of the Afridis — several hundred square miles of butchered, cursed terrain southwest of the Khyber Pass that few foreigners ever really penetrated, except to slip through surreptitiously.

"You know some Arabic," Wakhil stated.

I had told him that I had studied the language briefly in Egypt.

"Good. Then you will tell anyone who asks us on the road that you are an Arab. They cannot know that you are Ameri-

can. Otherwise do not talk or take pictures or look at anyone.
And don't ask for water. Afridi people — bad people, like
dogs. They are the agents of Najib [the Afghan Communist
ruler]," said Wakhil, lobbing a thick gob of spit on the ground,
as if to emphasize his disgust with the people we were about to
encounter.

Jihan-zeb just smiled and placed his finger over his lips,
warning me not to talk, then took my rucksack to carry. I was
grateful. (The rule among journalists was that if the mujahidin
offer to carry your pack, don't be a hero — accept the help. If
you refuse, later on when you really do need help, they might
not offer.)

They are "amongst the most miserable and brutal creatures of
the earth," wrote Winston Churchill in 1897, referring mainly
to the Tirah Afridis, after they had littered this plain with the
bodies of hundreds of British soldiers. "Their intelligence only
enables them to be more cruel, more dangerous, more de-
structive than wild beasts."

Of all the difficult places on the Northwest Frontier that the
British had to control, Tirah gave them the most trouble.
Their running battle with the local Afridis over safe-conduct
and the trade in weapons was never won, and occasionally the
Afridis would resort to such outrages as the kidnapping of a
seventeen-year-old English girl. Molly Ellis was abducted on
April 14, 1923, and released unharmed several days later, after the British had burned down the village of the kidnapper,
one Ajab Khan, who was a suspect in the murder of an English
couple three years earlier. Kidnappings still occurred here,
and that was why I had to be smuggled in and out of Tirah as
quickly as possible: an American journalist would require an
exorbitant ransom.

The greater Tirah was divided into two smaller valleys, the
Maidan and the Bazaar. The Bazaar was so named by the
British because of a tribal market there, which might not have

contained more than a few stalls. It was the more remote and inaccessible of the two, and in it tribal law still applied: there have been actual cases of adulterers being stoned to death in the 1980s. In 1984, a twelve-year-old boy was ordered by a tribal *jirga* (council) to execute a grown man who was the proven killer of his father. In an area not far away, after two teenagers had tried to elope, a *jirga* ordered the girl's father to shoot the boy and the boy's father to shoot the girl, and thus the matter was settled.

The Valley of Tirah Bazaar lived in a time warp. At least inside Afghanistan the population had been introduced, however rudely, to the modern world through the Soviet invasion and the refugee migrations and influx of Western-supplied weapons it provoked. But the Bazaar Valley, without a usable road until 1988, remained untouched. The mujahidin, the Afghan Communist regime, and the Pakistani government dealt with its miserably poor Afridi inhabitants exactly as the British had: through a pattern of raids, bribes, threats, and negotiations. "In these remote valleys, even more so than on Hadrian's wall in Britain, a thousand years pass as a dream," wrote Sir Olaf Caroe. "It has been but the fashion of arms that changes; Lee-Enfield going back to carbine, carbine to jezail, and jezail to bows and arrows."

The first sensation I had upon entering the valley was a pleasant one: that of being washed by soft, fresh breezes rolling over a yellow-green steppe. On each side of us as we plodded through fields of tall, withered grass was a long, low wall of chocolate-black hills. In the distance, like a two-dimensional cutout, was a crude mud brick fort with a square tower leaning slightly to one side as though it might tip over. I was tired, thirsty, and hungry, and the closer we came to that leaning tower, the farther away it seemed. Then suddenly we were passing it, and other mud brick forts — exactly like the first one and painted a fabulous golden yellow by the late afternoon sun — loomed ahead, punctuating the bleak, abstract land-

scape. The shrill sound of the wind in the grass was strangely
deafening in the otherwise silent terrain. The grass thinned
away and we were encased in a mist of fine dust. I felt I was
dreaming, and in my dream I was traveling along the Silk
Route of western China with Marco and Maffeo Polo. Had
they also been struck by the alienation of the central Asian
plateaus?

We marched steadily until late evening across flat stretches
of land broken every so often by a landslide several hundred
feet deep, which we had to walk down and then up again on
the other side. At dusk the sky turned a nacreous, heavenly
white for a few moments before going purple and black.
Groups of Afridis in white turbans were leading their sheep
and mules to stagnant pools of water to drink before disappearing behind the walls of those massive fortresses. We
avoided their suspicious glances. Like Lurang and Jihan-zeb,
they were all armed with assault rifles. I watched enviously as
two Afridi boys hauled up a bucketful of water from a well.
Sensing my thoughts, Wakhil tapped me on the shoulder,
clucked his tongue, and shook his head at me. Instead, the
four of us rested by the muddy bank of a pool after the Afridi
shepherds had gone. Lumps of animal dung floated in the
water; Wakhil, Lurang, and Jihan-zeb drank heartily. I filled
my canteen and dropped an iodine pellet inside when the
others weren't looking. According to the instructions, I had to
wait twenty minutes before drinking. Lurang jerked my shoulder with an open palm, gesturing to me to slurp directly from
the pool, as he did. When I politely refused, he turned his
head away in disgust, as though there were no hope for me.
As night fell and guns began going off in the distance, we
started walking again. I couldn't believe that the hike through
Tirah Bazaar had been much different for Alexander's soldiers over 2,300 years ago.

An hour later, in pitch darkness, we reached our first *chai-
kanah*, a mice-ridden wooden platform with benches and jute

beds where tea and biscuits were sold. A boy of about nine poured the syrupy-sweet green tea into ceramic cups on a rush mat. I had a pounding headache from thirst. Carefully, I gripped the cup's rim but it was still too hot for me to hold. I was so thirsty that I got down on my stomach and tried sipping the tea with my chin resting on the ground, but it was so hot I jerked back in pain. Almost in tears, I waited the long minutes for the tea to cool just enough to slurp it, scalding my tongue, until the boy refilled the cup. The biscuits were stale and dry. They must have been in their wrappers for years in the hot sun. After a few cups of tea I felt better and could enjoy the pleasant breezes and feeling of absolute peace and silence that overtook me, despite the echoing pop of rifles coming from over the border — not far away now, I hoped.

"We will spend the night near here and cross into Afghanistan in the morning," said Wakhil.

The tea boy led us to an Afridi fort a few hundred yards away. Wakhil explained that this particular Afridi family was of a clan that had a truce with Khalis's mujahidin, who were allowed to stay with them while passing through the valley. So the fact that we had interrupted our journey at this point was no accident.

Inside the mud brick walls of the fort was a dirt courtyard with rooms off to the side. Along the inner wall, jute beds and brass water pipes were set out. My mouth was choked with dirt and dust.

"*Salaam aleikum,*" shouted the dark, turbaned Afridi elders, who gripped each of us hard and took my gear off to a corner by the wall. They told us to sit on the jute beds and cross-examined us. Lurang and Jihan-zeb knew these men from previous trips. There was a distinct air of tense, exaggerated friendliness, in the way enemies and rivals in all cultures compensate for their hostility when meeting face to face. One of the Afridis, an obese fellow who never stopped coughing, spitting, and blowing snot out of his nostrils with two bare fingers, kept harassing me with the only English phrase he knew, which he bellowed over and over again: "How dooo you dooo! How dooo you dooo!" I was too tired and dirty to appreciate his awkward attempts at amicability, though, and I just nodded back at him with a forced smile. Before leaving Peshawar I had promised myself that no matter how physically awful I might feel during the journey, I would try my best never to act irritable in front of the mujahidin. This man gave me my first challenge.

Someone unfurled a large carpet in the middle of the courtyard, sending up small clouds of dirt. It might have been a cheap machine-made rug bought in Peshawar or Landi Kotal, but in the gas-lit darkness, surrounded by all the dismal earthen shades of dust, dried mud, and dung, it seemed magnificent. Round loaves of flat bread were thrown down, and a boy came around with a brass pitcher and bowl so we could wash our hands before eating. I'll never forget the damp, mildewy reek of the towel he gave me. It must have been wiped by hundreds of pairs of hands since it was last washed. We turned up our palms toward the starscape, moved them down over our faces in unison, and said "*Allahu akbar*," thanking God for the meal we were about to eat.

Except for a bowl of shriveled, overdone fried eggs swimming in thick oil, there was nothing on any of the plates that I could identify: no meat, chicken, or curd even. All the other bowls contained only oil and grease of differing shades of brown and green into which everyone dipped their bread. After green tea was poured from a blackened kettle, everyone said prayers again and the plates and carpet were quickly removed from the ground. One of our hosts filled a water pipe for the men to smoke while lying on the jute beds. There was a sweet, acrid odor to the tobacco; perhaps it had a trace of hashish in it. Wakhil, Jihan-zeb, and Lurang took only one or two puffs and then declined to smoke more. The Afridis then withdrew *naswar* from their shirt pockets — a potent Afghan chewing tobacco laced with opium and other stimulants. Several months later I tried some. One pill-sized ball placed along my gums was enough to make me dizzy and nauseated five minutes later. I never used it again.

The moon rose over the mud walls of the fort and shone into the courtyard like a searchlight, disturbing my sleep. Finally, I drifted off to the sound of distant gunfire, wild barking dogs, and Afridis coughing up and spitting the tobacco a few inches away from my head.

"Afridis bad people, very dirty people," Wakhil muttered while washing his feet, before saying his last prayers of the day.

The relationship between the mujahidin and their Pathan cousins the Afridis was full of so many layers of intrigue and games played within games that at times it seemed that every commander and *malik* (tribal headman) had his own foreign policy with regard to KhAD, the KGB, and the Pakistani intelligence service. Truces were so short-lived and based on such a degree of subtlety that each new fact or insight I gained seemed to contradict much of what I had heard before. After a while I gave up and realized that this whole tribal system I was studying was just what the dictionaries called anarchy.

To begin with, the Afridis are divided into eight separate clans, or *khels*. One clan, the Adam Khel Afridis, controls the weapons market at Darra. Another, the Kuki Khel Afridis living in the Valley of Tirah Bazaar, had made pacts with Najib's Communist regime in Kabul, hence the danger of transporting an American journalist through their area (though it was yet another, rival clan who had put us up for the night).

The pro-Communist Kuki Khel Afridis were led by Malik Wali Khan Kuki Khel, a man in his fifties with a dour expression stamped permanently on his face. I met him once briefly in Peshawar. When I asked him about accusations concerning the kidnapping of Khalis mujahidin by the Kuki Khel in the Bazaar Valley, Wali Khan Kuki Khel gave me a syrupy smile and said that such acts were rare and those responsible had had their houses burned down as punishment. Abdul Haq and his brother Abdul Qadir claimed that this was nonsense and that the *malik* was a liar.

"Kuki Khel people — stupid people," Abdul Qadir had said. "Wali Khan is a stupid man. He has the face of a rat coming out of mud. He is an agent of KhAD and KGB."

Qadir himself had the delicate, distinguished features of a Dürer portrait, enhanced by white sideburns and a fine gray beard. His eyes glowed with an intelligence that reminded me of a Talmudic scholar. But when it came to Afridis or other Pathans who had sided with the Soviets, every trace of humanity left him.

"In 1986, Kuki Khel people in Maidan Valley get nine hundred guns from Najib in Kabul," Qadir had told me. "They make trouble for mujahidin and mule caravans bringing supplies into Afghanistan. So I say to Wali Khan Kuki Khel, 'If you want to make trouble, I have artillery on this mountain and that. Mujahidin there will blow up your houses and your mosques and your schools.' So we bomb some houses of Kuki Khel and then there is no more trouble for our mujahidin passing through this valley. Kuki Khel become very easily afraid." Qadir sneered and spat a gob of *naswar* on the ground.

Though the Kuki Khel dominated the Valley of Tirah Bazaar, a family of Zakha Khel Afridis had been providing us with hospitality in the fort. The Zakha Khel were the most populous of all the Afridi clans, and their leader, Malik Nadar Khan Zakha Khel, was a colorful character whom I visited in his Peshawar and Landi Kotal homes. Nadar Khan Zakha Khel maintained a tenuous, on-again-off-again truce with the mujahidin. And because I wasn't sure what Qadir's attitude would be to my interviewing the Afridi leader, I kept my meetings with Nadar Khan a secret from all the mujahidin. It turned out to be a wise idea, I thought while lying on the bed in the Afridi fort.

Though Nadar Khan had a veritable palace in Landi Kotal, when in Peshawar — where he held court several times a week — he deliberately projected a relatively humble image in order to keep the respect of his tribesmen in the city, all of whom were very poor. His house was down a narrow alley with an open sewer in Peshawar's old quarter. In the early morning, as many as a hundred Afridis would wait in a dim, dirty anteroom to pay their respects. Plainclothes Pakistani police loitered there too, casting an eye on every person who went into the *malik*'s chambers; Nadar Khan's name was often mentioned in connection with all sorts of unsavory dealings on the Northwest Frontier. Outside his room stood four Afridi bodyguards with bandoleers and Kalashnikov rifles.

Nadar Khan was sitting on a soiled, unmade bed with a towel around his neck when I entered his air-conditioned room. On the table beside him was a half-eaten dinner, including a vat of sweets being devoured by flies. He didn't seem bothered by the intrusion, however. "*Salaam aleikum,*" he called to me, raising his thick black eyebrows with a lively smile. He was wearing a white *shalwar kameez* and yellow vest, and playing with prayer beads. I was struck by his impressive turban and *kullah* resting on a shelf next to a plastic, heart-shaped sign with gold lettering that said in English, "God Bless Our Home." A Western-style suit hung from a nail on the wall. On the floor in the corner was a cheap cardboard suitcase with a First Class sticker on it. In the eyes of his tribesmen in the anteroom, such objects implied a certain wealth and sophistication.

Nadar Khan had the dark skin and lilting, clicking accent of a Punjabi. He spoke passable English and was pleased to tell his life story to a foreign journalist. I was trying to cultivate Nadar Khan. This leader of eighty thousand Zakha Khel Afridis was a useful man to know: his word and written orders carried more weight in the Khyber Tribal Agency than those of the Pakistani authorities. When you traveled up the Khyber Pass in a vehicle owned by Nadar Khan, nobody questioned your permit, and the police just waved you on at the check-points.

To hear Nadar Khan tell it, he was an Afghan patriot who supported the mujahidin without restraint but who nevertheless, on account of his great political skill, was able to maintain cordial relations with the Communist regime in Kabul at the same time. Nadar Khan had lived nearly half of his fifty-nine years in Afghanistan and the rest of them in Pakistan, and he saw himself as the ultimate go-between, loyal to all sides without betraying anyone's confidence. Among the many gifts in his palatial fortress in Landi Kotal was a 9 mm nickel-plated Makarov pistol given to him by Najib when the latter was head of KhAD and a Belgian 7.62 mm rifle with a gold-plated inscription from "General Zia ul-Haq, President of Pakistan."

"All the mujahidin of the seven parties are my brothers," Nadar Khan said, "and we allow all the refugees to go through our land in Tirah. . . . The Russians are godless people. Our mothers do not weep when their sons are killed by Russians. Instead they are proud." He said that the kidnappings for ransom of mujahidin in the Bazaar Valley were the work of Soviet agents, perhaps of the Kuki Khel, which he had nothing to do with. "The KGB has its best agents in Washington, London, and Tirah," he advised me with a knowing stare. "The Russians and Najib try to influence us through scholarships and the supply of guns. We took the guns, of course, but did not play the game of KGB."

Still, Nadar Khan could not deny that he continued to own 150 acres of property in Kabul and Jalalabad that the regime had not confiscated. And he claimed to be in personal contact with Najib, and to be helping him arrange to leave office peacefully.

"Najib is little in mind, but he is not little in body," he said, laughing. "You know what they call Najib in Farsi? *Gow,* the ox. My son, Miraiz, I call him Little Najib. Look at him." Nadar Khan pointed out his teenage son, who, with his short, massive build, did in fact resemble the Afghan ruler. "I know Najib well," Nadar Khan went on. "His father used to work as a transport manager in the Kissakhani Bazaar here in Peshawar. His sister is the wife of Mamul Khan, a great friend of my father's. Najib will try to hold on in Kabul, but he will fail. Then he will come and live with me in my palace in Landi Kotal. This will provide a peaceful solution for Afghanistan."

Nadar Khan's fort in Landi Kotal, with its tomato patch, rose bushes, private mosque, and icebox stocked with Coca-Cola and Fanta, was certainly nicer than the place I was staying in the Valley of Tirah Bazaar. But the idea of the Afghan ruler's spending the rest of his days there struck me as comic. Inside its long walls, the fort had several locked gates, past which I was not permitted to go. Some of Khalis's mujahidin and Pakistanis said Nadar Khan kept smuggled Russian vodka and other contraband there. Once, Nadar Khan's tribesmen had kidnapped a Khalis commander in a reprisal for the destruction of a vodka consignment by the mujahidin, and delicate negotiations had been necessary to secure his release.

After I had interviewed the Zakha Khel leader, Abdul Qadir told me, "Nadar Khan is talking out of all sides of his mouth and he is only thinking of money." Qadir grimaced, as if he had just tasted something rotten. Though Qadir had a truce with the Zakha Khel Afridis and they were providing his mujahidin with food and lodging in Tirah, his feelings toward them were only slightly less hostile than those he harbored toward the Kuki Khel. "Now we must bargain with Nadar Khan. But after the war is finished, when mujahidin have power in Kabul, then we will deal with Nadar Khan and all of his people. The Afridis will be sorry that they ever made friends with Russia. Mujahidin suffer much and we forget nothing." Qadir added that he hoped the Soviets would bomb Landi Kotal, since that "would teach Nadar Khan and his people a lesson."

*

Lying in the jute bed atop my nylon sleeping bag that night in the Afridi fort, I knew that the hospitality extended to us was the result of chilling bargains over vodka and hostages and double-dealing with the Soviets, and that at some point in the not too distant future, Lurang and Jihan-zeb — or some other of Khalis's men — might come here to shoot and butcher the very people who had fed and sheltered us.

We were up at 4:30 A.M. and, thankfully, our Afridi hosts offered us only bread and green tea. It was still dark when we left the fort and began walking. After several hours we passed between two low mountains and entered a rock-strewn wadi shaded with mulberry trees. In a moment the Bazaar Valley was just a hazy memory, like a half-dream between sleep and waking.

The wadi led ever upward in a grueling, twisting incline, steep enough to make me out of breath, but not quite so steep as to provide any visible goal or summit. The trees gave me hope that a stream ran nearby, but there was none. After a while, Lurang and Jihan-zeb were practically pulling and dragging me along.

"A little more and we will be in Afghanistan," Wakhil said, trying to encourage me. He pointed to a vague area where the terrain leveled out.

Now Wakhil, Jihan-zeb, and Lurang quickened their pace, leaving me far behind. I struggled alone for half an hour until I saw the three of them sitting on a flat table of land in the distance. When I reached them I collapsed at their feet. They all laughed.

"Afghanistan!" Wakhil exclaimed to me, pointing a finger at the ground, which he stamped with his foot.

Behind me, the wadi we had just ascended fell away in a swirl of trees and gravel to reveal a panorama of mountains. For all their gray and dull green barrenness, they had a temperate, recognizable flavor. But ahead was something out of a sci-fi film: jagged ranks of sawtooth peaks that, despite the nearby web of lush riverbeds, seemed even more rain-starved than the land we were leaving. This was the so-called Durand Line, negotiated between the amir of Afghanistan, Abdur Rahman, and a special British envoy, Sir Mortimer Durand, in 1893 as the border that would separate Afghanistan from the Northwest Frontier of British India. The Durand Line is usually described in books as an arbitrarily drawn division that was not based on particular geographical features, so it was difficult to know when you had crossed it. But every time I went over the Afghan border, it seemed fairly logical and straightforward: the border ran along a watershed where the landscapes were noticeably different on each side. I saw no water here at the moment, but the autumn rains would bring plenty of streams, and the small plateau on which we were sitting would be where the waters split into two opposite, downward directions. We were now roughly twenty-five miles southwest of the border station at Torcham, beyond Landi Kotal. We had walked a total of twelve hours since the day before, zigzagging in a direction parallel to the border so that we might cross where there were no regime troops.

I groaned as Wakhil and the others stood up; that usually meant it was time to move on.

"No, you can sit for a while," Wakhil said. "We only go to pray."

4

Noble Savages

THE MUJAHIDIN dropped down on their knees and moved their hands lightly over the ground until their palms and fingertips were coated with dust. Holding their blackened palms before their faces, they each began to recite from the Koran:

> Believers, do not approach your prayers when you are drunk, but wait till you can grasp the meaning of your words; nor when you are polluted — unless you are traveling the road — until you have washed yourselves. If you are ill and cannot wash yourselves; or, if you have relieved yourselves or had intercourse with women while traveling and can find no water, take some clean sand and rub your faces and your hands with it. Allah is benignant and forgiving.

On this parched and stony plate of earth, without a trickle of water in sight, they smeared their temples and foreheads, purifying themselves with the dust. Then each, at his own pace, began moving prayer beads through his fingers, silently mouthing the words "*Allahu akbar*" (God is great) 34 times, "*Subhan il'aha*" (God is pure) 33 times, and "*Hamd-u-lilah*" (Praise be to God) 33 times, so that the name of God was repeated 100 times. Five times throughout the day they performed the service.

My interpreter, Wakhil, had studied Arabic in the course of becoming a *mullah*, but the other two could not have understood much, or any, of what they recited. (Pukhtu, though employing the Arabic script, is no closer to Arabic than French is to English.) But as with Hebrew in the mouths of many Jews of the Diaspora, the incomprehensibility of those harsh, ancient gutturals seemed only to increase the power of the language over my bodyguards, Lurang and Jihan-zeb, whose faces were flushed with awe and tranquility.

I had traveled in enough Moslem countries to cease being enamored of such rituals. I had already seen these prayers performed many more times in my life than their Christian or Jewish equivalents, and I no longer found them strange or exotic. Nor was I blind to the hypocrisies that so often accompanied religious fervor. To me, the monologue of the Koran had always symbolized the sterile authoritarianism of the East, where all public debate was drowned out. Arabic (and Persian too) was a language I disdained, even though I knew the alphabet and many simple phrases. Like Greek, Arabic struck me as a flowery, ostentatious language structured for poetry and demagoguery, but without Greek's flare for intellectual subtlety. Concerning the peoples of the Middle and Near Eastern deserts, I had always subscribed to the opinion of T. E. Lawrence, who in *Seven Pillars of Wisdom* wrote: "Their thoughts were at ease only in extremes. They inhabited superlatives by choice. Sometimes inconsistents seemed to possess them at once in joint sway; but they never compromised: they pursued the logic of several incompatible options to absurd ends, without perceiving the incongruity." In short, I was cynical toward the culture of Islam, and the more Islamic countries I visited and the more I listened to the relativist thinking of the region's experts in the media and the State Department, the more cynical I became — even though I knew my attitudes might be viewed by others as merely the prejudices and self-justifications of an American Jew who spoke Hebrew and had lived for several years in Israel.

Afghanistan, however, was a new and radical experience for me. The whole psychology of the Islamic faith was different here from how I had ever seen it. True, the awful denigration of women was both unjustifiable and tragic: male-dominated cultures tend to be emotionally underdeveloped as well as intellectually sterile. Still, because Afghans harbored no political insecurities and were more relaxed in their faith than Arabs or Iranians, Islam in Afghanistan manifested a certainty and unintimidating dynamism that did not exist in Iran, Pakistan, or any of the Arab countries I had visited. It was only in Afghanistan that I was able — at least I think I was — to see Islam objectively for the first time.

Religion in Iran and the Shiite suburbs of south Beirut possessed *fury*. In Iran, tens of thousands prayed en masse, reciting the words, syllable by heated syllable, in unison, begetting a collective hysteria reminiscent of the Nuremberg rallies. The cries of *Allahu akbar* carried a shrill, medieval, bloodcurdling ring. This was Islam's perverse reaction to the political challenges of the twentieth century: to the pressures of nationhood; to the West's military, economic, and cultural penetration of the Middle East; and to the creation of a Western-style Jewish state in its midst. But the young men with whom I was traveling in Afghanistan were, in an emotional sense, free and ignorant of those events. Afghanistan had never been industrialized, let alone colonized or penetrated much by outsiders. Unlike the Iranians, who *seemed* to pray just as fervently, the Afghans had never been seduced by the West and so had no reason now to violently reject it: Afghanistan did not require a resurgence of faith, for the Afghans had never lost it. Unlike most people in the Middle East, the Afghans were psychologically sure of themselves. Soviet bombs were the Afghans' first and only contact with the modern world. And even toward the Soviets, who had killed Afghans on a scale that rendered Western crimes against Arabs and Iranians statistically infinitesimal, the Afghans cultivated a simpler, less personalized hatred, one that did not reduce noncombatants to enemies the way the Middle Eastern terrorists did.

Away from the tensions of the refugee camps in Pakistan,

Islam had infused hope into the Afghan resistance without being too politicized by it.

In Pakistan, Islam was imposed from above, as a glue to hold together an artificially constructed nation of feuding ethnic groups. The religious passion that Zia sought for his people was something the Afghans had already inculcated in their bones without realizing it and without the need of an Islamic republic. Once inside Afghanistan, Islam, like so many of the customs of these mountains, existed in a time vacuum — in vitro, like a museum piece or laboratory specimen — purified of what the twentieth century had done to it in Pakistan, Iran, and elsewhere. Islam may not have responded well to modern pressures, but at least now I could respect it for what it was originally intended to be — something I couldn't do before.

Racked with thirst and fatigue, I watched in admiration as my companions spiritually and, it seemed, physically refreshed themselves with that dust. Of course, my respect was based on what I already knew about these young men rather than on what I was actually seeing. The image of Pathan tribesmen in Afghanistan rubbing their faces with dust and mouthing the name of Allah one hundred times was graphically indistinguishable from the many images of Moslem fanaticism. But because I had spoken with these mujahidin, and knew why they smiled and what they laughed at and what made them angry, because of the well of gratitude I felt when Wakhil said, after his prayers, "Don't worry, Babar Khan, we will find water for you," I knew that prayer had softened them, not made them harder or more intolerant.

What I knew most of all was that for Lurang, Jihan-zeb, and Wakhil religion was a private matter, just as it is for most Americans. They never spoke about it to me unless I asked, and they never proselytized. When I told Wakhil that I was Jewish, his only comment was: "Jews and Christians are people of the Book." (Another mujahid had said, "Are Jews anti-Soviet?" After thinking for a second, I said yes.) At no time did these so-called Moslem fundamentalists make me feel uncomfortable. Never were they overbearing. These were not the sorts of perceptions that would have survived the brutal reductions of the television camera, the narrow boundaries of hard-news writing, or the quantifications of the think-tank analysts in Washington and London. What the American public really needed to know about the guerrillas it was supporting with billions of taxpayers' dollars could never be provided by many of the people being paid to tell us.

It was only a fifteen-minute walk to water, which was provided at a camp of Gulbuddin Hekmatyar's mujahidin. How like Hekmatyar to have a base just inside the Afghan border! He could then make the claim of having fighters inside while still being far removed from the fighting. Hekmatyar's party (the *other* Hizb-i-Islami) was the only one of the seven resistance organizations that truly deserved the label "fundamentalist," inasmuch as it was anti-Western and totalitarian. Because of its formidable public relations machine in Pakistan, which was funded by Zia, the party garnered frequent attention in the foreign press, despite the fact that the allegiance of its commanders to Hekmatyar was dubious and its field presence inside Afghanistan and influence in the refugee camps overrated. Were Hekmatyar eventually to triumph, it would happen only through Pakistani support and intervention.

Up close, Hekmatyar's base resembled a stage set for a guerrilla camp rather than a real one. Rarely had I seen mujahidin who looked so well rested and clean, with perfectly wrapped turbans and new shiny leather bandoleers and *shalwar kameezes*. The buildings they inhabited were made of real stone rather than the mud brick and canvas of the other mujahidin camps, and on the floors were expensive, hand-stitched oriental carpets. They had new field phones, walkie-talkies, binoculars, ceramic plates, and fresh dates to eat, courtesy of Hekmatyar's Saudi patrons. I filled my stomach with the dates, which Wakhil, Lurang, and Jihan-zeb refused to touch. Hekmatyar's men displayed an intense interest in my canteen and rucksack. They wanted to know where they could buy such equipment.

"Tourists," Wakhil muttered angrily as we left Hekmatyar's camp, after I had finished eating the dates. "From now on, you will meet real mujahidin."

We followed a wadi for the next few hours until we had to climb a mountain just to meet our trail again. "Mines," explained Wakhil. That part of the wadi was strewn with them, and it was safer to go around it, even if that meant climbing up one thousand feet and then down again. It occurred to me that the mujahidin were usually not the victims of mine blasts because they had mapped out all the trails in their minds. The peasant farmers, and their children in particular, were much less knowledgeable about the trails and the mines than the mujahidin.

Then the easy part ended.

Just as I was getting tired, Lurang, wearing a sadistic smile, pointed to a line of hills that rippled upward until they merged with a steep escarpment covered with thorns and cactus that led to a ridge about ten thousand feet up. This was the first of a series of mountain walls that would take us to the sixteen-thousand-foot, ice-flecked granite platforms of what the international maps called Safed Koh (Persian for White Mountain), a range that formed the border between Nangarhar province and a sliver of Pakistani tribal territory surrounded by Afghanistan on three sides.

Babur, the Mongol king and poet, wrote: "The Safed Koh runs along the south of Nangarhar . . . no riding-road crosses it; nine torrents issue from it. It is called Safed Koh because its snow never lessens; none falls in the lower parts of its valleys, a half-day's journey from the snow-line. Many places along it have an excellent climate; its waters are cold and need no ice." Instead of calling it Safed Koh, Pathans use the Pukhtu word for White Mountain, Spinghar. The waters Babur referred to were in the valley on the other side of the series of hills we had to cross.

At the top of the first hill I fell to the ground under a rucksack that suddenly felt as though it were weighted with stones. Except for the dates and the grease-soaked bread at the fort in Tirah, I had not eaten for thirty hours. I had finished the last of the canteen water, and we were still several hours from the cold waters of the valley. My eyes stung from salty sweat. Without being aware of it, I was licking sweat from my forehand in order to soothe my throat, irritated from dust and lack of water. As I came across the ridge before beginning another climb, one of the straps of my rucksack tore. I cursed. Jihanzeb grabbed it by the other strap and surged ahead up the hill with the others, laughing at my weakness. Like the Tibetan lama who led Kim into Kashmir, the Pathans were *hillmen*, growing in strength in proportion to the difficulty of the terrain. Even Wakhil, so small and vulnerable looking in Landi Kotal, seemed to acquire stature as he *drew a deep double-lungful of the diamond air, and walked as only a hillman can. Kim, plains-bred and plains-fed, sweated and panted, astonished.*

I was so hungry and tired that I was hallucinating into *Kim*.

At the top of the next brow I allowed myself to drop to the ground a second time, thinking we had reached some sort of summit and would now be able to descend into the valley. But we were only on another shaved green platform below the main spur, and there was no shade. Again Kipling's novel came to mind: *Here one day's march carried them no farther, it seemed, than a dreamer's clogged pace bears him in a nightmare. They skirted a shoulder painfully for hours, and, behold, it was but an outlying boss in an outlying buttress of the main pile!*

The next few hours were a blur of agony. On the downhill march my companions left the trail and bounded earthward on a forty-five-degree angle over a treacherous, rocky slope, rifles and my rucksack clanging against their shoulders, while I hobbled along the path, knees quaking, thinking that if mountain goats could talk and think like men, they would be equal to the mujahidin. Then a trickling noise sent chills through my body: the sound of running water. In the failing, dust-stained light I could make out an assemblage of pudding-stone houses at the bottom of the hill that merged with the dun-colored soil like sand castles on a beach. The trail became so steep and my knees so sore as I descended toward the village that I slid the last fifty yards through the packed dust into a mud embankment, which was channeling the spring water I had heard into a young fruit orchard. I must have looked like a chimney sweep.

A pitcher of water appeared magically out of the twilight, held by an old man with a stringy gray beard and a *pakol* on his head. He squatted down in the mud and handed it to me.

As I started to drink he began yelling at me, raising a finger in the air. "*Khabarnegah, khabarnegah!*" It was the Pukhtu word for journalist.

"We told this man you are a journalist," explained Wakhil, who along with Lurang and Jihan-zeb was washing his feet and hands in the irrigation ditch in preparation for evening prayers.

The old man exploded into a loud babble of Pukhtu that sounded like an insult. His contorted, sunburned face was inches away from me, suspended in the enveloping darkness. Every time I took another gulp of water or rinsed my face and hands he shook his head in a mocking manner. When Wakhil came over after the prayers were finished, the old man was silent for a moment, then started screaming again.

"He says his name is Gholam Issa Khan." Wakhil had to shout so that I could hear his translation above the graybeard's ranting. I struggled to retrieve my notebook. Two loud, simultaneous voices now pounded at my head. I was covered with dust and lightheaded from hunger. This incident gained a mystical quality in my mind; it was like listening to the voices of your own conscience.

"The Communists don't like my God and his messenger,"

the old man said. "They tried to wipe out my way of life. But my God gives me strength. My God always helps me. America is godless but America is good because America gives me guns to fight Communists. After we drive the *shuravi* [Soviet forces] out of Afghanistan, we will drive them out of Bukhara and Samarkand and Tashkent too. *Allahu akbar!*"

"How old are you?" I asked. I wanted to get his story straight from the beginning. The old man thought for a moment. I wondered if anybody had ever asked him this question.

"Forty," Wakhil translated.

"Forty? He looks like seventy."

"These people are not like you," Wakhil said. "They don't know exactly when they were born. Why do you always ask such questions about numbers and dates? What does it matter?"

Wakhil was angry. Maybe the man really was forty — or at least thought he was. Lurang and Jihan-zeb were both ten years younger than I, yet they looked older.

The old man continued to shout: "Taraki people tried to rape my wife, to stop me from praying. I have thirty hectares. Taraki people want to take ten hectares away from me. They say my daughters must go to Communist school. I say I kill you first!" He shook his fist. "*Shuravi* come with planes, helicopters, *boom, boom*. This, this" — he pointed in all directions — "all finished. We go to Pakistan. Then mujahidin come, *shuravi* leave. We make all this, this" — again he pointed — "all over again. Again bomb, again make."

The graybeard jabbed furiously at my notebook, as if to say, "Write, write." I wrote. Then for the first time he smiled. I took out my camera and aimed it at him.

"*Ne, ne*," he shouted, covering his face with his hands.

"You must not take this man's picture," Wakhil said. "This man says his picture is only for God to see."

Behind the graybeard's frantic bursts of speech lay a familiar, well-documented story. Had I been traveling in South Africa, the West Bank, or Lebanon, where quantitatively the destruction and suffering were a mere fraction of what it was in Afghanistan, I would not even have taken out my notebook, because the contents of his story would already have formed part of the well of knowledge available to all serious newspaper readers. In those places, books were written about nuances because the basics were already known from the daily press. In Afghanistan, the basics had yet to be proclaimed. So the most fundamental feature of its history, which has never been fully appreciated, must be set down here.

While the country had always been horribly poor, dirty, and underdeveloped, Afghans had never known very much political repression until after the April 27, 1978, coup that brought the sixty-one-year-old poet and self-declared Marxist idealist Nur Mohammed Taraki to power. Until the 1970s, Afghanistan was relatively civilized by the standards of Amnesty International. The soldiers' knock on the door in the middle of the night, so common in many Arab and African countries, was little known in Afghanistan, where a central government simply lacked the power to enforce its will outside Kabul.

Taraki's coup changed all that. Between April 1978 and the Soviet invasion of December 1979, Afghan Communists executed 27,000 political prisoners at the sprawling Pul-i-Charki prison six miles east of Kabul. (That's 7,000 more people than were killed during Israel's 1982 invasion of Lebanon.) Many of the victims were village *mullahs* and headmen who were obstructing the modernization and secularization of the intensely religious Afghan countryside. The keystones of Taraki's revolution were land reform and the extension of secular education into the villages. By Western standards, this was a salutary idea in the abstract. But it was carried out in such a violent way that it alarmed even the Soviets, who through Taraki wanted to transform Afghanistan into a satellite.

"Land reform" to the graybeard Gholam Issa Khan and to Din Mohammed, Abdul Haq, Abdul Qadir, and others meant soldiers breaking into houses, raping or trying to rape the women, defecating on the dishes, executing the local *mullah* and headman, and confiscating land in a haphazard manner that enraged everyone, benefited no one, and reduced food production. It was the Cultural Revolution and the Chinese destruction of Tibet all over again, with hundreds of thousands of people affected. As in China and Tibet, it was perpetrated in darkness, with barely a scratch of interest from the normally aggressive Western media. The mujahidin revolt against the Kabul authorities and the refugee exodus to Pakistan were ignited not by the Soviet invasion, as most people in the West suppose, but by Taraki's land reform program, which represented the first instance of organized, nationwide repression in Afghanistan's modern history.

Taraki fell in mid-September 1979, toppled by his fellow Communist conspirator Hafizullah Amin, who was described by foreign diplomats as a "brutal psychopath." He had Taraki strangled and Taraki's family thrown into Pul-i-Charki prison. The mujahidin rebellion gathered strength as a reaction to Amin's crescendo of purges, mass executions, and land confiscations. It was a war that pitted an urban elite against rural peasants. The East bloc, contrary to its stated ideology, was behind the urban elite. "During 1978 and 1979 the people of Afghanistan were forced into a bloody struggle to defend themselves against incorporation into a new form of colonial empire ruled from Moscow," wrote Henry S. Bradsher, a former Associated Press correspondent.

When the Soviet army invaded on December 27, 1979, it was not so much a bold, new aggression as a last-ditch effort by the Kremlin to save a nascent satellite from being overthrown by Moslem guerrillas, as a result of the overzealousness of the Kremlin's own hand-picked men. To an extent, one could argue that the Soviet Union won and lost Afghanistan in 1978 and 1979, when few in the West were paying attention. The more than one million deaths and the planting of millions of land mines in the 1980s were merely part of the long, drawn-out, bloody aftermath of an already foregone conclusion.

Taraki's and Amin's oppression had depopulated Gholam Issa Khan's mud brick village and sent him and his kinsmen to refugee camps in Pakistan. The two leaders were Khalqis, sons of poor families who were members of an extremist, Pukhtu-speaking Communist faction called Khalq (Masses). The Soviet invasion replaced Amin with a more suave, moderate brand of Afghan Communist, Babrak Karmal. Karmal, then fifty years old, was born into a wealthy Kabul family and had been educated in the capital's foreign schools. He had helped form Parcham (Banner), an urban, Dari-speaking Communist faction that favored a more conciliatory approach toward the peasants. It was sometimes said that had Karmal and his Parcham allies been in power in the late 1970s instead of the more brutal Khalqi fanatics, land reform might have been implemented more intelligently, the mujahidin revolt might have lost momentum, and Afghanistan might have evolved into a quiescent Soviet satellite state like Bulgaria.

Karmal released political prisoners and relaxed the repression. But it was too late. Gholam Issa Khan and tens of thousands of others like him had already joined such mujahidin groups as Jamiat and Khalis's Hizb-i-Islami and had liberated large chunks of the countryside. Karmal's Soviet backers responded with mines, aerial bombardments, and ground troop assaults. Gholam Issa Khan's village had been destroyed and rebuilt several times before I saw it. It was uninhabited. But now, with the guerrillas in complete control of the area, Gholam Issa Khan and a few of his kinsmen and their wives came back periodically throughout the year to plant and harvest wheat, maize, and some other crops. The graybeard's story was a dramatic one. Still, with so much land to traverse and so relatively few journalists inside, I could have been the first to stop at his village and talk to him.

*

Gholam Issa Khan took us to an earthen house supported by
hardwood beams. A ladder led to an upper level, where jute
beds were arranged around a dusty carpet. Under the dim
white light of a hissing gas lamp, one-eyed Jihan-zeb, using a
rusted needle and thread, began repairing the torn strap of
my rucksack without my asking. He looked up and smiled at
me. I felt shamed, helpless, and grateful, all at the same time.
Someone brought moldy, moth-eaten pillows for us. Through
the beams, I saw a brilliant, breathing starscape. As sore and
dirty as I was, I felt like a baby in a cradle and nearly fell asleep.
A boy came with a brass pitcher of water and loaves of flat
bread in a bundle of cloth. I moved over to the edge of the
carpet when the boy brought a large bowl of thin, sour goat's
milk curd, called *shlombeh*. We took turns drinking from it. The
boy came with a second bowl and then with a kettle of green
tea, all of which I slurped greedily. I remember the aromatic
smell of burning deodar wood from the fire. After the boy
cleared the carpet, Wakhil, ever the *mullah*, led the group in
prayers.

In the middle of the night, I was awakened by the drone of
helicopter gunships dropping "fishing flares" in the black sky
over the mud brick village: huge, space-age insects disturbing
the silence. The Reagan administration's delivery of over a
thousand Stinger antiaircraft missiles to the mujahidin since
1986 had forced the Soviets into flying only after dark or at
high altitudes. My stomach knotted. Gholam Issa Khan lifted
his head for a moment, looked around, then fell back to sleep
with a dismissive wave of his hand. The helicopters were a
nightly occurrence for him. The others just grunted.

Morning found us in a paradise lost. This lush valley, ar-
rayed with walnut, mulberry, black plum, and oriental plane
trees and noisy with sparrows and magpies, had become a zone
of death. Bomb-cratered fields lay fallow. Antipersonnel
mines lay not far from the path. Once-soaring minarets were
cut off at their midsections, and village after mud brick village

that we passed through was nothing but a roofless jigsaw of collapsed walls adjoining mounds of rubble. I had seen similar places in eastern Turkey leveled by earthquakes: pathetic little toy towns that looked as though an unruly child had smashed them during a tantrum. But here was something else: clusters of tattered white flags flying on swaying bamboo poles signifying the graves of *shaheedan* — mujahidin martyred by the Soviets and Afghan Communists.

Still, as Wakhil never stopped pointing out, the province of Nangarhar was a beautiful land. Arriving from the arid north, Babur had observed: "In Nangarhar another world came to view — other grasses, other trees, other animals, other birds, and other manners and customs of clan and horde. We were amazed, and truly there was ground for amaze."

We stopped by a stream, and Jihan-zeb constructed a bath for me with a pile of stones. I took out my spare *shalwar kameez* from my rucksack and changed while in the water. Soaking wet in my new clothes, I washed the others by smashing and rubbing them against the stones. The men didn't wash, but they looked and smelled the same as when they left Peshawar: nothing at all seemed to affect them.

Walnuts and dried mulberries appeared with the curds at meals now. And maize too, which Jihan-zeb slowly turned in the fire. He held his whole hand in the flames for several seconds, turning the corn and smiling at me. Barking in Pukhtu, he beckoned Wakhil to translate.

"Jihan-zeb asks if you know why mujahidin are brave and feel no pain."

"No, why?" I asked.

"Because mujahid is a man who has already given himself to God. Though he still breathes, he is like the dead. He isn't afraid."

Jihan-zeb smiled again. His simpleminded expression was like that of a fanatic. He reminded me of the Iranian youths at the Gulf war front, with headbands bearing the inscription

"Ready for martyrdom" — the kind who, in slightly altered circumstances, were capable of switching from naïve kindness to cruelty, and butchery even.

In some cases, the mujahidin had been guilty of just that.

The guerrillas routinely executed enemy pilots upon capture (until American advisers prevailed upon them to at least interrogate the airmen first). In a region of Paktia province controlled by a Khalis commander, Jallaluddin Haqqani, they once took a group of Afghan Communist troops prisoner, lined them up in a ditch, and shot them in the head. After the negotiated surrender of the Communist border post at Torcham at the beginning of 1989, mujahidin alleged to belong to the Khalis organization killed the disarmed Communist soldiers and mutilated their bodies. Still, in most cases, the guerrillas held prisoners, whether Soviets or Afghans, and forced them to survive in the same Spartan manner as their captors. Documented accounts of mujahidin savagery were relatively rare and involved enemy troops only. Their cruelty toward civilians was unheard of during the war, while Soviet cruelty toward civilians was common. On January 16, 1988, for instance, after Soviet troops and an Afghan Communist militia unit captured the village of Kolagu in Paktia province from the mujahidin, they bound together twelve villagers, seven of whom were children, inside the local mosque before they burned it to the ground; nine of the twelve died. (Amnesty International later confirmed the details of the incident.) "Civilian massacres [perpetrated by Soviet and Afghan Communist troops] like the one at My Lai were the norm rather than the aberration," said David Isby, a military analyst and the author of several books about the war in Afghanistan.

To judge by the overall record, Jihan-zeb and his fellow resistance fighters were not fanatics but simply coarse peasants reacting to the invasion of their land in an uncompromising way. Because the Afghans lacked the material wealth that people elsewhere are terrified of losing, they were able to go on fighting and suffering. That is how they saved Afghanistan from the humiliating fate of so many countries in Eastern Europe. (Whether the Afghan Communist regime falls is to some extent beside the point, since the countryside will always be held by the resistance.)

By the standards of the Middle East, the mujahidin were paragons of virtue. Yet because they were so primitive, they were assumed to be barbaric. And the *glasnost*-happy Soviet media were masters at playing on this confusion of characteristics, weaving into their reports of Soviet battle losses a sequence of manufactured tales of mujahidin savagery.

The landscape became waterless again as we plodded through a rolling sandstone desert that made me think of mounds of ground curry. Then we began climbing up sandy slopes sprinkled with thorns, cactus, and the odd pine tree or two. Another day of thirst and sore knees — the fourth of our trek — brought us through the tree line to the Spinghar command post of the Khalis mujahidin.

Small bands of guerrillas were spread out in canvas pup tents over the chain of snow-dusted granite peaks and plateaus. From there they could look down on the Kabul–Jalalabad–Torcham highway, the ten-thousand-man Soviet armored division at Samar Khel, and the Soviet-occupied city of Jalalabad in the vast plain thousands of feet below.

It was a perfect guerrilla setup: from the air, the tiny green tents were practically indistinguishable from the stubble of dark lichen. The mujahidin had mounted captured Soviet-made heavy machine guns in ditches dug into the spurs, from where they could bag a low-flying gunship with a lucky shot. (It was near here that Khalis's men had shot down and captured the first Soviet pilot of the war, in July 1981.) The region's commander, Habibullah, lived with eleven other men in a tent about fifteen feet long and seven feet wide.

In the space of a few hours, I had gone from extreme heat

to extreme cold. My sweat-soaked body was suddenly shivering under my cotton *shalwar kameez* and the woolen *patou* that Wakhil wrapped around me. I was reminded of Arnold Toynbee's description of Afghanistan: "a Turkish bath on a gigantic scale, with the chilly room at an altitude of 7,000 feet and upwards, opening out of the steam room at 3,000 feet and under." Just as we arrived at Habibullah's tent, dark clouds tumbled over the plateau and the sky exploded in thunder. The first hailstones hit the ground, and the dozen men huddled inside with *patous* to keep warm. The temperature was now below freezing, and the mujahidin were without socks, boots, jackets, and sleeping bags. As they watched the sharp pellets of ice rattle on the ground, they smiled and looked grateful. Wakhil explained to me that the mujahidin called hail "Allah's mine sweeper," since the force of the pellets was often enough to set off the butterfly mines.

It was pathetic. Though by the late 1980s U.S. taxpayers were aiding the Afghan resistance to the tune of $400 million annually, the guerrillas still had no mine-clearing equipment, and the walkie-talkies that Commander Habibullah used to communicate with his units throughout Spinghar and adjacent valleys were cheap transceivers whose signals the Soviets could easily intercept. Out of habit, the mujahidin still relied on runners carrying handwritten notes through the mountains, a method that provided much tighter security. When better quality Japanese transceivers finally did arrive, they came with English-language instructions that nobody in these mountains could understand. You would have thought that someone in the massive American bureaucracy dealing with the largest covert operation since the Vietnam war would have had the instructions translated into Pukhtu and photocopied. The aid program certainly seemed more impressive from Washington than it did from Spinghar.

The racket of pellets on the canvas grew louder, and wind ruffled the tent, which was beginning to feel like a ship at sea.

The mujahidin inside ranged in age from teenagers to old men, and they all had been living together on this isolated peak for years already. In guerrilla armies there is no recruitment period, and some of the men had been away from their families since 1978, when the Taraki regime first forced them underground. I noted the disparity in their ages but was not particularly conscious of it, since they themselves didn't appear to be. They all wore the same *shalwar kameezes* and *pakols*. The younger ones had lived through the same experiences as the old men, and although they lacked white hair and wrinkles, the look in their eyes was just as old.

The hail turned into intermittent freezing rain. As evening fell, the oldest-looking mujahid, white-bearded Yar Mohammed, silently walked out of the tent to the edge of the escarpment, where the gusts of icy wind were fiercest. Split curtains of cloud flew quickly across the fairy tale light of the heavens, as though in a scene from the Bible. The old man sat on a clump of white hail and rinsed his bare feet with a pitcher of cold water. Then he bowed down on his knees in the wet ice and began to repeat *Allahu akbar* thirty-four times, his hands and forehead falling to the earth, where he kept them fastened while softly, almost inaudibly whispering the name of God to himself. He was absolutely rigid against the wind. Though barefoot and without a *patou,* he never once shivered. Inside the open-flapped tent, tucked deep in my sleeping bag, I shivered just looking at him.

What could you say about this spindly old man quietly praying barefoot in the ice? Compare him to a sword swallower or a yogi who walks over hot coals? As with Wakhil, Lurang, and Jihan-zeb praying in the dirt, a visual report of this man's behavior would only portray him as a fanatic.

Mujahidin life, and that of the Pathans in particular, was stark. Likewise, my thoughts and experiences over these last few days were intense but not varied — like the act of survival itself. Variety was more easily conveyed in journalistic prose than intensity because variety was horizontal, and reporters were conditioned to cover stories horizontally, aspect by aspect. But what did you do with people who were essentially uncomplicated? The mujahidin had few aspects to their personalities, but each aspect required boring deep down to a level of experience that went beyond speech itself. "Damn it, there's nothing you can say about the muj. You have to feel them," said Tony O'Brien, a photographer friend.

No one else paid much attention to Yar Mohammed's praying. The mujahidin, even when in a cohesive group like this one, often prayed alone, whenever each man felt like it. One after another they performed their evening prayers, if not alone, then in groups of two or three. Some shouted; others, like Yar Mohammed, just whispered. Up here on this plateau, in the hail and freezing rain, each man communicated with God in his own style. The chanting crowd in the mosque was absent, and the Koran seemed less like a monologue. This was as close to democracy as one was likely to get in central Asia.

In the gas-lit darkness, we sat around the sides of the tent and ate a meal of flat bread, raw turnips, onions, and green tea. Away from the villages there were no goats and therefore no curds. The only luxury was the water pipe, assembled from a brass pitcher and bamboo pole. After the repast, Commander Habibullah read a passage from the Koran while we all listened. It was one of the few occasions when everyone prayed together.

Habibullah was constantly busy, writing messages, communicating by walkie-talkie, or going off to a nearby tent on an inspection or to confer. He appeared efficient, competent, and unfriendly — disdainful of the world I seemed to represent. Only very late at night did he agree to talk to me.

Habibullah, one of Abdul Qadir's top lieutenants, had a dark Indian's complexion, a long black beard, and an aquiline nose. He reminded me of a Sikh warrior rather than a Pathan, and in the dim, smoky light he looked like a Greek or Syrian saint in an early Christian fresco. Habibullah was twenty-six years old and from the Kuchi tribe, a nomadic branch of the Pathans. Being a Kuchi explained a lot about his demeanor. The British writer Peter Levi, in an erudite travelogue about Afghanistan, *The Light Garden of the Angel King*, described the Kuchis this way: "Kuchi means travelers and they are hard to know. We found them stoical about disease and distrustful of the local doctors, and in their tents their behavior was regal." Erect and motionless, Habibullah spoke impassively through Wakhil's translation.

As in the case of Gholam Issa Khan, in the late 1970s Taraki's Communist regime seized Kuchi land in Nangarhar and hauled the local *mullah* and headman of Habibullah's nomadic encampment off to prison. They were never seen again. Many of his kinsmen fled to refugee camps in Pakistan. Habibullah joined Khalis's Hizb-i-Islami to fight the Communists south of Jalalabad, near the town of Rodat Baru, where his family used to live. He described how Soviet troops entered the Kuchi camp in 1982, "robbing houses, killing the goats, taking money and the cows." Then this Kuchi area was bombed from the air, and all the irrigation canals were destroyed. "Less than ten people out of two thousand are still left there. Many are in Peshawar, many we don't know if they are alive or dead."

About that time, Habibullah returned temporarily to Pakistan, where he married. He now had a wife and two children living in a refugee camp outside Peshawar. Amid strangers in the impersonal, barrackslike arrangement of the sprawling camp, his wife was obliged to wear the veil, something Kuchi women didn't have to do in Afghanistan, where everyone in the encampment was a close relative. Living as a guerrilla, Habibullah had seen his wife and children only a few times over the years, and he worried about them. He said over a third of the members of his extended family had been killed, "but if we stopped fighting and went to live in the camps in

Pakistan, we would all become refugee slaves and the Communists would have everything."

Habibullah was not vehement or even enthusiastic about what he said. There was an almost bored look in his olive-pit eyes. *Jihad* was obviously no joy for him, but a fundamental duty that grew out of the unfortunate circumstances of his life. Oppression had forced Habibullah — against his better nature, it seemed — to hate. The Afghans, I was beginning to notice, were not really good haters, not like the kind that existed in Iran, Lebanon, and other places Moslems felt themselves to be oppressed. The differences between those places and Afghanistan were, among other things, politics and urbanization. The mujahidin were not politicized to the degree that Arabs and Iranians were. The Afghan fundamentalists were mainly simple village people, not an angry peasant proletariat that had fled to city slums in search of jobs, as in Iran and Egypt, and in the process had sacrificed their cultural underpinnings. Habibullah had lost a lot, but one thing he hadn't lost was a sense of who he was.

Scurrying field mice and the drone of helicopter gunships again disturbed my sleep. When Habibullah saw my fear he laughed. It was the only time I ever saw a smile cross his face. He explained to Wakhil that the gunships never came in low over Spinghar anymore because of the enemy's fear of Stingers. "We don't have Stingers here," Habibullah said. "But we always say we do when communicating by radio, which we know they intercept."

After daybreak the bombs came. The earth vibrated from the thousand-pounders dropped by the fighter jets overhead. Clouds of dust from exploding earth filled the air. The nearest bomb hit several hundred yards away from us and, as it turned out, nobody was hurt. It had been a useless exercise: the jets had taken off from the military air field at Jalalabad, dropped their bombs from about ten thousand feet, and flew home.

The jets were flying so high that from the ground they appeared no larger than specks. Even with television-guided missiles — which these planes were not equipped with — hitting a target as small as a pup tent from that altitude is exceedingly difficult. It was another potent illustration of how the Stingers had changed the face of the war. Weighing only thirty pounds, the heat-seeking antiaircraft missiles were mobile and cost only $75,000 apiece, and in two out of three times that they were fired in Afghanistan, a Stinger destroyed a Soviet jet or helicopter that cost about $4 million each. So the Soviet and Afghan government pilots weren't taking any chances.

Wakhil and I said our goodbyes to Lurang and Jihan-zeb, who would now rejoin Habibullah's forces on Spinghar for guerrilla sorties in the Jalalabad area. We were headed down into the Kot Valley toward that city. Habibullah gave us a new guide, a raw-boned old man whose name I never found out and who I thought, gratefully, would be unable to move along at the same demanding pace set by Lurang and Jihan-zeb.

I was wrong.

The trek from Spinghar was all downhill and took only five hours, which must have been like a sprint for the mujahidin but was among the most difficult of the marches I made inside. The geezer practically jogged the whole way, holding his Kalashnikov in his hand rather than using the shoulder strap. The entire journey was in a canyon floor along a treacherous mountain stream. After days of walking for hours on almost no water, suddenly I was deluged by it. As we descended toward the plain, the weather became hot again, yet the spring water was as cold as melting snow and filled with sharp stones and pebbles. And it was moving fast. We had to ford the stream twenty-three times (masochistically, I was keeping count). My feet were numb inside my soaking running shoes, but I needed the traction to keep from falling in the water — anyway, our guide was not going to wait for me to take my shoes off and put them on again. Near the bottom of the canyon Wakhil noticed several butterfly mines that the mujahidin had surrounded with stones so a passer-by wouldn't easily stumble onto them. In such circumstances there would often be other mines in the vicinity that they hadn't spotted. The old man casually waved at us to come ahead and jogged on, and so did we. After a while I got so tired and out of breath that I stopped thinking about mines. If I was fated to step on one I would, and that was that. My principal fear was the immediate one: falling behind Wakhil and our guide.

The Kot Valley unrolled like a plush green carpet at the foot of Spinghar, a jungly world in sight of the snows. We alighted under a large plane tree on a raised table of earth about a hundred feet over the valley, providing a prospect from which to espy the terrain we were about to enter. A local farmer laid out a rush mat and Turkoman rug for us. His son, wearing a gold Sindhi cap, brought ceramic cups for tea. I took off my shoes and smelly socks and let the hot sun dry my feet while I drank tea under a blue sky on a rug I would have been proud to have in my living room back in Greece. It was the kind of moment that a traveler files away in his mind in order to impress people later on. But what I also remember about that moment was what the farmer told Wakhil about all the irrigation ditches that had been blown up by fighter jets, and the flooding in the valley and malaria outbreak that followed. Malaria, which on the eve of Taraki's Communist coup in April 1978 was at the point of being eradicated in Afghanistan, had returned with a vengeance, thanks to the stagnant, mosquito-breeding pools caused by the widespread destruction of irrigation systems. Nangarhar was rife with the disease. This was another relatively minor, tedious side effect of the Soviet invasion that lacked drama and would only have numbed newspaper readers if written about or even mentioned in passing — which it never was.

We crossed rice, grain, and maize fields, walking along rebuilt irrigation embankments and down dusty trails partially shaded by apple and apricot trees. It was hot and, for the first time since I left Peshawar, a bit humid too. Almost every mud brick dwelling we saw had been hit by a bomb. Yet more civilians lived here than elsewhere in the Spinghar region, and women in colorful *chadors* were ubiquitous in the fields, separating the strands of grain and carrying bundles of it on their heads. Only since the end of 1986 had refugees started to come back to the Kot Valley from Pakistan. The upsurge in cultivation was the result of one thing: Stingers. High-altitude Soviet bombing notwithstanding, the missiles were providing enough air cover to frighten away low-flying gunships, allowing some peasant farmers to return and start growing crops. Relief workers in other parts of Afghanistan where the mujahidin had Stingers had also noticed this phenomenon. The antiaircraft missiles were actually putting food in people's mouths.

We rested again in an apple orchard, and a farmer brought us the best meal I had eaten so far in Afghanistan: curds, lentils, greasy fried eggs, apples, and green tea. The heat, the greenery, the water slowly trickling in the stagnant canals, and the timelessness of the setting evoked a town in the Nile Delta in Egypt.

Our guide took Wakhil and me to meet the commander in the valley. His name was Ashnagur. He was tall and lanky, and with his rifle, bandoleer, and high, bright green turban wrapped tightly around his head he resembled an Afridi bandit. Ashnagur had the visage of a hawk, with a long hooked nose, huge forehead, and black beard. He seemed cocky and reckless. Besides the rifle, he had an old Spanish Star pistol stuck inside his belt with the safety catch off. He was surrounded by about thirty young boys, all armed and constantly staring at him, even though I was the one who was surely the novelty. It was a charisma that rubbed off on me too. Ashnagur hugged me and explained — without my asking — how he would send a prearranged coded signal on the walkie-talkie to

Habibullah, announcing my safe arrival. Then he smacked his huge calloused hand on the ground and said, "Sit. I am here to answer your questions."

Ashnagur was twenty-eight years old, the only child of a peasant couple in a Peshawar refugee camp. Since almost every other Pathan I ever met had at least half a dozen brothers and sisters, growing up as an only child here struck me as a much more intense experience than in my own culture. I wondered if his extreme sociability was a way to compensate for a lonely childhood.

Now Ashnagur seemed to have thirty siblings, all younger and looking up to him as the adored older brother. There was something scary and magical about this band of mujahidin. They suggested a Gypsy troupe, a Central American terrorist outfit, a Puerto Rican street gang, and the orphan thieves of *Oliver Twist* all rolled into one. Their Kalashnikov rifles and grenade launchers were emblazoned with purple and red talismans and pompoms. In place of dull brown *pakols,* some of the boys wore colorful bandannas around their heads. One boy carried an old megaphone for Ashnagur to shout orders through during a battle, but there were no medical supplies except for a half-used and expired package of cold pills. Others had rag-wrapped bundles tied on branches over their shoulders that contained lumps of American-supplied C-4 plastic explosive for nightly sorties against Soviet and Afghan regime installations in the area. Proudly, Ashnagur took out a fistful of the substance, stuck a copper wire into it that was affixed at the end to a "time pencil," and blew up a section of mud embankment to demonstrate the explosive power. The boys, who must have seen him do this many times before, nevertheless watched with awe. Isolated in this lush central Asian valley, with all their family members dead or in refugee camps, the boys had dreamed up their own rich pantheon of gods and sacred objects, including Allah, C-4 plastique, magic charms, and Ashnagur. For these homeless boys, Ashnagur was everything: older brother, father figure, and supreme role model.

There was one old man in the unit, sixty-year-old Said Hamidullah. Trachoma blinded him in one eye. He told me that one of his three sons had been killed here in 1986 during a Soviet ground assault. "As long as I can still see out of the other eye I will fight and kill Russians," he shouted at me in a hoarse, eccentric tone. "In the Gulf, Moslems are killing Moslems. The Palestinians are all Communists. Ours is the only true *jihad*." None of the teenagers laughed or at any time seemed to make fun of him.

They all lived off the land, eating wild maize, rice, fruit, raw turnips and onions, and the occasional egg or bowl of curds given to them by the local farmers. Almost every evening after dark they set out for the Jalalabad plain to blow up a small bridge or a section of road or just to take a few pot shots at an enemy base, since at this late stage in the war, neither the Soviets nor the Afghan regime's troops ventured from their bases. A siege mentality had overcome them.

Wakhil and I stayed with Ashnagur's unit for the better part of a week. I heard gunfire and the thud and shake of artillery throughout each day and early evening, and several times Soviet aircraft bombed the valley to no great effect. One evening, the boys in the unit brought me a chicken to eat, but it tasted rotten and had a maggot inside. I went behind a tree to vomit. Wakhil remonstrated me for insulting our hosts. I apologized. Another night, I was sound asleep under a plane tree when, at about four A.M., we were all awakened by the rumble of feet and the clanging of rifles. *Clack, clack, clack* — bullets slid into breeches as the mujahidin prepared for a firefight. My stomach turned. I rolled off the jute bed onto the ground. My ultimate nightmare was being killed or captured in an ambush by Communist troops, who from time to time found it necessary to prove that they were still to be taken seriously. It was a false alarm. Another guerrilla unit had just arrived from an

all-night trek and had forgotten to give the password. Everyone laughed, and I felt like a fool again, lying on the ground,
shaking.

Ashnagur conducted most of his sorties near the Soviet base
at Dihbala, a complex of sandbagged bunkers at the edge of
the Spinghar foothills that looked out on the Jalalabad plain.
The pattern was always the same. At dusk, the mujahidin
would eat a meager meal on the ground and then pray while
Ashnagur split the plastique into small pieces and prepared
them with the copper wire and time pencils, which had break-
able seals releasing acid that burned down the wire. The
march to the road linking the Soviet base with Jalalabad took
several hours. As usual, a bridge or section of the road would
be blown up and the guerrillas would beat a fast retreat. The
pace was impossible, so I went only partway to the target,
staying behind with a member of the unit. I heard the explosion and a volley of shots fired from the nearby enemy position
in response. Then the young fighter I was with badgered me
to run as fast as I could behind him. He cursed me all the way
back to Ashnagur's base area. Still, the others who had carried
out the sabotage operation arrived back first. Thank God Abdul Haq wasn't there to see me, I thought. The entire experience had the humiliating quality of army basic training. Each
day, more and more of me was being broken down.

When I staggered back I saw Ashnagur's boys collapsed on
the jute beds. Dawn had peeled away the darkness from their
faces to reveal glazed, jubilant expressions. Backfire from a
malfunctioning grenade launcher had blistered one boy's face.
Ashnagur gave him a cold pill. The boy, his eyes dazed and
watery, smiled and swallowed the pill with a serious expression, as if it could actually help. I gave him one of my painkillers. The others cleaned their rifle barrels and grenade
launchers with kerchiefs wrapped around branches. This was
the base of rural resistance upon which more impressive actions of other, more famous commanders rested.

*

Abdul Haq, the most important mujahidin commander in the Kabul area during most of the war,
takes a break in the field. *(Tony O'Brien/The Picture
Group, Inc.)*

Clashes between turbaned guerrillas, armed with only Lee-Enfield and Kalashnikov rifles, and Soviet tanks were not uncommon. *(Wide World Photos)*

Gulbuddin Hekmatyar, a fundamentalist and anti-Western extremist, received most of his aid from the United States and Pakistan. (© *John Gunston*)

Pir Syed Ahmed Gailani was a leading moderate in the mujahidin alliance. He was not popular among many rebel fighters, who considered him part of a dying aristocratic order. (© *John Gunston*)

Above: Abdul Haq *(left)* and Amin Wardak plan an operation against Kabul, the Afghan capital. Wardak quit Pir Syed Ahmed Gailani's rebel organization and joined Haq in late 1987. *(©John Gunston)*

Left: Yunus Khalis, a crusty Moslem preacher, fielded the strongest mujahidin army in the Jalalabad region. *(©John Gunston)*

Left: Abdul Haq's oldest brother, Haji Din Mohammed, was the man whose respect Haq desired most. (© *John Gunston)*

Below: Abdul Haq, in the dark vest and light *shalwar kameez*, lectures one of his fighters in the mountains of eastern Afghanistan. *(Tony O'Brien/ The Picture Group, Inc.)*

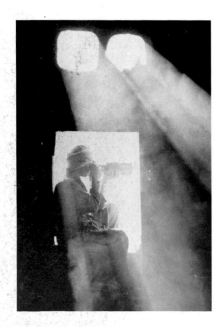

Left: John Wellesley Gunston was the most intrepid of a brave group of photographers who covered the war from inside Afghanistan throughout the 1980s. *(© Ken Guest)*
Below: In 1987 Congressman Charles Wilson (D-Texas) rode into Afghanistan on a white horse. Wilson was known on Capitol Hill and on the Northwest Frontier as the mujahidin's best friend in the House of Representatives. *(Wide World Photos)*

The author, in native dress, stands above a rice paddy on the Pakistan-Afghanistan border before climbing the Safed Koh mountain range into Afghanistan. *(Tony Davis)*

This village on the strategic Salang Highway was
destroyed during fighting between Soviet tank forces
and Afghan rebels in early 1989. The highway is the
principal supply route between the Soviet Union and
Kabul. *(Wide World Photos)*

Despite the constant fatigue and physical discomfort, I rarely felt cynical or let down. Because of the war, Afghanistan offered a form of travel that had all but died out in the last part of the twentieth century. I considered myself privileged to be crossing frontiers without the need of a passport and trekking over new and fascinating landscape that had not been altered by modern development. As selfish and retrograde as this attitude was, it was irresistible. I never felt uneasy, either, despite being at the mercy of a band of seared, scrappy young men.

As fighters, Ashnagur's band may not have been the most impressive, but they and the other mujahidin I met embodied characteristics that were unique in the Third World, and my awareness of this fact kept my enthusiasm from flagging. Not only were they fanatical Moslems who were exceedingly tolerant of nonbelievers; they were also probably the only group of their kind with whom a Western woman would have been absolutely safe. (Several female journalists, who would not necessarily think of themselves as tough, traveled with the guerrillas.) I saw no hint of overt homosexuality or any kind of sexual deviation, though, as in all cultures, such things undoubtedly existed.

Rarely in Afghanistan or the Northwest Frontier did I encounter a mujahid with a lewd look in his eyes, as if he were staring at someone through a keyhole — an expression I had seen throughout the Middle East. Displays of excessive politeness toward Western women, also common in that part of the world, were absent among the Pathans. Abdul Haq treated the occasional female journalist as if she were one of the boys — primitive though his attitude was toward women of his own culture. After Abdul Qadir had had the opportunity to pass through Bangkok, I asked him if he had taken advantage of the city's easily available sexual delights. "You think I am a donkey," Qadir hissed, as if I had insulted him.

You could come up with various explanations for the genuine respect accorded to foreign women by Pathans, as well as for the Pathans' apparent lack of sexual frustration and conflict when away from their wives for months at a time. A university-educated Pathan in Peshawar told me the fact that the Pathans were never urbanized, as Arabs and Iranians were, may have something to do with it. The exigencies of war may be another reason. In *The Danger Tree*, a novel about the World War II desert campaign in Egypt, the British writer Olivia Manning observed:

> Here in the desert, either from lack of stimulus or some quality in the air, the men were not much troubled by sex. The need to survive was their chief preoccupation. . . . In spite of the heat of the day, the cold of the night, the flies, the mosquitoes, the sand-flies, the stench of death that came on the wind, the sand blowing into the body's interstices and gritting in everything one ate, the human animal not only survived but flourished. Simon felt well and vigorous and he thought of women, if he thought of them at all, with a benign indifference. He belonged now to a world of men; a contained, self-sufficient world where life was organized from dawn till sunset. It had so complete a hold on him, he could see only one flaw in it: his friends died young.

Except for the desert sand, of which there was less in Afghanistan, it would have been an accurate description of the Pathan world in the 1980s.

Up to a point, that is. For the aura of masculinity and self-containment is common to men at war in general. But how many warrior societies were so primitive, so free of Western influence, and so chock-full of literary references?

At the turn of the century there were the Cossacks, the fabled horsemen of southern Russia. To Russian intellectuals like Tolstoy, the Cossack was a man of "primitive energy, passion, and virtue. He was the man as yet untrammelled by civilization, direct, immediate, fierce." That, at least, is how Lionel Trilling once described Tolstoy's attitude toward the Cossacks, comparing it to that of Isaac Babel:

> We have devised an image of our lost freedom which we mock

in the very phrase by which we name it: the noble savage. No doubt the mockery is justified, yet our fantasy of the noble savage represents a reality of our existence, it stands for our sense of something unhappily surrendered, the truth of the body, . . . the truth of open aggressiveness. Something, we know, must inevitably be surrendered for the sake of civilization; but the "discontent" of civilization which Freud describes is our self-recrimination at having surrendered too much. Babel's view of the Cossack was more consonant with that of Tolstoy than with the traditional view of his own people [the Jews]. For him, the Cossack was indeed the noble savage, all too savage, not often noble.

No, the Cossack of a hundred years ago was not often noble. The horseman of the steppes was the instrument of czarist violence against the Jews, raping and murdering women and children in sadistic pogroms. This was the problem with Babel's worship of the Cossacks. But to imagine the Pathans going into a village in Afghanistan and doing the same things strains credibility. Were this ever to occur, it would be so at odds with Pathan behavior that other Pathans would unite to condemn it.

For decades, Western journalists, relief workers, and other intrepid romantics had scoured the East in search of an exotic human specimen who was undefiled by the bastardizing influences of the West, yet was also without the perversions and hypocrisies for which the East was famous. The Afghan war brought their search to an end; on the Northwest Frontier they rediscovered Kipling's Pathans.

For the Americans who went to the Northwest Frontier in the 1980s, the attraction was particularly intense, perhaps because, unlike generations of British schoolboys brought up on Empire, Americans came late to the discovery that Kamal and Mahbub Ali and the characters in Kipling's stories and poems were not Arabs but Pathans — and set apart.

"At first, I knew only that Kamal and his fellows were some unusual kind of Indians, rather like our own Indians of the American West, devoted to brave and warlike deeds. . . . Then

I began to have a dim idea of the great tribal brotherhood which sprawled across northern India and Afghanistan," wrote the American diplomat James W. Spain in his memoir *The Way of the Pathans.* Actually, the Pathans were more like our cowboys than like American Indians; they lived by the law of the gun and had an unambiguous code of honor, Pukhtunwali, whose preeminent precepts are *nang* (pride), *badal* (revenge), and *melmastia* (hospitality).

Distinct from all other Moslem peoples in the Near East, the Pathans were essentially democratic and egalitarian, with political life dominated by the *jirga,* a kind of ancient Athenian parliament of tribal elders, and no tradition of especially cruel, autocratic rulers. Yet like the Arabs, they lived a harsh, sterile existence that was nevertheless baroque and romantic: "They have bred poets as copiously as they have bred warriors," Spain said. The Pukhtu ballads of Khushal Khan Khatak, reeking as they do of blood and flowers and noble deeds, are as Arthurian as those of the greatest Arab poets. The Pathans, then, were an American romantic's dream come true: as exotic as the Arabs, but without the Arabs' reputation for authoritarianism. The Pathans were *men.* As some Americans on the Northwest Frontier saw it, you didn't have to be an aesthete or moral relativist like those goddamn Europeans who worshiped the Cossacks and Arabs to justify them.

As the young mujahidin in the Kot Valley looked up to Ashnagur, Ashnagur — and Habibullah too — looked up to Abdul Qadir. Qadir, Abdul Haq's brother, was the chief guerrilla commander in Shinwar, the region of Nangarhar closest to the Khyber Pass. Ashnagur and Habibullah talked about Qadir as though he were some kind of god. "Qadir is our father, our brother. We follow him everywhere. He teaches us about religion. He is a wise judge," Ashnagur once said. In reality, what prompted these accolades was Qadir's social status: he was an educated man from a wealthy landowning family among poor peasants like Ashnagur and Habibullah. Whenever Qadir translated the newscasts on the BBC World Service into Pukhtu for his field commanders, an awed look came over their faces. They were obviously impressed with his education and knowledge of English. And Qadir was generous — always passing out wads of afghanis to the mujahidin and the peasants of Shinwar.

I got to know Qadir on my second trip inside, which Abdul Haq had arranged. Qadir's thirty-eight-year-old cousin had died of a heart attack two days before our departure for Afghanistan, and Qadir walked into the stone dwelling where we were staying near the border with tears in his eyes. "This fate comes from God," he said to me, boring his eyes deep into mine. "All of us must face it someday."

Qadir himself had serious kidney and liver problems, the same illness that had killed his father and that Abdul Haq suffered from too. Qadir, unlike Haq, was a chain smoker and *naswar* addict, chewing gobs of the opium-laced stuff throughout the day, and as a consequence was always coughing and spitting. He was thirty-five and easily looked fifty. He complained of stomach and chest pains before we even started out on our journey, and I wondered how he was going to climb the fourteen-thousand-foot pass that lay ahead of us. I also wondered how this fretful physical wreck of a man could maintain the respect and adoration of the likes of Ashnagur and Habibullah.

Qadir was in a particularly foul mood that day. Chewing *naswar* and puffing on a water pipe, he said sarcastically: "Where is Gulbuddin Hekmatyar? I thought he was Zia's big mujahid! Gulbuddin is afraid to cross the border. You know what Zia told Charlie Wilson [a Democratic congressman from Texas and an enthusiastic supporter of the mujahidin]? Zia told him, 'I will give you Jalalabad as a Christmas present, with Hekmatyar in charge.' Why do you Americans believe all this bullshit? Jalalabad will not fall so soon. The mujahidin are not ready for conventional battles. I know, because I and 'Engineer' Mahmoud [another Khalis party commander] will take Jalalabad when we are ready." Qadir then went outside to pray and sip tea on a carpet. Listening to the birds at sunset, he closed his eyes and seemed to enter a kind of nirvana.

The next day, taking a route different from the one I had traveled with Wakhil, we climbed the highest pass in the Spinghar range. At the foot of the fourteen-thousand-foot pass, before beginning the ascent, Qadir squatted on the ground and vomited, and in addition had an attack of diarrhea. But after a few minutes of groaning, Qadir slowly got up, draped a cloth over his *pakol* to further protect his head from the sun, and proceeded to climb the mountain, arriving at the windy, icy summit — the Durand Line — only a few minutes behind me. And, despite all the tobacco smoking he did, Qadir was not breathing hard. "This is good," he said, looking down the other slope at a lovely forest of firs, cedars, and spruces. "Now that I am in Afghanistan I feel better." From that moment on, I had trouble keeping up with him. Like Wakhil and every other mujahid I knew, Qadir grew in strength with the difficulty of the terrain while I always weakened.

His tenacity was unquestioned. In November 1986, Qadir led seven hundred guerrillas, clothed only in open leather sandals and cotton *shalwar kameezes*, against upward of two thousand Soviet and Afghan regime troops in a snowstorm near Dihbala. The battle was a stand-off. Several of Qadir's men had to have their frostbitten toes amputated afterward.

Other aspects of Qadir's personality were less entrancing. His strengths and weaknesses derived from the fact that he was a typical Pathan. Traveling with him was like going back to the days of Chaucer's knights; meals with him were medieval spectacles. As he was the leading guerrilla commander for the region, Shinwar peasants were expected to kill a sheep or goat in his honor. Every evening we would enter a new village and sit outside under the stars, talking, smoking a water pipe, and waiting for the meat to cook. Then Qadir, at least a dozen other mujahidin, and the village notables would enter the house and stack their guns against the mud walls, sit around the carpet, and silently devour a repast that would include a sheep or a goat, chicken livers, rice, onions, cucumbers, tomatoes, mangoes, and bananas. (Whether you were a journalist or a fighter, you always ate better when traveling with a big commander. The problem was trying not to break wind, something that Pathans consider to be far ruder and funnier than we Westerners do. An American relief worker did so in the presence of Abdul Haq, and the mujahidin spoke of the incident for months.)

Qadir even had a court jester, a sixty-year-old turbaned Afridi who was fat, didn't carry a gun, and seemed to have no discernible function except to tell stories and jokes. Journalists dubbed him "Haji Ball Grabber," because one of his pranks was to pretend to shake your hand while lunging for your testicles.

It was a leisurely stroll into Afghanistan with Qadir. He slept late and every night sat down to a huge feast. He had been in Peshawar for several weeks and told me he would need several more, to talk to Ashnagur, Habibullah, and other field commanders before planning a series of attacks against Soviet and Afghan regime positions near Jalalabad. This was in June 1988, after the Soviet withdrawal had started, when pundits in America were speculating about the possibility of a mujahidin assault on the city of Jalalabad itself. But the war seemed to Qadir like a sport. He fought and risked his life at his own pace and didn't consult much with other big commanders about what he was doing, as they didn't consult with him. This was why the assault on Jalalabad didn't come until February 1989, and partly why it failed.

Qadir was like an English country squire taking up the hunt. But finally, after a month of sleeping late and leisurely consulting with his subordinates, he surgically blasted the Afghan government post of Achin into near oblivion.

It was at Qadir's headquarters, an eyrie of tents and heavy machine guns looking out onto Soviet and Afghan regime positions at Dihbala, that I got sick. It was dysentery. I couldn't stop vomiting and had diarrhea. Unlike Qadir, however, I lacked the strength to climb a mountain.

Everyone I knew got sick in Afghanistan, and many of the books written about the country seemed to revolve exclusively around the writer's illnesses and constant physical discomfort. Because of its humor and brilliant, tongue-in-cheek conclusion, the British travel writer Eric Newby's 1958 classic, *A Short Walk in the Hindu Kush,* is the finest book of this genre. Having just scaled a twenty-thousand-foot peak despite awful weather and illness, and with little to eat, Newby and his companion, Hugh Carless, met up with the world-famous explorer Wilfred Thesiger on their trek back to Kabul. "Pansies," Thesiger called them, watching Newby and Carless inflate their air mattresses on the stony ground.

Losing weight and dehydrating fast, I had no choice but to go back to Peshawar. Trekking was impossible, but riding for seventy-two hours on a mule without a saddle while suffering from dysentery proved to be far more difficult than walking the same distance in good health. It was hard to hold down any liquid in my stomach, especially since the green tea began to taste like urine and the tea boys insisted on serving it in small cups half filled with sugar. I could focus only on the negative aspects of Pathan existence. How sterile their life was! Everyone wore unkempt beards and seemed to go for months without sex. Wherever I looked there were wild herbs growing on the mountainsides, suitable for all kinds of exotic teas, but the Pathans preferred only this weak, awful stuff. Unlike the Arabs, they disdained coffee and, of course, alcohol too.

Then the mule boy accompanying me, Farouk Ali, did something that surprised me. He grabbed a pink rose that was growing all alone on a rock face and stuck it behind his ear and smiled, wearing it like that the rest of the day. Ill with nausea, sunstroke, and dehydration, choking dust and sandstone and thorn bushes all around me, I was deeply affected by the sight of that rose and the extravagant gesture Farouk Ali made with it. It was like a revelation. This was a culture that had produced no painting or sculpture of any kind and boasted little original music or dance. Though Peshawar was the principal city of the Pathans, the Peshawar Museum was filled with Buddhist, Moghul, and Persian art only. But the Pathans did write poetry:

> Be they Roses, or Violets, or Tulips:
> By their sight is my heart now soothed to rest.
> May I devote myself to the Creator of these works,
> Since from his mighty hands such beauties have been
> produced.

Those were the words of Khushal Khan Khatak. The wearing of a pink rose by an uneducated mule boy was, for me, a sign that the poetic impulse ran deep in the culture.

Of course, Arab and Persian culture offered similar contrasts between the barren and the baroque. But with the Pathans those contrasts seemed to be starker and more dramatic. On a later trip inside Afghanistan I stayed at a guerrilla base that was under constant mortar bombardment where the mujahidin raised petunias and had paid the equivalent of $175 — a fortune by Afghan standards — for a songbird.

The little tea or water I could keep down was not enough to soothe my throat, which grew more and more parched. Then my throat became so dry it was almost too painful to swallow, and pressure built up in my ears as if I were in an airplane. At a tea stall I noticed a rotting watermelon skin, and my self-discipline broke down. Just the thought of more green tea or water was enough to make me gag, but I knew I could hold down a watermelon. I began crying, almost, for a piece, but there was no more. Evidently, watermelons could be had in war-torn Nangarhar, but finding one at a tea stall was a matter of luck. The idea of rinsing my desiccated mouth with the juice began to obsess me, however. I began to imagine mountains of watermelons and waterfalls of watermelon juice. Then I started counting the hours to Landi Kotal, where I could buy a watermelon. Or a Coke. Fifty hours to go, forty-five . . . I was lost in childhood memories of root beer and cream soda flushing through my mind. It was comic. All restraint had dissolved. Afghanistan had completely broken me.

The pain of thirst was so all-encompassing that I was barely aware of the welts that were forming on my buttocks from the hours on the mule. I was becoming so dehydrated and overheated that just the sound of trickling spring water sent chills of relief through my body, and rinsing my fully clothed body in the cold streams was pure sensual annihilation.

And so was the photograph of my family by the Aegean Sea. Opening his eyes wide, Farouk Ali pointed at the blue water in the background. The sight of my wife in shorts and without a veil appeared to have no effect on him. Never having been out of Afghanistan and the Northwest Frontier, he had never even seen a lake, let alone a sea. The sight of what, for a Pathan, was the equivalent of a naked woman did not stir him as much as the idea of a large body of water. Given my thirst, I could understand his emotion.

Then came the Valley of Tirah Bazaar. At a small camp of Khalis mujahidin we picked up two bodyguards for the journey through Afridi territory. It took eight hours on the mule during the hottest hours of the day, stopping not once for water. Because of my illness, I was now a whimpering idiot.

In Landi Kotal, I bought Farouk Ali and myself four watermelons and six Coca-Colas. Suddenly he seemed as thirsty as I was. He had never complained, yet now he was devouring the watermelons and Cokes faster than I. We both slurped and drank until there was nothing left. After I paid him for the mule, Farouk Ali went back into the desert toward the Valley of Tirah Bazaar and Afghanistan. Back to that same thirst and other deprivations.

The ability to endure, year after harrowing year, such a monastic existence, as barren and as confined by self-denial as that of the most disciplined desert anchorites, constituted the most lethal weapon the Pathans had in their battle against the Soviets. Had the Afghans acquiesced to Soviet rule without a fight, no doubt there would have been more watermelon and other fruit, and perhaps even a bus and paved road in Nangarhar. And there would not have been any mines. The idea of fighting for political freedom is an easy one to grasp until you see in the flesh what the cost is.

Of course, I didn't have to get dysentery to figure this out. But, in the manner of the surgeon learning about mines in the operating room, being sick in Afghanistan provided me with an experience through which I was better able to appreciate the concept — and the price — of freedom as I never had before.

5

The Growth of a Commander

A S   W E   A L L   K N O W, memory is selective. Individuals, like tribes and nations, continually revise their own pasts to conform with current self-images. This was especially true for the Pathans. "Facts," observed a British friend, "were so interwoven with fiction on the Northwest Frontier that one might as well unstitch all the carpets in the Khyber bazaar before finding a stitch of truth."

Between trips inside, I fell into a pattern of seeing Abdul Haq at least two times a week. I have only Haq's word for the seminal events of his youth. But that was all I wanted. It was his attitudes and image of himself, rather than the bare-bones literal truth, that I was after.

Haq's headquarters in a guarded Peshawar villa was one of the few places in the Third World I'd seen where real work — rather than the usual conspiracy-mongering over endless cups of tea — seemed to be done, where I knew that I was taking up valuable time. In the waiting room I always saw a group of mujahidin nervously clutching notes, waiting to see "Haji Sahab" (Mr. Haji). One entered Haq's private office only after removing one's shoes. Apart from that, his office had a surface resemblance to that of any businessman or lawyer in the West. Haq would usually be talking on one of his two desk phones while simultaneously reading a report and writing notes on a separate sheet of paper. Next to the two phones were a small globe and a red desk lamp. Papers were stacked at neat right angles to the other objects on the desk and separated into "in" and "out" piles. Behind the desk on the wall was a large map of Soviet posts in Kabul. (In the adjacent "war room" was a nine-foot-high Soviet wall map of Afghanistan, with a sandbox that had markers for planning battles: this was the room where John Gunston's pictures were displayed.)

Haq, always dressed in a gray *shalwar kameez* and vest — the equivalent of a pin-striped suit in the West — would be on the phone for a few minutes after I came in the office. Inevitably, a succession of mujahidin would file in, take seats opposite him, make a request, and give him a note to initial before being ushered out to receive a stack of money from Haq's Tajik accountant. The tone of each man was submissive. Listening to their requests, Haq looked discerning, impassive, and slightly smug, as if he knew beyond a shadow of a doubt that he could accurately size up the character and actions of every man under his command. His was a face that at times reminded me of Marlon Brando playing Don Vito Corleone in the opening scene of *The Godfather.*

Profusely apologizing for the interruptions, Haq would hobble over to the couch opposite me, order tea, and patiently submit to my queries about his life. He took only one lump of sugar in his tea and didn't smoke — unusual for an Oriental male. Scratching his beard, he would joke: "The eyes of a journalist scare me almost as much as the eyes of a doctor with a knife about to cut into my foot."

Abdul Haq was born Abdul Rauf on April 23, 1958, in Nangarhar province west of Jalalabad. But he spent his first years in the faraway southern province of Helmand, near Iran and Pakistan, where his father, Mohammed Aman, was the representative of a Nangarhar construction company. A clash of wills between the two dominated Haq's first childhood memories. In his mind, he and his father were the only actors on stage. The rest of the family didn't exist. The eerie Helmand steppes provided a beautiful yet threatening background.

"I was on a bus with my father," Haq said. "For hours I was

asking him questions. I don't remember about what, but I kept asking them. He got so tired of my questions that he started screaming and slapped me. Everybody on the bus was a stranger. We didn't have any friends in Helmand. I was four. It is my earliest memory.

"Another time, my father was driving his jeep up a hill near our house. It was evening and he was tired. On either side of the road were mud walls. I stood in the middle of the road and refused to let him pass. He started screaming at me, but I wouldn't get out of the road. I hugged the ground with my body. Finally, he drove around me and crashed the side of the jeep into the wall. I was five, I think.

"I wanted to go to school like my older brothers, but my father told me I was still too young. I was only five and you had to be seven. I got so mad that I tore up my brothers' school books. So my father took me, unregistered, to the school. I remember once the teacher fell asleep. Maybe he was tired or sick, but I thought that rude and I went over to the teacher's desk and hit him hard over the head with a stick to wake him up. The teacher ran after me but I got away. I was always a little devil.

"My father liked to see children fight. I remember he would throw a coin up in the air and my brothers and I would scramble for it. I worshiped my father. I was six when he died of kidney disease. He was fifty-one. We left Helmand and went back to Nangarhar. We had no family in Helmand. In Nangarhar we did — lots of aunts and uncles and cousins to play with. We owned land and a big house and garden, and everybody in the village knew us. We always had lots of guests. This gave me a great sense of security after my father died. I found that I was part of something. From then on I had no doubt who I was."

Haq was wealthy by Afghan standards; nevertheless, when in Peshawar he lived in one room with his wife and two children in the same crowded house as the families of his two older brothers. Though he confided in foreigners and felt alienated from the rest of his family, he could not stand to live apart from any of them.

Haq's family is of the Arsala Khel, a subdivision of the Jabbar Khel, which is a leading landowning clan of the Ahmadzai — the great Pathan tribe that historically has been in conflict with the Durrani kings (also Pathans), who ruled Afghanistan from the middle of the eighteenth century through 1973, when King Zahir Shah was deposed and went into exile in Rome. The Jabbar Khel consists of over fifteen hundred prosperous families, who in days gone by robbed travelers on the Kabul–Jalalabad road. Jabbar himself is buried near the main road, and his grave is, according to one legend, a place of evil and a haunt of robbers and wolves. Haq's hometown of Fatehbad is synonymous with the deaths of many British soldiers during the disastrous British retreat from Kabul in January 1842. But in the last hundred years the clan has gained a reputation for government service. Haq's great-grandfather on his father's side was Wazir Arsala Khan, a foreign minister of Afghanistan. Haq's cousin Hedayat Arsala was until 1988 an officer of the World Bank in Washington, D.C. The first time I met Haq, in his car after the mine injury, Hedayat Arsala was by his side, having flown over from Washington as soon as he heard about the accident. Haq, the maimed warrior in a *shalwar kameez,* and Hedayat in a gray suit and tie, looking like an international banker — it made for a deliciously interesting contrast and testified to the reserves of love, tradition, and talent in this Pathan family.

"I know little about the history of my family or my people," Haq said. "I feel humiliated that it is foreigners like you who have to tell me about the history of the Pathans. The problem is that I spent so much time fighting and in jail that I never had a chance to read books. When this war is over all I want to do is read about my own culture, nothing but read, so that I'll know what I was fighting for."

As a little boy in the Nangarhar village of Fatehbad, Haq went with his older brothers every morning at 5:30 to pray in the local mosque. Then came six hours of Koranic school, followed by lessons with a private tutor. "The *mullahs* were strict and kept us busy till the evening. If we talked or were late, we'd get a hard slap across the face. There were only the *mullahs*. The government in Kabul didn't exist for us.

"But we had a house in Kabul and spent the summers there. Kabul was cooler than Nangarhar. I love my village a hundred times more than the city. I hated to buy things from strangers and go into stores where we didn't know people.

"Everyone in my village was Moslem. It was something that you didn't think about or question. That's why the fundamentalists are so strong now against the Communists. To destroy one ideology you need another. I remember when I was eight I started at the lycée. One of the teachers, who I now realize was a Communist, told us we must go to war against Pakistan for Islam. So I asked, 'What about Panjdeh?' [Russia had taken this town in northwestern Afghanistan in 1885.] I had seen it on a map. The teacher ignored me. So I kept asking the same question over and over. Finally, the teacher hit me, so I hit him back. Then my classmates and I dragged him outside and dry-shaved his head. I was taken to the principal's office and suspended from school for a time. But my family didn't punish me. This was my first political experience.

"When I was a little older, about twelve or thirteen, I was taken with some other boys to be tutored by Yunus Khalis, who was a close friend of the family. He joked a lot, made me laugh, and gave me little presents. Khalis was good with children. I adored him and looked up to him."

Khalis, a renowned Islamic scholar and mathematician from the nearby town of Khogiani, ran a publishing house that printed the first Pukhtu translation of several Koranic commentaries from the original Arabic. The idea of such a scholar finding pleasure teaching unruly teenage boys was typical of Khalis, a salt-of-the-earth type with a ready sense of humor who was completely lacking in pretense. (Years later, Khalis would arrive barefoot to his first meeting with the natty UN special representative to Afghanistan, Diego Cordovez. In Khalis's hand was a rusty nail, which he used as a toothpick.) I'll never forget watching Khalis in his Peshawar headquarters while one of his commanders playfully yanked at his long red beard, which Khalis had just redyed with henna to impress his teenage wife. Khalis laughed loudly the whole time, slapping the man on the back. Afterward Khalis sat down next to me, smiled, and patiently answered my questions about Islam, which he lamented was "totally outside the thought pattern of the West, making it difficult for Americans to understand our struggle, even though they are helping us with arms." This is an ayatollah? I asked myself. A foreign policy bureaucrat in Washington might say he was. But had Khomeini ever let an American reporter into his presence and behaved like that? The answer, of course, was no.

Back in 1973, when King Zahir Shah was overthrown by his first cousin and former prime minister, Mohammed Daoud, fundamentalists like Khalis and Haq's older brothers, Din Mohammed and Abdul Qadir, cheered. Zahir Shah had held the throne for forty years, since he was eighteen, and to the fundamentalists he was a corrupt profligate who fiddled while Afghan Communists busily burrowed into the state bureaucracy. But the fundamentalists feared Daoud even more. He was known to be a friend of the Soviet Union and stood for a stronger, more efficient central government.

Daoud's coup was made possible by the assistance of cells of junior officers controlled by Parcham (Banner), the less extreme of the two branches of the Afghan Communist party. Parcham's influence in the army's lower echelon complemented Daoud's own clout among the generals. The combination made for a bloodless coup, in which all potential resistance was snuffed out. Because the Parcham Communists were crucial to Daoud when he first assumed power, he let them dominate the ruling revolutionary council. Eventually, Daoud purged the Parchamis from the council and tried to steer a less pro-Soviet path. As a result, not only were the disaffected Khalqis — the more extreme of the Afghan Communists — busy plotting against Daoud's government, but the Parchamis were too.

To Khalis and Din Mohammed especially, the Kabul government under Daoud was a godless force seeking to extend its dominion into the countryside in order to subvert age-old religious and tribal traditions. As reactionary and paranoid as this vision may have seemed in 1973, subsequent events were to bear it out completely, when the more extreme Khalqis overthrew Daoud. The most powerful mujahidin groups in the 1980s were the fundamentalist ones, simply because the fundamentalists were the first to decipher the course of events in the 1970s, and therefore the first to act.

Abdul Haq continued his story the next time we met: "Just after Daoud came to power, I remember we had a teacher at our school who, like the other one, tried to introduce Socialist ideas into the class. I objected to this." Haq formed a delegation that protested to the headmaster and demonstrated outside the school. "My family had a few acres of land, so I had a little money to spend on making posters and placards. I was arrested." That was the end of Haq's formal education.

"I learned how to use a Lee-Enfield rifle and explode dynamite at an early age. It was an easy way to hunt and fish and kill cats. I once killed a hundred fifty cats with dynamite," Haq bashfully admitted. "I attacked my first police station when I was sixteen. It was easy, but we didn't know what to do once we were inside. One of us was captured and tortured. I promised myself that I would never do anything like that again without planning every detail in advance. It was about then that I took the name of Abdul Haq, so I wouldn't get my family into trouble. But for months at a time I would use the name Saleh to confuse the police. I had other names too during that period. I can't remember them all.

"The first time I was caught with plastic explosive I told the policeman it was soap. He said, 'All right, light a match to it. We'll see if it's really soap.' I lit the match, and of course it didn't explode. It was a type of plastique called *kama,* which only explodes if it is lit from inside. You can hold a match around the edges all day and nothing is going to happen.

"I used to hide large amounts of it in a shop. Then one day the police came and took away the shopkeeper. The plastique was taken too. Nobody ever saw the shopkeeper again. I never knew exactly what happened, whether the police had found the plastique or whether the shopkeeper was arrested for something unrelated. No, I didn't feel guilty. I didn't will the police to arrest him. If I was the one arrested, who was going to weep for me? By this time — it was 1976 — my family was split up and Khalis and Din Mohammed and Abdul Qadir were all in hiding or already in Pakistan. No, never in my life have I known any self-doubt."

Before his twentieth birthday, Haq was involved at the fringes of two coup attempts against Daoud, shuttling messages and explosives between various rebel officers in the Afghan military. Haq was an early bloomer: a roughneck who thought quickly and clearly on his feet, undoubtedly blessed with an extraordinary natural intelligence — the quintessential guerrilla. He was becoming every bit an equal to those who had once inhabited the jungle of Algiers and were now dismantling Beirut, places where the competence of the inner-city combatants was much higher than the crude, comic-opera attempts of the Pathans, who fought well only in their mountains.

In April 1978, Haq slipped and fell off a friend's roof. So when the police caught up with him near Mirwas Maidan in downtown Kabul, with an unloaded gun he had just purchased, it was impossible for him to run away. "I just said, 'Bullshit,' and threw the gun at one of the policemen as hard as I could and then punched him in the face."

Haq was thrown into Pul-i-Charki. (Daoud had built the prison, and there, as fate would have it, Daoud would spend his last days, together with his family.) In the cell across from him was the infamous Khalqi leader Nur Mohammed Taraki. Haq studied his face for hours at a time. "So that's Taraki, I said to myself, the top Communist. Everybody in the prison knew who he was. No, I never spoke to him. I only stared. He was old. I thought, He's not so goddamned tough."

One overcast day the soldiers came to remove Taraki's handcuffs. It was the morning of April 27, 1978. Haq would never forget the moment. The Khalqi's expression was fixed in stone. One minute a prisoner, the next the keeper and tormentor of other prisoners. Taraki inhabited a world of power and violence and terror; maybe it was all the same to him. Whatever his emotions were, he kept them hidden. The eighteen-year-old fundamentalist guerrilla, who to the new Communist ruler of Afghanistan was just another prisoner, read nothing in the old man's face. Taraki was murdered the next year by fellow Communist Hafizullah Amin, the same man who had let him out of prison that morning.

"A few hours later we were all freed. The warden said, 'Everybody out and fight the Daoud regime.' The next day I was arrested again and taken back to Pul-i-Charki. This time I was not allowed a radio or my Koran. I had to sleep on the cement floor. That's where I pissed, since I was no longer permitted to use the toilet." Others were soon being tortured. A broken Fanta bottle rammed up the anus was the most common method. Months later, when Soviet advisers came, the guards were taught how to wire the rectum, in addition to the ears, nose, and testicles, so they could administer electric shocks. When they came to take a man away, he gave his clothes and whatever else he had to the other prisoners. The man then simply vanished. The family was told nothing, not even that the man had been arrested in the first place. All that remained of him were his clothes, worn by other men who would give them away a second time when their turn came. Whenever the prisoners heard the rumble of trucks and buses outside, they knew that a lot of men were to be taken away at once to the "firing range." Sometimes they were killed with machine guns in the courtyard. Over a seventeen-month period, Taraki killed roughly twenty thousand people in this manner, more than the number of Egyptians and Israelis who died in the 1973 Middle East war. To Afghan Communists, this was the Saur Revolution, named for the Moslem month that corresponded with April 1978, when they removed Taraki's handcuffs.

When guards came to take away Haq, they placed a black hood and sheet over his head and body. "I gave one man my watch and another my *shalwar kameez*. I figured they were going to kill me." Instead, they shoved him into an automobile, and after driving for about forty-five minutes they took the hood off. "I was in the parking lot behind the Interior Ministry and KhAD headquarters. Okay, I said to myself. Now they're going to torture me. I knew this was where the special cases were brought. But they just held me for three months. I was treated better than in the prison. Then one night, around two A.M., they put me in a Volga and drove me to my sister's house and released me." As is so often the case in Afghanistan — where men keep in close contact all their lives with second, third, and fourth cousins through extended tribal networks; where blood is not only thicker than water but as persistent as the law and politics too — a distant relative was found who in turn had a relation at the Interior Ministry, and with their help, plus a $7,500 bribe, Haq was released. He was "young and just irresponsible," Haq's relative told KhAD officials during the negotiations.

"A few days later I escaped to Pakistan," Haq said. "That's when I really started fighting."

Abdul Haq spent only two weeks in Peshawar before joining the forces of an older and already established mujahidin leader, Jallaluddin Haqqani, who had just opened a front against Taraki's regime in Paktia, an eastern province south of Nangarhar, along Afghanistan's border with Pakistan. Jalla-luddin taught Haq how to fire and repair all types of machine guns and other ordnance that Haq had not yet encountered.

But fighting with Jallaluddin had made Haq realize "how stupid the mujahidin were. We would build huts that leaked snow from the roof. We would start a fire and burn our faces while feeling cold on our backs. We would go for days without food, when a little planning would have allowed us to eat whenever we wanted. We suffered for no reason because we had no experience in surviving for long periods outside in the snow."

Haq left Jallaluddin after a few months and started his own front in Nangarhar, where Khalis's Hizb-i-Islami enjoyed strong local support, thanks to the stunning personal example set by Khalis himself in the *jihad:* here was a man in the seventh decade of life, with one kidney, who nevertheless sported a pistol in his belt and had lived outside in the snows of Nangar-har with Din Mohammed since the first year of the fundamen-talist revolt against the Daoud regime.

Haq harbored deep love and respect for his older brother and Yunus Khalis, but he was not blind to their faults. Din Mohammed and Khalis both had plenty of faith and heart, but that's all they had. In the eyes of Western diplomats they may have been fundamentalist radicals, but Haq saw them as overly conservative and hopelessly out of date when it came to devel-oping a strategy that would allow the mujahidin to survive against a modern superpower's army.

"I knew I must start a front on my own in Kabul," Haq told me. "Khalis had nothing there at the time. All of our strength was in Nangarhar and Paktia. Khalis and my brother said, 'No, the government is going to kill you. You are too young and don't know what it is to fight the regime in Kabul. You are not ready to fight there.' I had lots of arguments with them about it. It was the first time I ever fought with them. Finally I said, 'Look, I'm going to start a front in Kabul whether you want me to or not. Can you help me with money or arms?' They said no. I got really angry and told them that the machine guns and other arms I captured in Nangarhar were mine to keep, and I was going to take the guns with my friends to Kabul. I left Peshawar without saying goodbye. I was really mad. I felt deserted."

Abdul Haq once claimed to have started his Kabul front with three other mujahidin and 300 afghanis (under $5 at the time). No doubt he exaggerated. Nevertheless, in his mind it was something he accomplished on his own, without the help or encouragement of those he had always loved and looked up to. He had at last broken away from the family fold. Years later, when Western analysts discerned that Haq had kept his distance from the family interest in Khalis's Hizb-i-Islami, they couldn't have known how right they were.

Of the three original fighters who crossed into Afghanistan with Abdul Haq in the first weeks of 1980, two are now dead. One of the two was a Kabul police officer, Zabet Halim, who defected with arms, a car, and several other men and joined up with Haq in the forests of Paghman, west of the city. More weapons came from Haq's other brother, Abdul Qadir, who had more confidence in Haq than Din Mohammed or Khalis had. Qadir had smuggled the guns across the border from the arms bazaar at Darra without Din Mohammed's knowledge.

Haq's mujahidin then numbered about a dozen. They lived in the fields, in the snow, and attacked small Communist posts in the outskirts of Kabul. Halim's stolen car was used to make night forays into the city — easy at the time, since this was before the Soviets had established a formal security perimeter.

Haq spent his time in the capital meeting with the few friends he could trust, to explain what he was trying to do and to ask for their help. He also sent messages to Khalis and Din Mohammed, begging them to reconsider. He needed more arms and more money. No answers came. He eventually cut off all contact with them.

The culture Abdul Haq was operating in, though riddled with treachery and intrigue, didn't include a modern, sophisticated underground guerrilla network. Haq didn't learn such a technique on his feet, either: even a few small mistakes in 1980 would have cost him his life. He just seemed to know instinctively what an intelligence network was. Later in his career he would use file cards for everything, but that was because his mind seemed to be divided into airtight compartments, each keeping track of a different underground operation simultaneously. His ability to think analytically was his single greatest asset, even more developed than his talent with explosives.

"I realized that not everyone can pick up a gun and fight. Not everyone was a tough guy like me. But everyone could do something. Those who had money could buy boots and field jackets for us. And those who couldn't fight and didn't have money could just work their way up behind desks in the government and listen — and tell us what was going on. You have to make even the weakest and stupidest people feel they have an important job to do. That way everyone will help you."

The first months of 1980, as the Red Army was implanting itself in Afghanistan, parading up and down the main roads with tanks, showing the flag — in effect telling the citizenry that armed, popular resistance was a quaint, romantic notion that just didn't work in the real world of massive Soviet arms — Haq spent more of his time talking than he did fighting. It was an elementary apparatus he was setting up: clandestine groups of five or less, all people he knew, who in turn would organize similar groups of people they could trust absolutely.

One secret group did nothing but print leaflets. Another distributed them. Another passed messages between printer and distributor. One unit hid the explosives while another transferred them to a third, which carried out the operation. No group knew very much about what the others were doing. Haq invented a language of code words, coded clothing, even an umbrella code for street signals. One month, someone holding a black umbrella meant an operation was on, while the next month the same color meant it was postponed. Because such a basic intelligence system had never been attempted with any discipline in Afghanistan before, and because the Soviets weren't expecting one, it was effective.

A confidant of the guerrilla leader said, "Haq knew that for such people to succeed they needed to live in nice houses in nice neighborhoods — like Chardihi, south of the city — and have nice cars and nice clothes, so they would look like people who had enough money to bribe their way out of the army and would never be stopped or suspected by the police. He also knew that such groups of people may go months at a time doing nothing at all for the network, yet still had to be maintained, still encouraged, still given pep talks — and still *paid*."

The short time Haq was in Nangarhar before starting the front in Kabul, he had established a rudimentary network in Jalalabad that he had turned over to "Engineer" Mahmoud (another Khalis commander). Mahmoud did nothing with it: never contacted the people, never paid them. So that underground fell apart and Haq got very angry at him. The other mujahidin, including other top Khalis commanders, had no concept of what a network was all about.

Intelligence work took a good deal of money, since operatives had to be paid. Haq, because he was a clear thinker, was a good talker and persuader. With the coming of the Soviets, his reputation as a brawler and young rebel was suddenly converted into hard currency as someone with experience at what the Afghans needed most. So the money came. It came from

Haq's friends' fathers who were merchants and traders. It came from Abdul Qadir, more sympathetic to Haq than Din Mohammed, who ran a smuggling network between Afghanistan and Pakistan. And it came from a handful of wealthy, patriotic families willing to give money rather than fight or lose their business with the Communist government.

In July 1980 the BBC reported that a large number of mujahidin were harassing the Soviets in Paghman, west of the capital. "There were only thirteen of us in Paghman," Haq told me. "The rest were in houses in Kabul. The BBC exaggerated, but it felt great. It felt like we were really doing something." The same month Haq took shrapnel in the head and returned to Pakistan for the first time since he had argued with his oldest brother and Khalis. (It was the first of many shrapnel wounds Haq would suffer. In the mid-1980s, when he traveled abroad to meet President Reagan and Prime Minister Thatcher, the fragments in his body set off airport metal detectors.)

"I shouted at my brother. I was very rude. I was supposed to respect him but I didn't. I was full of pride because I had proved him wrong. Hizb-i-Islami asked me to come to the headquarters. I refused. Khalis called me. I shouted at him too. Then one day I was sitting on a carpet drinking tea with Qadir when Khalis came into the room and sat down. I didn't say hello to him. He grabbed me hard and shouted at me and told me not to be so proud. He admitted he had been wrong about me. I agreed to go with him for two days up to Swat [a mountain valley and resort area in northern Pakistan]. It was my first vacation since I was a child. I felt better. That was when Khalis said, 'All right, whatever you need, the party will help you.' "

Haq gradually built up an underground network of several hundred safe houses involving thousands of Kabul citizens, who with little advance warning could distribute leaflets throughout the city within hours. And this was in addition to the seven thousand fighters Haq had in Paghman and the other mountain regions overlooking the capital. Haq pioneered the technique of using dummy mujahidin convoys as decoys to ambush Soviet armored troops. He taught his men how to hold their rocket fire until the helicopter gunships were practically on top of them. Wherever he moved in the mountains around "Russian Kabulistan," he sent out lateral — as well as forward and backward — patrols to make certain he himself was never ambushed. Any of his men who wasted ammunition shooting at birds or other wild game — an Afghan tradition — had their rifles confiscated. Mujahidin who aroused his wrath often got his big, hairy fist in their face. Haq was still very much the little devil who had smacked the teacher. His short fuse made him at once feared, loved, hated, and respected.

Haq's underground units made their reputation with the kidnapping in Kabul of General Yevgeny Nikolaivich Akhrimiyuk, a relative of the late Soviet leader Leonid Brezhnev. General Akhrimiyuk was reported to be the head of the KGB in Afghanistan during the Daoud era and, in 1983 when he was captured, was one of the senior advisers to the Afghan puppet ruler Babrak Karmal — though officially he just advised the government "on geology."

General Akhrimiyuk's Afghan driver of four years secretly worked for Zabet Halim, the police officer who defected to Haq when the latter first organized the Kabul front. One morning, the driver picked up the general outside the entrance of the Ministry of Mines and Industry in Kabul and headed for the airport to meet the general's wife, arriving that day from the Soviet Union. On the way, the driver casually asked the general if it would be all right to give his brother a lift to the bus station, since his brother had to go to Jalalabad. General Akhrimiyuk said no, it would not be all right. The driver expected this and had thought of something else.

The driver mentioned to the general that he had accidentally left the trunk open. Before the general could protest, the driver pulled over to the side of the road on a street near the

Ministry of Defense. As the driver got out to close the trunk, another man jumped into the car through the open door and pointed a cocked pistol at the general's head. The driver, who had not left the trunk open at all, quickly got back into the car and drove out of the city, to a rendezvous with Haq's men in Paghman. After three days there, they took General Akhrimiyuk to an area bordering Pakistan, where they held him for eight months.

There was talk of exchanging him for fifty of Khalis's mujahidin being held prisoner in Kabul. But as the talks stalled, Haq said he began to feel a little sorry for the general, who was old, sick, and had been badly wounded in an antipersonnel mine explosion during World War II. General Akhrimiyuk whimpered constantly about his wife and family, but despite continued questioning, stuck to his cover, refusing to discuss anything except "gas and petroleum." The mujahidin allowed the general to write a letter to a high-level Soviet official, begging him to negotiate a release, but nothing happened.

"I was always against torture," Haq said to me. "And this guy was old. I went to Strasbourg, where I told the European Parliament that we don't kill prisoners. Then I picked up a newspaper and read that my party had killed him. It was Khalis who ordered him killed. I got really mad at Khalis but he just said, 'He was dying anyway.' I should never have let Akhrimiyuk get out of my hands. They held him for months and didn't even get any information out of him. What did I have him kidnapped for?"

Within Afghanistan and among the Afghan refugee community on the Northwest Frontier, Abdul Haq's reputation grew. On November 21, 1985, Dr. Najib replaced Babrak Karmal as Afghanistan's Communist ruler, and Haq faced a new challenge. Najib, born in 1946, was almost twenty years younger than Karmal, more lethal, and more dynamic. A medical doctor trained in security work by the KGB, and head of KhAD from 1980 to 1985, Najib had been described by the Afghan prime minister at the time, Sultan Ali Keshtmand, as a "strong and penetrating weapon of the Revolution." Najib, more than any other Afghan, was responsible for making KhAD the feared and effective enterprise it was. Under his command, KhAD grew into a force of twenty-five thousand, with a budget larger than that of the Afghan regular army. KhAD took over all aspects of the arrest and interrogation of political prisoners, with the jurisdiction of the police restricted to common criminals.

As soon as he replaced Karmal, Najib — who would later change his name to Najibullah (*ullah* means "of God") in an attempt to gain religious support — made a whirlwind tour of the government-controlled areas of the country, making resolute statements about "national reconciliation." Despite the bullish, thuggish caricature the West had of him, Najib was more than just a secret police heavy. He was a talented political survivor, far more deft than any of his Communist predecessors in juggling the carrot of reconciliation and better economic conditions with the stick of absolute terror against the mujahidin and those who supported them.

"Najib was moving very fast," Haq explained. "It was crucial that I break his spell quickly, to show the citizens of Kabul that he was just another Soviet puppet, no better than the previous ones at controlling the mujahidin."

The last half of 1986 was to be the most spectacular season of Haq's career as an urban guerrilla. Those months solidified his reputation as one of the big three mujahidin commanders in all of Afghanistan, along with the more senior Ahmad Shah Massoud in the Panjshir Valley and Ismael Khan in Herat. Only Haq, however, had his main base of support inside the Afghan capital.

The first of his targets during that time was the Sarobi dam and power station, which supplied Kabul with much of its electricity. Haq's planning started in late June, seven months after Najib had taken power. "I had lots of problems just to get over the mountains north and east of Kabul. The dam was protected by minefields and deliberate flooding. The bridge over the Kabul River and all the trails leading to the bridge were patrolled by government troops. We moved only at night. Everybody had to closely follow the man in front of him so only the lead man — who knew the trail well — was threatened by mines. We used layers of cloth and foam to cushion the horses' hooves so they wouldn't make noise and alert the soldiers. We walked for several nights like this. Because we had to travel light, we carried only tea, cucumbers, and some bread to eat.

"When we were a day and a half from the dam we stopped and sent out a recon team. They returned after three days without enough information. I got mad and sent out another team. Three more days went by before the second team returned to tell me we needed at least a thousand kilos of plastique to really do the job. Great. I had looked everywhere just to find two hundred fifty kilos.

"Next we had to clear a path through a minefield. We worked for twelve nights, from eight in the evening to three in the morning. I used a pocketknife, dragging it gently over the dirt. When the knife hit metal you heard a click and chills went up and down your back all the way from your fingernail — it was a mine. Every night we advanced another ten meters."

Destroying the dam with 250 kilos of explosive was impossible. So Haq decided to put all of it in one place, a control room near the top of the dam. Getting in was easy: it was the only one of three control rooms that was empty and unguarded. After the minefield, security at the dam site itself was like everything else in Afghanistan — a mess.

The July 20, 1986, explosion did not destroy the dam, but it wrecked the control room, the bridge atop the dam, and the machine for lifting the gate of the dam. It also cracked one of the three pylons supporting the dam and killed about a dozen technicians and government soldiers. It plunged the city of Kabul into darkness that night and caused minor flooding in the surrounding area. For three months, until the dam was completely repaired, sporadic power blackouts plagued the capital. The damage was estimated at over $2 million.

Less than six weeks later, at ten in the evening on August 27, 1986, Abdul Haq struck again. His men blew up the ammunition dump at Qarga, west of the capital, the headquarters of the Afghan Eighth Army Division and the single largest Soviet munitions depot in the country. A massive fireball rose over a thousand feet into the air, and the concussions that followed made windows vibrate throughout Kabul. Smaller explosions continued into the morning.

Haq and his men set off the explosion with only two 107 mm Chinese-made rockets, mounted on crossed sticks and attached to two taped wires hooked up to a plunger. But the planning took three weeks.

"I had to find out exactly where the ammo dump was on the base," Haq said. "We didn't have aerial photographs, which meant we had to find out from contacts in the Afghan army. Then I had to measure the distance to a launch site, since all we had were four rockets that weren't guided by radar." Finding a launch site was difficult because the free-flight range of a 107 mm rocket is only about two miles before it starts angling. There was no place that close to the dump that was very far from a government post.

"I sent out ten people to walk the distance, counting their steps in their heads. They all came back with different numbers. I added them all up, divided by ten, and went with the average. I had four rockets. All I really needed was one hit.

"Because government posts were all around, we couldn't just set up a rocket launcher. We needed diversions." So Haq's men initiated small attacks on government posts in the

Paghman region near Qarga. "When there was shooting everywhere, we brought in the rockets."

The first two missed the target. Then his men fired the second two, and still nothing happened. Later, black smoke started to rise in the distance. "The black turned to green, and then to bright yellow, lighting the whole sky. We were five miles away, but it was difficult to breathe because of the smoke. I was scared and laughing at the same time. 'Oh, my God,' I said to myself. 'What did I do?'

"We ran away. Everybody was watching the blasts. Nobody noticed us."

The Qarga base reportedly housed a number of surface-to-air missiles, and Haq suspected that these caused the huge yellow fireball. He took color photographs of it and hung them in his office. Haq had tipped off a British diplomat in Kabul who had a video camera. He recorded the explosion from the roof of the British embassy; the video made the rounds in Peshawar in 1987.

What Haq did not do was take one of the handful of television cameramen resident in Peshawar with him on the operation. This allowed several other mujahidin groups and commanders also active in the Kabul area to claim credit for the Qarga blast. And a British documentary highlighting the exploits of Ahmad Shah Massoud included the video footage of the Qarga explosion without mentioning Haq's name. In the rumor-filled, conspiracy-ridden atmosphere of Peshawar, and in the American Club and the Bamboo Garden in particular, different stories emerged about how the attack was actually carried out. One hyped version had it that mujahidin had dispatched trucks filled with plastique to crash through the gate of the army base protecting the ammunition dump. When Haq claimed that he was responsible for the blast, and did it with 107 mm rockets, most people — given his reputation — believed him.

After the Qarga operation came other attacks. On November 23, 1986, a bomb made of gasoline, fertilizer, and gunpowder exploded near the Ministry of Education, where Najib was attending a party conference. Five members of his entourage were reported killed. On December 14, a tunnel leading to the turbines of the Sarobi dam and power station was blown up, causing power cuts in Kabul. In addition, there were periodic downings of Soviet and Afghan military aircraft over the Kabul region through the end of 1986. Haq either planned or played a role in all of those incidents. In 1987, the Communist regime's military situation kept getting worse, until October, when Haq stepped on a mine.

Peshawar, May 18, 1988. Abdul Haq was walking barefoot up and down the stairs of his office, exercising his legs and trying to build calluses on the stump of his right foot. Eid el Fitr, the great feast that ends the month-long Ramadan fast, had just concluded. Three days earlier, the Soviets had started their withdrawal from Afghanistan, and foreign correspondents who had flooded into Peshawar to cover the story were already leaving: Afghanistan was again being forgotten. Haq looked tired. He had been in his office most of the holiday, the second most important feast in the Moslem calendar, and had seen little of his family and only one or two visiting journalists. He was in the process of sending fifteen hundred new men into the field over the coming days, and that meant meeting with dozens of subcommanders, issuing orders, and handing out money — in other words, starting new underground operations. Haq had bought no new clothes, something Moslems traditionally do for Eid el Fitr. On this night, however, he had arranged a dinner in the carpeted room above his office for a few friends. We all reclined against cushions and talked for almost four hours. We were served plates of grilled meat and chicken, yogurt, *firni* (custard flavored with ground pistachios, almonds, and cardamom), *mantu* (pasta filled with meat and spiced with cumin, chili peppers, and coriander), many salads and cooked vegetables, and heaps of Kabuli rice sprinkled with raisins and scented with saffron and black cardamom seeds. There was plenty of Coca-Cola too, something you rarely got from the Khalis mujahidin. In the sky Venus formed an equilateral triangle with the tips of a crescent moon, evoking Islam's most powerful and mysterious symbol. The details of that night are hard to forget.

Throughout the meal, Haq massaged his foot. It had not healed well, he complained. A recent jaunt across the border into Kunar province revealed that he still had difficulty climbing mountains: "After five hundred yards I begin to feel pain." Haq was not in a good mood. He felt frustrated and tied down. His real reason for inviting us was to hold court, to unburden himself of his fears, and to lecture us about how the Pakistanis and the alliance of mujahidin political leaders — including his brother Din Mohammed and Khalis — were playing into Soviet hands by contemplating an all-out attack on Jalalabad.

Despite exercise, Haq was still overweight, and with his beard, his gesturing, outstretched hands, and the mounds of food on the table, I had a vision of an angry Henry VIII. "You want to know why it's dumb to attack Jalalabad?" Haq thundered. "Because it's dumb to lose ten thousand lives. There's no way the mujahidin can take the city now. It's surrounded by a river, mountains, and minefields. And if we do take it, what's going to happen? The Russians will bomb the shit out of us, that's what." Which is exactly what was to happen after the mujahidin captured the northern city of Kunduz that summer; the Soviet air force bombed Kunduz until the guerrillas withdrew to their previous positions a few days later. "And if they don't bomb the shit out of us, then we have Jalalabad and they have Kabul — parity, two Afghan governments. Then there will be pressure for us to negotiate. No, we must take no cities. Take everything but." Haq shook his fingers. "Jalalabad should fall last, not first. Abdul Qadir and 'Engineer' Mahmoud know this. Only the politicians don't. It's so stupid . . . You want me to show you what's going on in Jalalabad? Come on, I'll show you." Lumbering down the steps, he dragged us into his war room, with the wall-size map of Afghanistan stolen from the Ministry of Defense in Kabul.

"Yeah, the Russians withdrew from Jalalabad." Haq bashed his fist against the map. "All the Western journalists covered that. And after, five hundred Russians were sent back there from Paktia. Where were the stupid journalists when that happened, huh? The Russians may be withdrawing, but they're also moving troops around. They want everyone to think they're out of Jalalabad, so the mujahidin will be expected to take it. They're bluffing us, and the alliance is going for it."

Haq hated the seven-party alliance, officially known by the misleading title Islamic Unity of Afghan Mujahidin. "I've never been to alliance headquarters. I shed blood in Afghanistan, not in a conference room in Peshawar." Someone at the table asked Haq what he thought of the alliance's cabinet-in-exile, in which his oldest brother, Din Mohammed, was the defense minister. Haq was silent, then said, "I guess it's better than Najib's cabinet."

It wasn't just a matter of temperament, of being a soldier accustomed to action all his life and scorning a bunch of squabbling politicians. It was something deeper, something Haq didn't much like to talk about but couldn't help talking about once you got him going on the subject. Haq just wasn't comfortable with Moslem fundamentalism. "I don't think we need it," Haq had once told John Gunston. "Always in the history of Afghanistan the people have resisted any kind of force. The British learned this, and now the Russians have. If our people are forced into something they don't want, the fighting will continue. What we need instead is a broad-based government."

However, the seven-party mujahidin alliance was dominated by four fundamentalist groups — those of Yunus Khalis, Gulbuddin Hekmatyar, Jamiat leader Burhanuddin Rabbani (for whom Ahmad Shah Massoud fought), and Rasul Sayyaf. Relations between these men were not always easy. Hekmatyar was genuinely hated by the other three leaders, and especially by Haq. Haq said, "Gulbuddin's problem is that he kills more mujahidin than Soviets." Though he would never openly admit it, Haq was disappointed at the failure of an August 1987 assassination attempt in which Hekmatyar was nearly blown up by a car bomb in Peshawar. (It was never clear who the perpetrator was; the Soviets, the Afghan Communists, and every mujahidin group besides Hekmatyar's own had strong reasons for wanting Hekmatyar dead.) Some people tried to persuade Haq that, for the good of Afghanistan, *he* had to be the one to kill Hekmatyar, for only he had the skills for carrying out a successful and clean assassination. Moreover, according to this logic, whoever the other resistance groups believed had brought off such an assassination would see his prestige and clout rise sharply. Haq rejected this advice out of hand.

As a commander, Haq ultimately directed his wrath against the Pakistanis — specifically, the Inter-Services Intelligence Agency (ISI), Zia's version of the Central Intelligence Agency, if you can imagine the CIA equipped with a conventional military force all its own. American taxpayers were footing the bill for the weapons the mujahidin were receiving, but ISI decided how those weapons were to be distributed among the various commanders and mujahidin parties. This was part of the bargain the United States struck with Zia for enthusiastically providing the guerrillas with a rear base in Pakistan. And it wasn't just that Zia — and his clique that continued to run ISI for months after his death on August 17, 1988, in a plane crash — favored Hekmatyar. More to the point, ISI gave weapons to the commanders and parties it could control, and to the commanders who let ISI do their military planning for them. Haq wouldn't stand for this. He held ISI in low regard: he thought its agents were a bunch of meddlesome Punjabis who were trained in military academies and knew nothing about guerrilla warfare in Afghanistan. Didn't ISI spend time and money to blow up a bridge near Kandahar that the Soviets had stopped using months before? Wasn't ISI gung-ho for attacking Jalalabad? As Haq, among others in Peshawar, pointed out: why should the Pakistanis, who never won a war, give orders to the Afghans, who never lost one?

The Americans were of no help to him, Haq told us over the long dinner that night. Despite bankrolling Zia to the tune of hundreds of millions of dollars annually, the American intelligence community knuckled under to ISI, convincing themselves that Hekmatyar was not half as bad as everybody said he was. In the process Haq got shortchanged. (This was paradoxical, since he had been the first mujahidin commander ever to meet with President Reagan and with Prime Minister Thatcher, in the mid-1980s, a time when the fighting was not going well for the resistance.)

I sympathized with Haq. To travel from Peshawar to the American embassy in Islamabad — Pakistan's make-believe modern capital, which resembles a sprawling American suburb — was to enter a world light-years removed from the war in Afghanistan. Here diplomats served up a defense of Hekmatyar built on nothing, it seemed, but a fragile edifice of clichés:

Sure, he's ruthless. But killing Russians is nasty business, isn't it?

True, he's divisive. I'll give you that. But that's why people aren't objective about him.

At least he's charismatic. He has a vision of what he wants to do with Afghanistan, something the other mujahidin leaders lack.

Killing Russians was nasty business, sure. But the available evidence suggested that Hekmatyar was killing fewer of them than he claimed, while being responsible for killing other mujahidin — and Western relief workers and journalists too. The Paris-based group Médecins sans Frontières (Doctors Without Borders) reported that Hekmatyar's guerrillas hijacked a ninety-six-horse caravan bringing aid into northern Afghanistan in 1987, stealing a year's supply of medicine and cash that was to be distributed to villagers to buy food with. French relief officials also asserted that Thierry Niquet, an aid coordinator bringing cash to Afghan villagers, was killed by one of Hekmatyar's commanders in 1986. It is thought that two American journalists traveling with Hekmatyar in 1987, Lee Shapiro and Jim Lindalos, were killed not by the Soviets, as Hekmatyar's men claimed, but during a firefight initiated by Hekmatyar's forces against another mujahidin group. In addition, there were frequent reports throughout the war of Hekmatyar's commanders negotiating and dealing with pro-Communist local militias in northern Afghanistan.

As to Hekmatyar's vision of Afghanistan's future, he and his lieutenants openly admitted wanting a centrally controlled theocracy dedicated to fighting both "Soviet and American imperialism" which bore a striking resemblance to Ayatollah Khomeini's Iran.

The American diplomats, meanwhile, discounted Khalis's organization because Khalis was just an "old man lacking Hekmatyar's political talent." As to Khalis's frequent trips inside to visit his troops, one diplomat remarked, "I wonder what he does in there, talk to God?"

In truth, American analysts didn't actually believe half the things they said about Hekmatyar, or about Khalis even. The U.S. government, specifically the CIA, was tied to Hekmatyar because all Washington really cared about was its future relationship with Pakistan. Washington had always thought of Afghanistan as a primitive tribal society of marginal importance that even in normal times fell within the Soviet sphere of influence. And once Soviet soldiers were physically out of Afghanistan, American policy makers were quite willing to see that primitive land and its tribal people again through the narrow lens of their ally Pakistan.

What hurt Haq was not that America should care more about Pakistan than Afghanistan; a clever analyst, he realized the logic of this. What hurt him was that, having personally led the struggle on the ground to eject the Soviets from Afghanistan's capital city, he was a daily witness to the colossal waste of American money and weaponry, thanks to the narrow-mindedness, incompetence, and corruption of Zia's henchmen in ISI. This is what should have bothered the average American taxpayer too, since the Reagan administration was spending billions on arming the mujahidin through Pakistan, compared to only tens of millions for the Nicaraguan contras.

Abdul Haq instinctively knew what it took a reporter several months of living in Peshawar and traveling inside to grasp: beyond President Reagan's and President Zia's basic determination to force the Soviets out of Afghanistan, many, if not most, of the individual policy decisions that came under the framework of that brave goal were wrong ones. Hadn't the CIA station chief in Kabul, following the Soviets' December 1979 invasion, declared that the Afghans had no chance; that it was all over but the shouting; that in six months the Soviets would control the whole country? Hadn't the Americans dithered for years before providing Stingers and other sophisticated light weaponry to the mujahidin because certain elements of the American intelligence bureaucracy were convinced they had no chance? And hadn't the Americans decided to throw the whole operation of the war in the lap of ISI, with little independent intelligence of their own except for satellite photographs and a handful of diplomats restricted to Kabul city?

In the end, the mujahidin's willingness to suffer to a nearly unimaginable degree eventually overcame, and thus masked, the awful mistakes of American and Pakistani policy makers. As an angry Haq told a British official in Pakistan a few weeks after our dinner: "Don't lecture me about why the Russians are leaving Afghanistan. They are leaving only because we spilled our own blood to kick them out."

Something else regarding the United States hurt Haq. "None of my mujahidin ever hijacked a plane, killed or threatened journalists or relief workers, or in any way created headaches by extending the war to innocent foreigners." Then why was the United States, he seemed to imply as we rose from dinner, allowing the Pakistanis to back the one leader of the seven who had been accused of doing all of those things except hijack a plane?

Believing himself to have been "abandoned" by the United States and Pakistan, Haq worked on his own to topple Kabul. As befitted a man whose forte was intelligence work and sabotage, his was an extremely subtle and fragile strategy that made relatively little use of violence. He was aware, unlike the men at ISI, that the citizens of Kabul did not automatically support the mujahidin, and that if the mujahidin were foolish enough to launch rocket attacks in heavily populated areas, the capital's inhabitants could quickly turn against them. Another problem, as John Gunston confirmed right after his daring trip inside the city, was that Hekmatyar's Pakistani-financed public relations machine — which the Soviet media did all it could to encourage — guaranteed that Hekmatyar had more name recognition among Kabul's citizens than either Haq or Ahmad Shah Massoud. And since Hekmatyar's image was that of a fundamentalist demon, the people of Kabul weren't entirely sure they wanted Najib overthrown: better the devil you know than the one you don't.

To counter this bad public image, Haq increased the frequency and circulation of "night letters" (leaflets distributed by his underground network throughout Kabul). The first of these that he sent out after the start of the Soviet withdrawal said, among other things:

> We . . . have instructed our mujahidin groups around Kabul to be very precise in their [rocket] attacks, and we have strongly urged and ordered them not to attack any areas in which there

are civilians. Despite that, there may be some groups that may have fired rockets at some areas by mistake, for which forces under my command are not responsible. . . . The objectives of our mujahidin are the military bases of the Soviets and the [Afghan] Communists. Because it is difficult to aim these rockets precisely, we are appealing to families who live near these bases to leave the area so they will not be hurt.

Haq's public relations campaign was not limited to the civilians of Kabul, but to the regime's soldiers and members of Najib's government as well. Eight years of building an underground network had yielded him many useful sources of information within Communist-controlled Kabul, allowing Haq to publish "situation reports" that were at times more informative than the weekly reports distributed by the U.S. embassy in Islamabad.

According to Haq's sources, the Afghan Communists were so bitterly divided that much of their time was spent plotting against each other rather than fighting the guerrillas. You would have thought that given the withdrawal of Soviet troops and the upsurge in mujahidin rocket attacks on Kabul during the summer of 1988 that the two factions of the Afghan Communist party — the working-class, Pukhtu-speaking extremists of Khalq and the more sophisticated Dari speakers of Parcham — would close ranks against the common enemy. But the hatred and treachery between the Khalqis and the Parchamis were so fierce that the withdrawing Soviets had to spend considerable time and energy just to keep them from slaughtering each other.

As ruthless as President Najib's reputation was (he ran KhAD for five years), he was actually the leading moderate among the Communists. Najib, of middle-class origins and with a university education, was a typical Parchami. He was willing to negotiate with mujahidin commanders, if only to split the resistance further, as part of a deftly executed policy of trying to keep a pro-Soviet regime alive and functioning in

Kabul. Najib's nemesis was the Afghan interior minister, Sayed Mohammed Gulabzoi, who was a Khalqi. Like many Khalqis, he was semiliterate, from humble origins, and an extremist who believed that the soft, vacillating Parchamis had to be liquidated in order for the Afghan Communist party — officially known as the People's Democratic Party of Afghanistan, or PDPA — to deal effectively with the guerrilla threat. To think that the Khalqis on their own could slug it out with the mujahidin after the uniformed Soviet troops left, without even the pretense of a diplomatic strategy to wean away disenchanted resistance commanders, was insane. "You can't explain it rationally," said one Western diplomat who shuttled between Kabul and Peshawar and who backed up Haq's account. "Put it down to centuries of inbreeding."

Taraki and Amin were Khalqis, and their rule of Afghanistan in 1978 and 1979 was so brutal that it sparked the original mujahidin rebellion that forced the Soviets to invade. A decade later, as the Soviets were pulling out, a Khalqi coup against Najib's regime was a Kremlin nightmare. Given the rude fact of Khalqi control over the Interior Ministry, which boasted its own elite paramilitary units known as Sarandoy, the Kremlin had no choice but to think on its feet and massage Khalqi ambitions, protecting Najib at the same time.

Haq's informers reported the following sequence of events:
In early 1988, in an attempt to cut off a Khalqi coup plot against him, Najib had Gulabzoi removed from his post as interior minister and maneuvered to have the vacant Defense Ministry portfolio filled by a Parchami ally. Gulabzoi reacted by flying to the Soviet Union, where he lobbied the Kremlin for twenty-one days to dump Najib. The Kremlin appeared to go along, telling Najib to appoint Gulabzoi's Khalqi comrade General Shahnawaz Tanai as the defense minister. Najib refused. The first week in August, Soviet Foreign Minister Edvard Shevardnadze had to travel to Kabul just to twist Najib's arm. When even that failed, the Soviets trotted out Major General Kim Tsagolov to give a press conference in Moscow, stat-

ing that Najib lacked popular support and that his government could not survive the Soviet troop pullout. Finally, on August 16, Najib made the Khalqi general Tanai the new defense minister. But at the same time the Soviets gave Najib thirty new bodyguards. To try to keep the two Khalqis, Gulabzoi and Tanai, on speaking terms with Najib, the Soviets forced the three Afghans to meet with one another for two hours daily.

Even so, according to Haq, on September 9, 1988, the Soviets just managed to prevent a Khalqi coup against Najib. The Soviets clearly had had enough of Khalqi intrigue. In early November, Gulabzoi was taken at gunpoint from his Kabul home and put on a plane to Moscow, where he went into a kind of exile in reverse, as the Afghan ambassador to the Soviet Union.

With Gulabzoi out of the way, the Kremlin now tried to knock Parchami and Khalqi heads together and concomitantly improve the regime's image by appointing an Afghan prime minister who was not even a member of the Communist Party, nor associated with either of its two warring factions.

The new man, Hassan Sharq, was a laundered Communist — someone recruited years before by the KGB, as securely in Moscow's pocket as Najib or Gulabzoi. Yet, because Sharq was not officially a Party member, he was paraded before the world as the compromise figure needed to end the mujahidin siege. Only the most naïve and sympathetic foreigners were fooled, such as UN special negotiator Diego Cordovez, who actually described Sharq as the most sensible man in Afghanistan. But Cordovez was alone in his judgment. The mujahidin rejected Sharq, as did the Pakistanis and the Americans. Even the media caught on to him rather quickly. In an early November column in the *New York Times*, A. M. Rosenthal labeled Sharq a Moscow-controlled appointee with absolutely no credibility. (Useless as a public relations tool, and with no power base of his own, Sharq was soon removed as prime minister.)

*

The roll of events in Kabul told Haq that, given the fragility of Najib's regime, the time had come to do what he had done when he first set up the Kabul network: meet with people, argue, negotiate, and persuade. On weekends (Thursday afternoon through Saturday, since the Moslem Sabbath was Friday), Haq began disappearing from Peshawar, traveling with his bodyguards over roads the guerrillas controlled, to meet with regime army commanders who wanted to defect. Haq argued that they should stay in place, listening and passing on information to the mujahidin, and bolt only when he gave the word. Haq also met with disgruntled Communist Party members who were Khalqis. Such meetings were not difficult to arrange. The level of treachery between Khalq and Parcham was so deep that for one to conspire with the mujahidin against the other was natural.

Haq kept up the military pressure during the middle of 1988 through a series of surgical rocket strikes on Kabul airport, which further demoralized the Communist Party and military establishments. In the third week of June, Haq's men bombed eight Su-25 fighter jets on the ground, a loss valued at roughly $80 million — the most costly destruction of equipment in any single attack during the war. The mujahidin had got lucky: one of the rockets struck a jet dead-on, igniting a chain reaction of fires and explosions that engulfed the seven other planes.

"We could fire thousands of rockets everywhere in the city every night and then march in and take over," Haq said. "But you would kill hundreds of thousands that way." He figured that, considering the political situation in the capital, the best way to take Kabul was not to take it at all: better to let it implode through the cumulative weight of Khalq-Parcham infighting, well-timed rocket attacks and defections, and the picking off of all the government posts circling the city, blockading it step by step. Lack of food and electricity was something the population would not like but would understand. Indiscriminate rocket attacks, however, they would not understand. And mass support for the mujahidin was crucial if the Communist power structure was to cave in. When that collapse looked imminent, then — and only then — should the guerrillas negotiate with the regime. The regime might be expected to accept any kind of a deal at that point. Of course, had Haq's advice been taken, the mujahidin would likely have made better military progress than they did immediately following the Soviet withdrawal. (Haq was naïve in only one respect: he didn't foresee that the Soviets would spend billions — rather than the anticipated hundreds of millions — of dollars to keep the regime in power, while the Americans would deliver only a fraction of that amount to the mujahidin in 1989.)

Haq argued that Massoud, who had a military plan of his own for taking Kabul, had less support and fewer contacts in the capital than he did. It wasn't that Haq, a Pathan, was resentful of Massoud, a Tajik. After news arrived in Peshawar that Massoud had ejected the Soviets from the Panjshir Valley, Haq offered a self-deprecating smile and said, "Good for Massoud. Maybe I'm just a wimp and he really is a better commander." But Haq genuinely felt that Massoud's strategy forced him to rely more on conventional military means, which meant a greater loss of civilian life. Nevertheless, after years of shortchanging Massoud and Haq, ISI suddenly decided to become more generous toward the Tajik commander.

In early 1989, Haq's weapons supply was cut off completely. Without weapons to dole out, he began to be deserted by mujahidin. Even Gunston, sensing the growing importance of Massoud over Haq, began making trips inside with the Tajik instead. Haq turned out to be the Afghan Cassandra, whose prophecies were always right but never believed by those charged with spending American taxpayers' money. Haq not only suffered but was punished because of the truth he uttered.

ISI, whose policy and personnel remained the same for

months after Zia's death, was evidently taking no chances. Its men mistrusted both Haq and Massoud for their audacity in running their own wars. But at least Massoud appeared to see the bloody conquest of Kabul as the climax of *the* war. Haq's position was too subtle for ISI. He held that the war was, to a certain degree, already over, even though the mujahidin lacked the capability for an all-out conventional assault on Kabul — as well as on Jalalabad and other cities — without a heavy loss of civilian life. Haq believed the end would come through patience, sabotage, and careful, surreptitious manipulation of the Kabul regime. But ISI, echoed by the Americans, was thinking more along the lines of events in Berlin in 1945. They wanted *Götterdämmerung* in Kabul and Jalalabad (the city closest to the Pakistani border) to be bloody and humiliating for the Communists. Indeed, the Americans were willing to let the Pakistanis install Hekmatyar as their surrogate afterward if that was the price to pay for the pleasure of seeing the Soviets "clinging to their helicopters," after the fashion of forces departing from Vietnam. Of course, that's not how it turned out.

Haq labored on. He still had his own resistance fighters and his unique underground network. In late 1988, he put the finishing touches on architectural plans for major new mujahidin bases west and east of Kabul, complete with caves, air ducts, fuel and grain stores, workshops, and a hospital, and all protected by antiaircraft cover.

"Grain stores are the most important thing," Haq told me. "When Kabul does fall, there are going to be shortages of everything, maybe even a famine. We have to start planning now. I don't want chaos, like in Kunduz, or else the Soviets will take it right back, like they did there."

But ISI and the other resistance commanders in Peshawar were not thinking along those lines. Some American officials dismissed Haq as "yesterday's man." Haq sensed this. "The

Pakistanis, the Americans — they don't like me," Haq muttered. When bitter, he could be pathetic, like an overgrown sulking little boy. When angry, he could be frightening; at such times, you thought only of what his fist could do.

As at the start of the war, when he left Khalis and his older brother in a huff and stalked off to launch a front in Kabul, Abdul Haq at the time of the Soviet withdrawal was once again completely on his own.

~~

Haji Baba and the Gucci Muj

JUST AS Abdul Haq was, behind the scenes, the most respected of the Peshawar-based mujahidin, Rahim Wardak was
the most laughed at.

Haq, having never served in a formal army, had no rank and
did not psychologically require one. Wardak, a former general
in the Afghan army who defected while a military attaché in
India, had a very impressive-sounding rank and title: major
general and chief of the general staff of Mahaz-i-Milli Islami
(National Islamic Front of Afghanistan, or NIFA), one of the
moderate groups in the seven-party alliance. Haq's English
was often ungrammatical and full of swear words; Wardak's
was a polished, Sandhurst variety. Haq always wore the same
gray *shalwar kameez*. Wardak, a portly man in middle age
with black, gray-flecked hair, sported aviator glasses, pressed
American military fatigues, a scarf and matching beret in cam-
ouflage design, a pistol and a survival dagger. Wardak resembled not an Afghan guerrilla but a fashion model in a merce-
nary magazine advertisement. Flanked, as he sometimes was,
by a squad of NIFA mujahidin armed with Israeli-manufac-
tured Uzi machine guns, he and his men conveyed the aura of
a Latin American drug smuggler's army. Regarding the dagger that Wardak carried, Haq once remarked, "You want to
see a knife? I'll show you a real knife." He picked up a small
knife from his desk. "This is a penknife. I open letters with it.
That's more than Rahim Wardak does with his knife."

Wardak controlled no territory inside Afghanistan and rarely left Pakistani soil. He directed "battles" across the border with a frequency-hopping walkie-talkie given him by the Americans. But not even the Americans in Islamabad were fooled by him. Once when Wardak claimed to have rained two thousand rockets on Kabul, a check by the U.S. embassy revealed that only eight rockets had fallen on the city that week. Wardak called the December 1987 mujahidin siege of Khost, in Paktia province near the Pakistani border, in which he took part, "the biggest battle of the war." But a few weeks later, Wardak said Khost was "a joke," blown out of proportion by the media.

At the American Club bar, Wardak was considered "a goofy NIFA general." He was the extreme, comic embodiment of the British military historian John Keegan's dictum: "Generalship is bad for people. . . . The most reasonable of men suffuse with pomposity when stars touch their shoulders."

When reporters, diplomats, and relief workers in Pakistan thought of NIFA, Wardak naturally came to mind. He was an apt symbol for a party of mujahidin who dressed slick, talked fancy, did less fighting, and held less territory than the rough-hewn, tea-slurping fundamentalists of Yunus Khalis's party.

NIFA's founder was Pir Syed Ahmed Gailani (a Pir is a hereditary saint). Gailani, in addition to claiming direct descent from the Prophet Mohammed, was the leader of the Sufi Qadirrya sect, which has small groups of followers throughout the Middle East. While this sounds pious and impressive, the Pir's reputation on the Northwest Frontier was anything but. Some journalists, and mujahidin too, called him "the disco Pir." In the mid-1970s, while Khalis and others were fighting in the hills, Gailani ran a car dealership in Kabul. Rather than traditional robes, he preferred Savile Row suits, Gucci loafers, and silk scarves. John Fullerton, in a 1983 primer about the war in Afghanistan, described the Pir, in his late fifties, as "otiose, sedentary, sleepy-eyed and boastful." Later he developed cancer, and this necessitated frequent trips to London. But during the fasting month of Ramadan in spring 1988, the Pir's departure for London caused many to remark aloud, "Away from the eyes of the mujahidin, in England he doesn't have to fast."

Gailani's troops were known as the "Gucci muj." NIFA offices in Peshawar, Islamabad, and Quetta were staffed by mujahidin in designer sunglasses, running shoes, and sleeveless Banana Republic vests and fatigue pants. Some even wore expensive cologne and possessed Sony Walkmans, along with camouflage-patterned wallets and briefcases. They patronized the restaurants and coffee shops of expensive Pakistani hotels. NIFA offices were air conditioned, of course, and had refrigerators stocked with soft drinks. But the most significant physical characteristic of the "Gucci muj" was that their leading officials either had beards that were neatly trimmed — like the Pir's — or had no beards at all.

To visit a NIFA office was to be bombarded with complaints about American and Pakistani arms supply policy. Apparently, Zia was shortchanging the NIFA commanders, just as he was Abdul Haq, in favor of Gulbuddin Hekmatyar's Hizb-i-Islami. But instead of soldiering on, the NIFA mujahidin constantly whined about it. They saw themselves, correctly, as representing the Western values that America encouraged. Yet Pakistan's intelligence service, with U.S. acquiescence, was giving NIFA only a pittance in weapons and supplies. This was why NIFA, according to its own officials, was not more active in the fighting. The American and Pakistani answer was: "If NIFA showed more fighting ability, then it would get more weapons." To that, NIFA retorted: "If Hekmatyar takes power in a post-Soviet Afghanistan and turns the country into a version of Khomeini's Iran, then America and Zia will have only themselves to blame." (When Zia was killed in a plane crash, NIFA officials were quietly ecstatic.)

NIFA had only two leaders they could really boast about:

Amin Wardak and Haji Abdel Latif, two commanders with strong local support in their areas who fought well — without cologne or matching berets and scarves.

Amin Wardak, who was unrelated and unconnected to Major General Rahim Wardak, had been the guerrilla chieftain of Wardak province, southwest of Kabul, since 1978. For two years, Amin Wardak and his men had no contact with the Pakistan-based resistance parties, and completely on their own they wrested control of Wardak province from the Afghan Communists. After the Soviets invaded, Amin Wardak sent a group of mujahidin to Peshawar to negotiate with the parties in order to get more arms. A deal was struck with NIFA, only because of an old friendship between Pir Gailani and Amin's father. But the relationship quickly went sour. "We saw Gailani give power and money to people who weren't doing any real fighting, while we were doing to Ghazni [a major town south of Wardak province] what Abdul Haq was doing to Kabul," explained Amin's younger brother, Ruhani Wardak. "Gailani," he went on, "wanted a diplomatic strategy and we preferred to fight . . . And what about Rahim Wardak? Well, our people were getting killed while he was still a military attaché in India for the Communist government!"

Considering the contempt Amin Wardak had for Pir Gailani, it was amazing that the relationship lasted as long as it did. It wasn't until the beginning of 1988 that Amin Wardak formally broke away from NIFA and joined up with Khalis. The final straw was nothing that the Pir precipitated; rather, it had to do with Abdul Haq's injury. The medical compound where Haq was taken after he had stepped on the mine was in Wardak province, and so under Amin's control. Haq felt that he owed his life to him and showed his appreciation by sending Amin several truckloads of weapons and ammunition. Some bargaining ensued, and as a result NIFA was suddenly without one of its only two big commanders.

NIFA still had Haji Abdel Latif, though. Haji Latif was about

the last person on earth one would normally associate with the
"Gucci muj." He was in his eighties and, even more so than
Khalis, spent most of his time inside, fighting. Haji Latif had
a particularly unsavory reputation before the war. He had
served twenty-one years in prison on a murder charge and was
a strange sort of brigand: he was the leader of a gang of Kandahar cutthroats that functioned as a benevolent mafia, robbing rich merchants by making them pay exorbitant rates for
"protection" and, occasionally, giving some of the money to
the poor. NIFA officials defined him as a "Robin Hood figure."
His gang was called Pagie Louch, Farsi for "bare feet," because
along with special prayers and magic incantations, its initiation
rites involved walking barefoot on a bed of hot coals. New
members also had to suffer nails to be driven into their heels
without showing pain.

Switching gears from gang leader to mujahidin commander
was easy in Afghanistan, particularly in the southern desert
city of Kandahar, the wildest part of perhaps the wildest country on earth.

In a war that was in many ways the most dangerous ever for a
reporter to cover, Kandahar was the most dangerous theater
of the war. Its desert land was flat and cluttered with land
mines. When MI-24 helicopter gunships swept in low after
their prey, you could run but you couldn't hide. Because you
didn't have to walk, the Kandahar area was physically less
demanding than everywhere else in the country. But never in
the mountainous north did a reporter feel as scared and vulnerable as when jammed inside a Toyota Land Cruiser, slowed
down by deep pockets of sand, with Soviet helicopters in the
sky. The Kandahari guerrillas, more than the other mujahidin, had a reputation for reckless bravado. When mines and
helicopters were reported ahead, they slammed on the accelerator.

Kandahar really got to me; it wiped out what was left of my

so-called objectivity. Being there made me think that the Western media really were a bunch of pampered, navel-gazing yuppies, too busy reporting illegal detentions and individual killings in South Korea and the West Bank — before dashing back to their luxury hotels in Seoul and Jerusalem — to bother about the nuclearlike wasting of an entire urban center by the Soviet military. The throngs of reporters in places like Israel, South Korea, and South Africa, and the absence of them in Kandahar, or even in the Pakistan border area that abuts it, made me think that "war reporting" was fast becoming a misnomer.

Blazers were replacing flak jackets. The warfare most often videotaped and written about was urban violence in societies that have attained a level of development sufficient to allow large groups of journalists to operate comfortably. The worldwide profusion of satellite stations, laptop computers, computer modems, and luxury hotels with digital phone and telex systems was narrowing the media's horizons rather than widening them. If there wasn't a satellite station nearby, or if the phones didn't work, or if the electricity wasn't dependable, you just reported less or nothing at all about the place. Although the South Africans, for example, merely curtailed your movements, the Soviets tried to hunt you down and kill you. So you covered South Africa while at the same time denouncing its government for the restrictions it placed on your work. But you didn't fool around with the Soviets, because they were serious about keeping reporters out. I couldn't think about Kandahar; I could only rant and rage about it.

The modern destruction of Kandahar had its origins in the American decision to build an airport there in 1956. By the time the airport was completed in December 1962, at a cost of $15 million, it was already considered a white elephant. According to Louis Dupree, in his 1973 book *Afghanistan*, the airport, in theory, "would have been a refueling stop for piston aircraft on their way across the Middle East and South

Asia. . . . The introduction of the jet age smashed this dream before the completion of the project, and the magnificent facilities now sit, virtually unused, in the desert" outside Kandahar.

Of course Dupree, when he wrote that passage, had no way of knowing what was going to happen. It turned out that the Americans did not build a white elephant after all. Following the Soviet invasion, that airport, about fifteen miles southeast of the city, became the heart of the southernmost concentration of Soviet soldiery in the three-hundred-year history of Russian imperialism in central Asia. Not since Czar Peter the Great first moved against the Tartars had the Russians been so tantalizingly close to the warm waters of the Indian Ocean: five hundred miles across the Baluchi desert, to be exact; or, to put it another way, thirty minutes' flying time by strike aircraft or naval bomber to the Persian Gulf.

The Soviets garrisoned the airport and the nearby city against mujahidin attacks. Early in the war, when the attacks grew more bold, the Soviets, as they had begun to do in the Panjshir Valley in the north, stretched the definition of counterinsurgency in Kandahar to a point beyond any that the Americans in Vietnam had ever conceived of. They peppered the surrounding desert with tens of thousands of land mines, which they usually dropped from the air but sometimes shot from mortars. Soviet rockets fired from the city and the airport blasted the villages around Kandahar. These villages became lifeless archeological sites, overgrown with weeds and silent except for the buzzing of flies and wasps. But the Kandahari mujahidin were every bit as hell-bent as the Soviets. They zigzagged through minefields on the dust-packed, gravelly wastes with double-barreled 23 mm antiaircraft guns mounted on the backs of their pickup trucks, firing away at anything that moved in the sky. The guns made a harsh, piercing noise that felt like sharp metal inside your stomach, but the gunners never used ear plugs. In 1986, the year after

Charles Thornton of the *Arizona Republic* was killed in a helicopter ambush, when even the bravest journalists avoided
Kandahar, the fighting there became truly awful.

James Rupert of the *Washington Post* was one of a handful of
American reporters to visit Kandahar before the Soviet troop
withdrawal and the only one I'm aware of who visited the city
in 1986. His October 6 dispatch was the most graphic news
story about the war in Afghanistan by an American journalist:

> Kandahar at night is a lethal fireworks display. During a
> week-long stay here, I saw red tracer bullets streak through the
> streets each night, while green, white and red flares garishly lit
> up the landscape — all amid the crash of artillery shells, mor-
> tars and gunfire.

Rupert described a group of mujahidin listening to a radio
report about a bombing in Beirut. "Why do they always talk
about Beirut?" the man asked Rupert. "Kandahar had a hundred bombs last night." Rupert's story made little impact and
was quickly forgotten.

The following year, 1987, the situation in Kandahar wors-
ened still. A State Department publication noted, "By the on-
set of summer, the capital of southern Afghanistan and its
surrounding areas had become the scene of what has been
probably the heaviest concentration of combat of the war."
The Soviets, who by this time were starting to tell their own
people the truth about what was happening in Afghanistan,
brought an *Izvestia* correspondent to Kandahar in September.
He wrote that the city "is one big ruin. There is shooting all
the time. Nobody would give a brass farthing for your life if
you took it into your head, say, to walk down the street un-
armed."

In 1987, the Soviets carpet bombed Kandahar for months
on end. After reducing part of the city center and almost all of
the surrounding streets to rubble, they bulldozed a grid of
roads to enable tanks and armored cars to patrol the city in
sectors, indiscriminately destroying shops and homes in the

process. Then they tried to win back local sympathies through a rebuilding campaign. But mujahidin filtered back into the area and besieged Soviet positions. Probably more than ten thousand soldiers and civilians were killed and wounded in Kandahar in that year alone.

By 1988, the population of Kandahar, about 200,000 before the war, amounted to, by one estimate, no more than 25,000 inhabitants. The only people in the West aware of what was happening were officials in Washington with access to satellite photographs and Pakistan-based diplomats, journalists, and relief workers. The American media not only ignored the Kandahar story but in most cases probably weren't even aware of it. The grinding, piecemeal destruction of Afghanistan's second-largest city constituted an enormous black hole in foreign news coverage in our time.

Throughout the decade, Haji Latif was in the thick of this carnage, which meant that NIFA, whatever its reputation elsewhere, was a major player in the Kandahar fighting. One NIFA official was quick to boast about this: "We have the most fighters in Kandahar, so why don't the Pakistanis and the Americans help us more?"

It was questionable whether NIFA really did have the most fighters in Kandahar, since Khalis and the other fundamentalist parties had considerable presence as well. But beneath the claims were fascinating little truths that gave the Kandahar fighting an importance far beyond the quantity of blood shed there.

Ideology mixed with a moderate dose of self-interest drew Haji Latif and NIFA together. NIFA was in fact at its core a royalist party, favoring the return to Afghanistan of exiled King Zahir Shah. This sat well with Haji Latif, since the king had represented a loose, rather corrupt power structure that had allowed his banditry to flourish.

King Zahir Shah's forty-year tenure on the throne in Kabul — from his ascension in 1933 at the age of eighteen to the

1973 coup engineered by his cousin Mohammed Daoud, which toppled him — was by any reckoning a less than glorious time in Afghan history. Though Afghanistan enjoyed relative peace and development, it was the king's lazy, uninspired leadership that permitted the Soviets to gain a foothold inside the state bureaucracy. One Western specialist on Afghanistan, with reference to the king's philandering ways, puts it this way: "While Daoud and the Communists were busy building a power structure in Kabul, the king was busy following his dick around Europe."

The fundamentalist parties loathed the king with a passion, almost as much as they did the Soviets. For men like Yunus Khalis, Din Mohammed, and Gulbuddin Hekmatyar the king was the living symbol of the cowardice and moral corruption that had brought the godless Soviets down on the nation's head. Din Mohammed once explained to me: "How often, during his years of comfortable exile in Italy, has the king spoken out against the sufferings of our people and the crimes of the Russians? Thousands of Afghan children die, and what sacrifice has the king, in his Italian villa, made for the *jihad*? None." The political attitude not only of Khalis's party but of the other fundamentalist groups could be summed up in one phrase, which I heard often in Peshawar: "No king, no Communists!"

Afghan fundamentalists liked to compare King Zahir Shah to Shah Shuja-ul-Mulk, the early-nineteenth-century ruler of Kabul, who owed his throne to the British during their brief occupation and was therefore the puppet of a foreign army. The fundamentalists thought that King Zahir Shah was as bad as Babrak Karmal and Najib, the Soviet-imposed rulers. At a rally of fundamentalist parties on the Northwest Frontier in February 1988, I saw an impassioned mujahid grab the microphone and yell, "Death to Zahir Shah! So many mujahidin have been sacrificed for Islam that we don't want to be ruled by anyone except God!"

When the peasant fundamentalists of Yunus Khalis's Hizb-i-Islami looked at the mujahidin of Pir Gailani's NIFA they saw a group of pampered, Westernized, not particularly religious aristocrats who were sacrificing less for the *jihad* than they were.

Indeed, all of NIFA's top officials were related either to the king or to Pir Gailani. All were educated abroad or in the few Western-style schools in Afghanistan and Pakistan. They began their *jihad* after the fundamentalists (Pir Gailani didn't proclaim *jihad* until 1979). And their families were making much less of a sacrifice than the fundamentalists: whenever a mujahid from NIFA talked about his relatives, he mentioned brothers and cousins in the United States or Europe. Whenever one of Khalis's fighters discussed his family, he referred to brothers and cousins who were *shaheedan* (war martyrs) or were still fighting.

The hatred of the fundamentalist parties like Khalis's for the nonfundamentalist parties like NIFA was therefore easy to comprehend, since it had to do not only with politics but with class divisions as well. But this didn't mean that the mujahidin of NIFA weren't patriots too. By any standards other than Afghan ones, they were extremely religious — certainly more so than most Pakistanis, Arabs, or urban, middle-class Iranians I ever encountered. If not five times a day, they prayed three or four times. Whatever the Pir may or may not have been doing in London, his mujahidin in Pakistan and Afghanistan observed the Ramadan fast. The fact that many members of their families were abroad meant that they had other options; they didn't have to live in the heat and filth of Pakistan or risk their lives inside if they didn't want to. By their own lights, the NIFA fighters were indeed making a sacrifice; very few of them were pompous exhibitionists like Major General Rahim Wardak. And their hatred of the Soviets and the Afghan Communists was every bit as authentic as that of the fundamentalists, no matter what the fundamentalists themselves claimed.

But the NIFA guerrillas' hatred of the Soviets took a different form: it was fired by tradition, not religion. The difference between NIFA and Khalis's Hizb-i-Islami was that Khalis's men were revolutionaries, while the NIFA mujahidin were simple patriots. They wanted a restoration of the days prior to 1973, when Daoud's coup against the king set the country on the ignoble path toward communism. Khalis, on the other hand, wanted a new Afghanistan entirely: an Islamic republic, free of both king and Communists. Unlike Iran's Islamic republic to the west, it would not be repressive. Unlike Zia's Islamic republic to the east, it would not overflow with hypocrisy.

Because NIFA was willing to settle for less, and was also doing less of the fighting, it was more willing to talk to the enemy. As the Kremlin began to realize that communism, as an ideology, had no future in Afghanistan and the best it could hope for was a return to the status quo ante, NIFA and the other nonfundamentalist parties became even more inclined to make a deal. By late 1987, NIFA and Moscow were each willing to settle for a return to mid-1973 conditions.

This was why these parties were labeled moderate. The irony throughout the war was that, politically, the moderate parties were in sync with official U.S. policy, which stated that the Soviets must leave and that the Afghans should determine their own future, preferably along pro-Western lines. But it was the radical mujahidin, sworn to fight to the death and compromise be damned, who got American aid, and not the moderates, who echoed U.S. policy from closer to the sidelines.

As Khalis symbolized the religious and warrior strands of the Pathan personality, Pir Gailani symbolized another rich heritage — based on royalty, history, and myth — that was also Pathan. The Pir's only real political ally in Peshawar was Sibghatullah Mojadidi's Jabha-i-Nijat-Milli (Afghan National Liberation Front). Mojadidi had fewer troops in the field than NIFA. A standing joke in Peshawar was: "There are two things you never see in Afghanistan — Hindu graves and Mojadidi's mujahidin." Still, Mojadidi was more respected than Gailani. Though a staunch royalist distantly related to King Zahir Shah, Mojadidi — who carried a pistol in his belt and had once threatened to shoot Hekmatyar — had a record of opposing not only the Communists but the king too, whenever he felt the king was straying too far from Islamic ideals.

The march of current history had favored Khalis. As Abdul Haq first realized as a youngster, communism was an ideology so extreme that it required another ideology, equally extreme, to repel it. Khalis's politics proved more useful and virile than Mojadidi's and Gailani's. Mojadidi and Gailani stood for an Afghanistan that was disappearing, a country of chivalrous ballads, ancient myths, and genealogies in unlikely confrontation with brutal, mechanized twentieth-century totalitarianism.

Kandahar symbolized this brutal confrontation more than any other place, not only because of the intensity of the fighting there but because it was the ancestral home of Afghanistan's kings and the hearth of the country's cultural tradition. Isolated in the southern outback of central Asia, Kandahar's culture was pure Afghan, untouched by the culturally corrupting influences of Iran that had bastardized Herat or those of the Indian subcontinent that had bastardized Kabul. Kandahar in the 1980s represented past centuries being destroyed by this one.

Kandahar's glory began with one man on horseback. The man was Ahmad Khan, leader of the Abdali contingent in the army of Nadir Shah the Great, the Persian king whose forces had conquered Moghul India in 1739. Ahmad Khan and his Abdali kinsmen, though proud Afghans, were personally loyal to Nadir Shah, for even though the king had defeated them in battle, he generously incorporated them into his army. When, in his later years, Nadir Shah grew suspicious and brutal, he relied increasingly on Ahmad Khan and the Abdalis against his own Persian and Turkish forces, who he was convinced were out to kill him.

One night in 1747, sensing a plot against the king, Ahmad Khan and the Abdalis rode into the royal camp at Quchan, in eastern Iran, to protect him. At dawn, the sight of Nadir Shah's headless body greeted the Abdali force in one of the tents. Ahmad Khan and his four thousand horsemen fled the camp as the king's erstwhile followers looted it. Pursued by these hostile troops, Ahmad Khan sent a diversionary force to Herat and led the bulk of his cavalry southeast toward Kandahar.

"On his ride to Kandahar, Ahmad Khan thought quickly," Sir Olaf Caroe wrote in *The Pathans*. Kandahar was in a frontier zone between the Persian homeland and the Moghul territories to the east that the Persians and their murdered leader, Nadir Shah, had recently vanquished. In this sea of blood and turmoil, Ahmad conceived of an island of order: a native Afghan kingdom that would be sanctioned by whoever would now rule Persia, in exchange for which he would aggressively patrol the mother kingdom's new territories to the east. Pathan legend has it that just then he fell upon a caravan spiriting to Persia the very Indian treasures Nadir Shah had looted eight years earlier. This treasure included the Koh-i-noor diamond, which was to finance Ahmad Khan's new Afghan state.

Ahmad Khan was only twenty-four when he became King Ahmad Shah. In a camp outside Kandahar, as Caroe tells it, the other Abdali tribesmen "took pieces of grass in their mouths as a token that they were his cattle and beasts of burden." Because Ahmad Shah liked to wear an earring fashioned of pearls, he became known by the title Durr-i-Durran (Pearl of Pearls). Henceforth, he and his Abdali kinsmen would be known as the Durranis.

The Durrani empire, which would eventually become modern Afghanistan, began in Kandahar. From there Ahmad Shah Durrani conquered Kabul and Herat, and Meshed in Iran. He invaded India eight times, sacking the Punjab as far as Delhi. But it was always to Kandahar that he returned after his conquests, and that is where he is buried.

Ahmad Shah's empire in Persia and India began to crumble even before his death, but the Durranis were to rule Afghanistan until 1973, when Daoud deposed the last Durrani monarch, King Zahir Shah. Though political power in Afghanistan shifted to Kabul following Ahmad Shah's death, Kandahar remained the region where tribal support for the Durrani kings was strongest right into the 1980s. One nineteenth-century historian wrote that the Durrani tribes viewed Kandahar "with a species of reverence as being the burial-place of the kings and heroes of their tribe." This was why NIFA supporters, and Mojadidi too, were justified in claiming Kandahar as their city, the only place in Afghanistan where their parties were more significant than those of the fundamentalists.

My own fascination with Kandahar began with the name itself. According to Peter Levi, Kandahar is probably the only Greek place name to have survived in Afghanistan, stemming from the Arabic form of Alexander's name, Iskander. In 330 B.C., a year after his decisive victory over the Persian forces of Darius at Gaugamela, east of modern-day Mosul in Iraq, Alexander the Great led his army of thirty thousand men through what is now Kandahar. He left his elephants in the mud swamps west of the present-day city, then crossed the snowy summits of the Hindu Kush on foot.

I visited Kandahar briefly in November 1973, passing through by bus on my way from Herat to Kabul. I stopped for a night at a cheap hotel by the bus station near the city's Herat Gate. The darkness and my own discomfort — I was slightly ill and horribly cold in the unheated hotel room — gave the evening a surreal quality. All I could recall later was a wind-blown square filled with bearded men in high black turbans smoking a water pipe. I sometimes wondered whether that square in my memory survived the years of bombing.

More recently, I came to know Hamid Karzai, a thirty-year-old Kandahar native and spokesman for Mojadidi's Afghan National Liberation Front. Hamid was the son of Abdulahad Karzai, the *khan* (headman) of the Popalzai tribe, the branch of the Abdalis that produced Ahmad Shah Durrani. With Abdul Haq, Hamid Karzai represented for me all that was larger than life in the Afghan character. He was tall and clean-shaven, with a long nose and big black eyes. His thin bald head gave him the look of an eagle. Wearing a sparkling white *shalwar kameez*, he affected the dignity, courtly manners, and high breeding for which the Popalzai are known throughout Afghanistan. Hamid, unlike the crowd at NIFA, whose royalist sentiments and moderate politics he shared, was not a "Gucci muj." When he did wear Western dress, he preferred conservative blazers and slacks or a leather jacket. He moved between the Occidental and Oriental worlds without pretension or falsity. I remember him in his Peshawar villa, sitting on a carpet in a *shalwar kameez*, speaking Pukhtu with his turbaned Kandahari kinsmen, a copy of George Eliot's *The Mill on the Floss* nearby. Hamid was one of six sons, but the only one who had not gone into exile in Europe or North America and who aspired to succeed his father as head of the Popalzai.

Throughout his childhood, Hamid had resented the restrictions placed on him as the son of one of Afghanistan's most important men. He longed to escape Kandahar and the stifling routine of tribal ceremonies. He wanted to serve his country, but only as a diplomat living abroad in the West. His first shock and humiliation came as a student in India in 1979, when officials at the U.S. embassy in New Delhi informed him that the Taraki regime had imprisoned his father. A few months later, the Soviets invaded Afghanistan. "I suddenly realized how spoiled I was," Hamid told me. "I realized that I had been consciously rejecting all the things that were really important and now were lost."

A few months later, in 1980, Hamid visited a refugee camp near Quetta. As soon as he entered the camp, hundreds of Popalzai tribesmen gathered around him, smiling. "They thought that just because I was the *khan*'s son, I had the power to help them. I felt ashamed, because I knew I was just a naïve student who was spending his college years thinking only of himself and his ambition. I was not what they thought I was. My goal from that moment on was to become the man that those refugees thought I was. To become a man like my father."

The man that Hamid Karzai became was one who never tired of talking about the rich history of his tribe and the region of Kandahar. The story of the founding of the Popalzai — first told to me by Hamid — sounds like one of the archetypal tales in the Book of Genesis.

Abdal, the patriarch of the Abdalis (later the Durranis), died at the age of 105 and was succeeded by Rajar, who in turn passed over his oldest son and picked the younger but smarter Zirak to be headman. Zirak ruled for many years and had four sons. One day, near Kandahar, the family was breaking camp. By then Zirak was over 100 and too old even to move, let alone saddle his horse. He asked his oldest son, Barak, for help. Barak laughed and made fun of his father. The second son, Alik, did the same. The third son, Musa, told his father to get on a horse and follow him. When Zirak was not able, Musa kicked him and told him he must remain behind until the beasts devoured him. Popal, the youngest son, offered to carry his father on his back. Old Zirak never forgot the incident, and when he died at the age of 120, he invested Popal as head of the clan. Thus it was that Popal founded his own branch of the Abdali tribe.

The mythic, elemental quality of the story is enhanced by

the fact that, though the origin of the Popalzai is relatively recent — the late fifteenth century — nobody can accurately date when the events took place. It is such stories that, stylistically at least, lend credence to the notion that the Pathans are descendants of the ancient Hebrews. True or not, one could at least say that the desert surrounding Kandahar was to the Pathans what the wilderness of Sinai was to the Hebrews: the seed-ground where an assemblage of tribes grew into a nation. To Hamid Karzai, Kandahar was "the home of our original Afghan culture, the genuine Afghanistan."

A trip to Kandahar begins in Quetta, the capital of Pakistan's province of Baluchistan. Quetta and Baluchistan were to the Kandahar region what Peshawar and the Northwest Frontier were to the rest of Afghanistan: a rear base for mujahidin, war correspondents, and relief workers. And because everything about the Kandahar area was wild and exotic, even compared to the rest of Afghanistan, Quetta was wilder and more exotic than Peshawar.

As I looked down from thirty thousand feet on the flight from Islamabad to Quetta, Baluchistan resembled a series of boils and lesions on a scratched, sandpaper surface: the product of volcanic upheavals and tectonic shifts going back two billion years. Once on the ground, I continued to feel lost in space. There was a weird flimsiness to the setting. In 1935, Quetta was wiped out by an earthquake that killed twenty-three thousand people in the city and many more in the desert around it. In the 1980s, everything in Quetta seemed truly temporary, as unstable and prone to violent shifts as the ground I walked on.

The new Quetta was built on the ruins of the old one. The single-level unfinished cement houses looked like a theatrical set that could have been ripped out at any moment from the gray backdrop of hills beyond by blasts of plateau wind.

During the Afghan war, Baluchistan was especially impor-

tant strategically. It was the only remaining barrier that kept
the Russians from reaching the Indian Ocean — the ultimate
dream of the czars. Like so many strategic places, Quetta was
a shithole. Only in July 1988 was a decent hotel opened. Before that, you stayed at the New Lourdes. To flush the toilet in
your room you needed a raincoat and Wellingtons because the
water exploded in all directions. The place had no heating and
the boiler rarely worked, so during the cold plateau winter,
when temperatures dipped below freezing at night, you faced
the choice of a cold shower or none at all. The Bloom Star, the
only other hotel at the time, was just marginally better.

Baluchistan was the ultimate free-trade zone and smuggler's
haven: an unregulated void of hazy identity set between Iran,
Afghanistan, and the Pakistani province of Sind, with its back
to the Indian Ocean. Despite the awful accommodations, you
could get almost anything in Quetta — heroin, Japanese cam-
eras, cans of Heinz soup, relatively recent copies of *Gentlemen's
Quarterly* and the *Washington Journalism Review*.

Even the ethnic identity that gave the province its name was
at risk in the 1980s, as the influx of Pathan refugees from
Afghanistan tipped the demographic balance against the Ba-
luchis, a people of Middle Eastern origin who speak an Indo-
European language similar to Pukhtu. Because Quetta, with a
population of 250,000, was one fourth the size of Peshawar,
and because Baluchistan was inundated with close to a million
refugees from southern Afghanistan, the Afghan influence
on Quetta appeared even more dramatic than in Peshawar.
Quetta seemed to have *become* Kandahar, since a large portion
of Kandahar's prewar population now lived in or near Quetta.
With its Afghan merchants, Afghan carpet shops, and refugees smoking water pipes, Quetta blurred in my mind with the
Kandahar I had briefly known in 1973.

Everything about Quetta had an air of unreliability, and I
was apt to distrust much of what I saw and heard.

The first person I met there was Atta Mahmoud, a twenty-eight-year-old refugee from Kandahar, who lured me to his carpet shop. Inside, we sat cross-legged on the floor, sipping cup after cup of green tea. He wore a psychedelic black, green, and gold turban; his eyes were crazed. He implored with his hands as if speaking to a multitude and kept calling me Baba, which means father and is a sign of respect. But there was a fawning quality to his voice; his words had the tone of a sales pitch. Having had previous experiences with carpet dealers in the East, I was deeply suspicious, especially after Atta Mahmoud told me he had worked at the Sunshine Hotel in Kandahar before the war, and had sold drugs there to European hippies.

But Atta Mahmoud wanted to talk about Kandahar, not about carpets. "Kandahar city, Baba, is no more. No more, I tell you. There is not a street or a building standing, Baba. No more nut or apple trees. No bazaars. Just one meter of dust and new paved roads for Russian tanks and security patrols." This was the first eyewitness account I had heard concerning the destruction of Kandahar. I wanted more specifics, but he was hard to interrupt and his oration soon disintegrated into a mad tirade, much of it incomprehensible. "The only thing you can do with a Russian is slit his throat, Baba . . . If you don't want to slit his throat, you are a Communist."

He casually mentioned that his two small sons had been killed in a Soviet artillery bombardment of Kandahar the year before, in 1986. This seemed so horrible that I didn't know how to react, or even whether to believe him. I told him I was sorry, and then, in order to break the silence, I asked the price of some of his carpets. But he brushed aside my query, treating it as an insult. He said we could discuss carpets another day. I decided that this man was not after my money and that much of what he told me about Kandahar might actually be true.

Next I wanted to see Zia Mojadidi, who, though related to Sibghatullah Mojadidi of the Afghan National Liberation Front, was not connected with the party. Rather, he was a former faculty member at Kabul University and the local stringer for the Voice of America. Western journalists in Islamabad told me that Zia Mojadidi was a thoroughly professional reporter and the most reliable source of information in Quetta. But his phone was out of order, and the directions to his house were vague: "near the Helper's High School and the orphanage." After searching for half an hour and banging on several doors I found him — miraculously, it seemed to me. He looked like a professor, with thick glasses and a courteous, serious way of speaking. The room he took me to was completely bare, save for carpets on the floor. Since he did not show me the other rooms in the house, he gave the impression of living a marginal existence, and this made me uncertain. After twenty-four hours in Quetta, my instinct told me that if a man possessed no furniture, he also possessed no useful information. His precise speech dispelled some of my doubts, however. He did have information, and filled the holes in Atta Mahmoud's description of Kandahar with hard facts. Basically, Zia Mojadidi, the respected local journalist, backed up the carpet dealer Atta Mahmoud's story of how the Soviets were destroying Kandahar.

At a Red Cross hospital for war victims, my feet finally touched solid ground. Real people packed the corridors; bullets, mortar fire, and mine fragments had torn up their flesh. The day I visited there were 103 patients, and since the hospital had room for only 60, the staff had set up tents on the lawn. The surgeons were working nonstop. A nurse shaved a little boy's head in preparation for surgery. He shrieked with terror. Orderlies wheeled by with carts stacked with bottles of blood. The smell of disinfectant was everywhere. The situation was the same at the thirteen other hospitals in Baluchistan, I was told. But these patients, the doctors said to me, were the lucky few: the ones who had made the three-week trek on foot from Kandahar to the border and the grueling, bumpy drive from the border to Quetta without dying of their injuries or being killed by Afghan regime border guards. It was in the interest of the Communists that wounded civilians never reach the border alive; that way there would be no witnesses to what was happening.

I had never seen indications of this level of carnage in the hospitals I had visited in Basra, Iraq, in the company of a horde of other Western journalists writing about the Gulf war. Basra had a Sheraton, though. Quetta then had only the New Lourdes and the Bloom Star. Sure enough, when the swank Sareena Hotel opened in 1988, the number of journalists in Quetta increased dramatically. Still, stories about the Kandahar fighting in the American press and on television were practically nonexistent.

I wrote as much as I could about Kandahar for a radio network and a magazine. But the Red Cross hospital was as close to the reality of the fighting as I was able or willing to get at the time. I was scared. The vision of Charles Thornton, the *Arizona Republic* reporter who was killed by a helicopter missile just as he reached the top of a hill, made me think hard about crossing the border. But in 1988 I returned to Quetta and, swallowing my fear, was determined to reach Kandahar.

The NIFA villa, from where I began my trip to Kandahar, was in a Quetta suburb. It had only a few guns, but it was luxurious in comparison with more rough and ready mujahidin headquarters: there was air conditioning, marble floors, a tiled bathroom with Head and Shoulders shampoo, and a refrigerator filled with soft drinks and mineral water. Fashionable wicker furniture and a Persian carpet filled the living room. A Russian ceramic tea set from the czarist period sat in a cabinet against the wall. On the wall were photographs of King Zahir Shah, in exile in Italy. There was also a photograph of the Baghdad mausoleum of Sheikh Abdul Khader, reputedly the fourteenth direct descendant of the Prophet Mohammed and a distant relative of the Aga Khan and of King Hussein of

Jordan, the great-grandfather of Pir Gailani. (The Pir's family had migrated to Afghanistan from Iraq at the turn of the century.) Everything in this villa suggested comfort and privilege, but not even privately was I critical. Having gone into Afghanistan several times with the Khalis fundamentalists, I was grateful for the pampering. Whatever the fear and danger, I knew that being relatively clean and well fed would keep me happy for now.

A NIFA staff man brought me to the villa from my downtown Quetta hotel in a spanking new Land Cruiser with racing stripes, the latest addition to NIFA's car fleet. As soon as I arrived, I met the mujahid who was to be my interpreter, Mohammed Akbar. He was twenty-one, spoke excellent English, and was a sophisticated Kabuli to the core. Had the Soviets not invaded, he would undoubtedly have gone abroad to study in England or America. His first remark was to ask if I had brought a sleeping bag, toilet paper, and water purification tablets for the trip. I all but laughed aloud. The gulf between Akbar *jan* (Akbar dear), as his NIFA comrades called him, and Wakhil, Lurang, and Jihan-zeb — the interpreter and guides for my first trip with Khalis's Hizb-i-Islami — was vast.

NIFA supplied Akbar and me with a Land Cruiser (though not a new one), a driver, and several bodyguards. Kandahar was 150 miles northwest of Quetta. Before the war, the journey on the all-weather road took as little as six hours. By that idyllic standard, our route would be circuitous: straight on the all-weather road for 40 miles — halfway to the border — then northeast and east over the Baluchistan desert, hugging the Pakistan side of the border, then over the border into the Arghastan desert in a northwesterly direction, arcing north and west over Kandahar in order to enter the city's environs from the southwest. This meant eighteen hours of continuous driving. But compared to the previous year, 1987, and the year before that, our trip did not seem circuitous at all. Back then, the northern arc over and around the city was much wider, and the journey took several days. Despite the Soviet-driven orgy of destruction in Kandahar, the military situation in southern Afghanistan had been steadily shifting in favor of the mujahidin, and this was reflected in the traveling distance from Quetta to Kandahar.

A turning point in the southern front of the war was the capture of the Afghan border garrison of Spinboldak, on the main road between Quetta and Kandahar, by the mujahidin in early September 1988, a few weeks before my journey. The Spinboldak fighting cost, at the very least, several hundred lives between May and September. The two or three paragraphs about Spinboldak that could be found on the inside pages of American newspapers described the fight as between the mujahidin and the Afghan regime's forces. This was not exactly the case. The battle actually had little to do with the struggle against the Communists, and for that reason made for a revealing story about the guerrillas: it was the best case study of Pathan tribalism that the war produced.

On paper, the mujahidin of the fundamentalist parties, led by Khalis's Hizb-i-Islami, fought the forces of General Ismatullah Muslim of the Afghan regime's militia. In reality, it was a battle between the Achakzais and the Nurzais, two hostile clans within the Abdali (Durrani) tribal family. The Achakzais inhabited the plateau region between Kandahar and Quetta on the Afghan side of the frontier. As far back as the middle of the eighteenth century, the Achakzais had a tough, unruly reputation — even by the standards of the Kandahari Pathans. Ismatullah Muslim was a living monument to this tradition.

Ismatullah was a warlord who in 1984, unhappy with the amount of weaponry the mujahidin were giving him, promptly switched to the side of the Afghan Communists, who made Ismatullah a general and paid him and his Achakzais handsomely.

One of Ismatullah's first moves was to fortify Spinboldak, a sheer rock mountain rising from the flat desert. This offended the Nurzais, who claimed it as their territory and who held a pistol to the head of Yunus Khalis. Khalis's teenage bride was one of the twin daughters of Nadir Khan Nurzai, the head of the clan. Nadir Khan had reportedly blackmailed Khalis the day before the wedding, saying, in effect, "I'll give you my daughter only if you give me and my men weapons to fight Ismatullah."

It was evening when the Land Cruiser pulled out of the driveway of NIFA headquarters in Quetta. One of the gate guards splashed a pail of water against the rear windshield — a Pathan blessing for good luck on the journey.

Even before leaving the all-weather road we got a flat tire. The jack was too short, so the driver had to build a platform of stones for it. When the vehicle wobbled, the driver crawled completely underneath it to adjust the stones with his hands. He was smiling and laughing, oblivious of the danger. When we were up and running again, I noticed he was missing several fingers — the result of a mine accident, he told me.

We left the all-weather road halfway between Quetta and the border. Suddenly we were bouncing as if on a trampoline. The air inside the Land Cruiser was filled with a fine dust, though all the windows were shut. The tires kicked up a dust cloud so thick that our headlights did more harm than good, for light thrown against the dust cut down visibility. Off the track, I noticed that the dust had collected in high ridges, reminding me of photographs of the moon. I had seen dust this bad once before, in Tigre in northern Ethiopia. There the soil was eroded from drought and the neglect spawned by civil war. Here in Baluchistan we were in a desert where nothing had ever grown. It felt as though we were scratching our way across the burned, powdery crust of a giant pie that had been left too long in the oven.

"This is Baluchistan, but we call it Powderistan," Akbar joked.

After driving northeast along the border for several hours we crossed into Afghanistan at a point where NIFA had built a small, permanent camp for mujahidin coming in and out of the war zone. This was where the guerrillas picked up their weapons.

It was 2 A.M. and freezing cold as only the desert can be. The starscape was out of a fairy tale. There was no room in any of the mud huts so we slept outside, our faces covered in dust. I crawled deep into my sleeping bag, shaking from the cold. Akbar and the others had already fallen asleep. Away from their air-conditioned offices, the "Gucci muj" turned out to be just as tough as the Khalis boys, and in the case of the driver, just as reckless too. I wondered if back in Quetta and Peshawar their pretensions to fashion were merely an effort to look Western. Since we foreigners required "noble savages" to feed our own fantasies, what we really held against the "Gucci muj" was their yearning to be like us.

My first sight on awakening the next morning was the black NIFA flag snapping in the wind against the toneless predawn sky.

"Why is it black?" I asked Akbar.

"Because we are in mourning. Our freedom is lost," Akbar explained.

The flag of Khalis's Hizb-i-Islami was green, the symbol of Islam, the warrior faith of the future that seemed to give its fighters a kind of superhuman strength. The truth of each party was in the color of its flags, I thought: NIFA looked backward, lost in mourning over the past.

Over the border in Afghanistan, this desert region's name changed from Baluchistan to Arghastan. The landscape changed too, from deathlike to more deathlike. We were still scratching our way across the same greasy pie, but now the crust was a mere chalky film that covered our faces with white inside the Land Cruiser. Long ribs of cindery hills marked a horizon that appeared to curve, as though we were on a smaller planet. Between the lines of hills, carved as if by a knife, was only an ashy nothingness: not a single thorn grew here. I thought of the landscapes in Paul Bowles's novels, in which the abstract, cubist features of the Sahara are symbols of madness, nihilism, and sensual annihilation.

A moving cloud of dust kicked up by even a small motorcycle on this desert would be easily visible from the air. I listened fearfully, hoping not to hear the hum of a plane overhead.

A village of domed mud brick houses sprinkled a hillside just as we came over the horizon and got our second flat tire. If a landscape is bleak and primitive enough, I thought, the distant past starts to blend with the future.

In one of the houses we sipped our tea in a mud-walled room, leaning against pink cushions while our driver worked on the tire. The pink startled me: it was the first bright color I had seen since leaving Quetta.

We moved on across the ocean of sand, wrinkled occasionally by a bed of limestone or a long fang of cliffs. We came upon the only pit stop in Arghastan: a cluster of mud huts where a few Land Cruisers, Bedford and Japanese diesel trucks, and Yamaha motorcycles had gathered. Old men in turbans approached and kissed my hand. Most were mujahidin. The rest were traders transporting fresh produce back and forth across enemy lines. Fighters of the fundamentalist parties could be distinguished by the ghoulish Zia posters stuck to their truck windshields. Zia, with his deep-set bedroom eyes, looked like a vampire, set against a background with a plane exploding in midair. The caption read *Shaheed* (martyr).

Gruel bubbled in pots. Men repaired tires. Akbar and I bought and devoured about a dozen blood-red pomegranates. It was like a daydream: to be so thirsty and then have your thirst quenched in such a sensuous way, with sticky, tangy juice bleeding down the sides of your mouth onto the ground. Like the pink cushions, the red of the pomegranates clashed with the whitish hues of the landscape.

I noticed that while Akbar and I indulged ourselves in slurping fruit, our driver prayed in the corner of one of the huts. Next to him, other mujahidin drank tea, oblivious of his prayers. I turned around and saw a medieval diorama: three levels of mud rooms, in each of which a man kneeled in prayer on a carpet, wearing either a turban or a *pakol,* and next to him a tea ceremony was in progress. Whether moderate or fundamentalist, all the mujahidin eventually stepped off to the side to pray. As in the mountains of Nangarhar, the solitude of each man in prayer gave the act a power and meaning that I never saw before or since in the Moslem world. Akbar was the last to pray before we left. His sharp, hairless features were clenched especially tight, as though the pomegranates constituted a luxury forbidden by the *jihad* or NIFA's official state of mourning.

After a few more hours of plowing through the dust we began to hear that sinister, stomach-churning sound: the drone of airplanes. We were now closing in on the main "ring road," the paved track linking the three main cities of Afghanistan — Herat, Kandahar, and Kabul — from west to east. The section of the road linking Kandahar with Kabul was tenuously controlled by the mujahidin, so vehicles using it were often targets of helicopter strikes. The area around the highway marked the end of the Arghastan desert and the beginning of the Kandahar war zone. Before reaching the road we stopped at a village to inquire about the situation farther ahead.

The bath of dust continued into a carpeted room shaped like a church nave, where the villagers led us. They brought water from a stagnant irrigation ditch for us to wash with, then served us green tea and curd. The Kandahari curd was much better than its Nangarhar equivalent: it was thinner and flavored with crushed mint leaves. The sweet, acrid odor of a cheroot filled the room. It was late in the afternoon now, and we were told it was safe to cross the highway. Before we left, an old man who had been our host pressed me to stay as his guest for several days. I politely refused. After such kindness and hospitality, I wondered whether the danger ahead was only an illusion.

Here and there in the sea of dust I could discern the burned-out hulks of vehicles that had been hit by a missile or had run over an antipersonnel mine. We were now in the mine zone. The Soviet air force over the past few years had laid down countless — perhaps 100,000, perhaps a million — mines over hundreds of square miles around Kandahar. The landscape was utterly ruined, to the extent that its very existence consti-tuted a danger to living beings. Our driver with the missing fingers kept precisely to the tracks made by the previous vehi-cle. Veering off into the desert was no longer safe.

Then we reached the ring road.

In almost any other country in the world the sight of a des-olate, single-lane paved road, embanked a few feet from the ground to protect it from sand drifts and flooding, would be commonplace. But in Afghanistan this empty road was a stra-tegic route as well as the country's main highway, marked on international maps by a line almost as bold as that indicating the border between Afghanistan and Pakistan. The driver as-cended to the level of the pavement, turned left toward Kan-dahar, and pressed the accelerator to the floor. The sight of a helicopter now would probably mean instant death. But there was no helicopter or anything else in sight.

Two miles down the road we turned off and headed west across the desert. We were about fifteen miles north of Kan-dahar, which we would by-pass in order to enter it another day from a southwesterly direction.

The dust thinned and we could make out the hard limestone terrain in the falling evening light. From now on, the desultory rumble of exploding bombs was a permanent sound, except for an hour or two in the middle of the night. The driver speeded on, braking sharply every time we hit a pocket of sand. We were directly under the flight path between Kandahar airport and the Soviet air base at Shindand, south of Herat in western Afghanistan, in a stretch of desert strewn with wrecked vehicles blown apart by missiles or mines.

The drone of a plane penetrated the silence between the exploding bombs. I watched for a sign of recognition from Akbar or the driver, but there was none. Nervously, I asked Akbar about it.

"Just an Antonov transporting troops. They don't bomb."

I asked how he knew it was an Antonov, since the plane was flying too high for its contours to be seen.

"By the sound. After a while here you can tell each plane by its sound."

After climbing a steep, winding pass in total darkness we entered the Arghandab River Valley, and for the first time since leaving Quetta twenty-four hours before, I was among trees and crowds of people. The town of Arghandab, ten miles northwest of Kandahar, had been firmly in mujahidin hands since 1987 and had been rebuilt. The nearby beech and mulberry forests held the largest concentration of guerrillas in the Kandahar region. Each of the seven resistance parties had a presence here.

The journey so far had kept me in a state of dreamlike disorientation. Now, as I came out of the night into town, sights and sounds hit me. Tongas filled with veiled women clopped along. Market stalls were crowded. The Arghandab River, along which the army of Alexander the Great had camped, rippled peacefully. Drivers honked their horns for the right of way. The rumble of explosions had died down for the moment, and it was hard to believe that this village was a short hop from the devastation in Kandahar. Life here appeared so normal, and getting here, despite the breakdowns and dusty discomfort, had been relatively uneventful. Kandahar, which for so long seemed so distant, so impossible to reach, so dangerously enigmatic, was suddenly only a few miles away. And yet it felt farther away here than it did in Quetta.

I began to worry that I had misjudged the story's significance, that the level of fighting and destruction had been vastly exaggerated by the mujahidin, the war freaks, and the Afghan experts in their feverish effort to get the attention of the media and the outside world. As the Land Cruiser struggled through the brush and forded a series of swamps on its way to the NIFA encampment, I felt two kinds of fear: that there would be fighting, danger, and destruction, and that there wouldn't be any.

At daybreak I was shaken awake by the low-density thud of a mortar. The hollow, vibrating tenor of the sound meant that the fire was probably incoming, not outgoing. But the fact that it was hard to distinguish meant that the shells were landing at least a few hundred yards away, and it would be safe to make a dash to the latrine, which the "Gucci muj" had rigged up with a light bulb and toilet paper.

The beech and mulberry forest where NIFA made its camp was just north of a chain of piebald mountains, on the other side of which lay Kandahar. Since the Arghandab River Valley was full of mujahidin, as a matter of course Afghan government posts in the northern part of the city regularly fired their 102 mm shells (which have a range of seven to nine miles) over the line of mountains in the direction of Arghandab. The guerrillas replied in kind with their recoilless rifles and captured Russian heavy machine guns.

Coming back from the latrine, I was invited into the commander's tent for breakfast. Unlike Habibullah, the taciturn Khalis faction's commander on Spinghar who shared his tent with eleven other men, NIFA commander Ismael Gailani, one of the Pir's nephews, had a blue and yellow tent all to himself, doubtless purchased in a sporting goods shop abroad. Instead of the flat bread, raw onions, and green tea I ate for breakfast, lunch, and dinner at Spinghar, the commander asked me how I liked my eggs.

Ismael Gailani, in his mid-thirties, was a handsome Pathan with sharp, sculptured features, shiny black hair, and a thick, well-kept beard. His good looks were further embellished by brown-tinted aviator glasses, a matching brown *pakol, shalwar kameez,* and Banana Republic sleeveless vest — and an ostentatiously displayed Russian Makarov automatic pistol. The number of troops he led was small, but he traveled like a commander, with his own new Czech motorcycle, purchased on the black market in Kabul, and an escort pickup truck with a double-barreled antiaircraft gun mounted on the back.

My first impression of Ismael was not favorable. Like Abdul Haq, he looked stern and impassive when receiving his men. But while Haq's expression seemed a natural outgrowth of his thoughts at the moment, Ismael appeared to be striking poses. I assumed that Ismael, like so many foreigners and NIFA officials on the Northwest Frontier, was afflicted with a milder version of what Major General Rahim Wardak suffered from: he had convinced himself that he was a character in a movie.

Ismael told me he had attended university in India, had a wife and three daughters in London, and was extremely lonely here in Arghandab. These revelations unsettled me. Mortar fire was landing all around us. There was nothing vicarious about the danger he was in. The movie *was* real, though his own role in it had obviously been blown out of proportion. I had a wife and son in Greece, and explaining to them why I constantly traveled as a journalist to war zones was not always easy; explaining such a life to our Greek neighbors, who harbored little interest in the world outside their country, was nearly impossible.

Like Ismael, I judged myself a lonely person: at home, few comprehended the fascination of my work, and when traveling I was frequently in the company of people from non-Western cultures, with whom my relationships were, perforce, fleeting. But Ismael's loneliness had to be much greater. His family was larger than mine, he had been away from them for many more months, and he was in more constant danger than I was. Unlike Abdul Haq, he was much too Westernized to be emotionally compensated by the company of his manly fellows. Inside Afghanistan, the average NIFA mujahid was just as much of a backwoodsman as the Khalis fighters, and it was often just the accident of tribal loyalty that steered some Pathans toward NIFA rather than into the ranks of the fundamentalists. But Ismael, with his shampoo and his Walkman lying in the corner of his tent, was culturally some distance from his own troops.

"I can't explain to people in London what I'm doing here," Ismael told me. "My wife's friends tell her that I'm crazy. They tell her I could get killed. So when I'm in London, I ask them, 'Didn't you fight against the Nazis?' They answer, 'Yes, but we weren't occupied. Our children weren't threatened like in Afghanistan. So why don't you just make peace with the Russians? Why do you go on fighting?' How can an Afghan communicate to people who think like that?"

I began to understand that Ismael, in his own pampered way, was heroic, if in wholly different terms and on a more muted scale than Abdul Haq. Haq's heroism and the value he placed on freedom were instinctive reflexes. His bravery was as natural as the thorns that grew on the mountains in Nangarhar. Ismael, through conscious thought, had come to place a high value on freedom too. The modest heroism that he displayed — his permanent presence in Arghandab — he had willed at some personal cost. By the standards of Abdul Haq, the fundamentalists, and the Pathans, Ismael Gailani was not much of a commander, but by Western standards he was a person to be taken seriously.

I ate boiled eggs while the shells rained down on us.

"That last one was only one hundred yards away," said Mohammed Akbar, my interpreter from Quetta.

"One hundred yards is closer than you think," I said. "If that shell landed only a hundred yards away it would sound a lot worse."

The ground shook and dust flew into my tea. The noise was a long, condensed burst in my ears, as if the air was being sucked out of the tent.

"*That*," I said, trembling, "was a hundred yards away."

Ismael sat, relaxed and impassive. "This is what it's like here every day." He smiled, cleaning his plate greedily with his fork. We later discovered that a farmer plowing in the next field had been killed, and the mud-walled latrine I had used a few moments before had been riddled with shell fire.

In the midst of the mortar barrage, Haji Latif arrived. An impish grin was stamped on his leathery face as he hugged and kissed each one of us in turn, his black eyes full of laughter. He had a white beard and wore a black Kandahari turban with thin white stripes wrapped around his head, the ends falling to the middle of his thigh. The only "Gucci" touch was his black sneakers. But even those were 1950s playground style, and the white laces were untied.

With his smooth features and an assault rifle slung over his shoulder, Haji Latif didn't look like the eighty-three-year-old he claimed to be. Nor, with his squeaky voice and effeminate lisp, did he live up to his sinister reputation as a convicted murderer and gang leader before the war. Whenever he looked at me with his mouth hanging open, I thought he was going to start to drool.

I never heard the name Haji Latif uttered. Everyone called him Haji Baba as a sign of loving respect for his age.

"Are you really eighty-three, Haji Baba?" I asked.

"I was already a young man when King Amanullah went on his European tour, and I remember as if it were yesterday when Amanullah tried to fight his way back to Kabul from Kandahar. When Zahir Shah became king [in 1933] I was twenty-eight. All my friends have collapsed and died. With the help of God I am still strong and can fight Russians."

Haji Baba inspected the caged yellow canary and the patch of purple petunias that Ismael's men carefully looked after — this was as mortar shells continued to fall close by. Between the deep thuds of the shells came the high-pitched sound of the songbird, bringing a broad smile to Haji Baba's face.

"All the mujahidin in Kandahar have these birds," Akbar noted. "The sound they make is like poetry."

Having placed a few petunia seeds in his pocket, and satisfying himself that the bird and the flowers were being well cared for, Haji Baba reclined on a pillow and rush mat under a mulberry tree, pulled his knees up to his chin in a fetal position, and quickly fell asleep.

"Haji Baba doesn't sleep much at night, and because of his age he must take many naps," said Akbar.

The mortar attack continued unabated.

"Come here, listen to this," Ismael said.

He handed me the earphones of a captured Russian transmitter hooked up to an old Chinese generator operated by foot pedals. I heard two people talking to each other loudly in Russian for several minutes. According to the Soviets, and also to the U.S. State Department, there were no Russians left in the Kandahar area in October 1988, when I visited. Officially, the remaining Soviet troops had withdrawn with much fanfare and international media coverage a few weeks before. (Russians leaving Afghanistan seemed to be an easier and more interesting story for American editors to handle than Russians fighting in Afghanistan.) But these voices were proof that there were at least a handful of Soviet advisers left behind to help Afghan regime troops, and they were partial proof of the claim made by NIFA, the fundamentalist parties, and the journalist Zia Mojadidi in Quetta that at least five hundred crack Soviet soldiers had recently returned to Kandahar.

There was nothing surprising about this. Nor was it, technically speaking, a violation of the Geneva accords governing

Soviet disengagement; provided half their troops were out of Afghanistan by August 15, 1988, and the remainder by February 15, 1989, the Soviets could move troops in and out of cities as they chose. What bothered me about their presence was that either the State Department was lying about it for its own convoluted reasons or that U.S. intelligence was faulty.

When I returned to Pakistan I learned that the State Department's belief that the Soviets were out of Kandahar was based primarily on "satellite imaging" — a series of photographs from space that would show any unusual amount of air traffic in a given area. In fact, this technique was not foolproof, since several hundred troops could have filtered back into Kandahar over a period of days or weeks without satellite detection.

More troubling still was this: several times in Arghandab, and in Panjwai (another mujahidin stronghold southwest of Kandahar), I heard the horrific, piercing sound of Ismael's antiaircraft gun. The gunner fired only when a plane was in the air, and that was several times a day at least. The aircraft I saw — Antonov helicopters and various kinds of Soviet fighter jets — were usually ascending or descending in the vicinity of Kandahar airport, and none that I saw were hit. But later, in Pakistan, I learned that American intelligence had reported that heavy mujahidin pressure had deterred all enemy aircraft from landing or taking off from Kandahar airport during the entire period of my visit. This was untrue. When I asked whom the Americans were relying on for their information, I was stunned to learn it was their liaison in ISI, Pakistan's intelligence service.

ISI had developed a pattern of exaggerating the successes of the mujahidin who were deep inside. The reason was to justify Zia's strategy of arming his Peshawar pet, Hekmatyar, to the detriment of the other six resistance groups. ISI's motive was particularly strong. When it began to look as if Kandahar might fall to the guerrillas, ISI got nervous. Kandahar's conquest would strengthen the hand of royalist forces such as NIFA's, because it was in Kandahar that King Zahir Shah enjoyed his strongest support. ISI, intent on creating a fundamentalist Afghanistan in Zia's image, wanted Kandahar to fall only if the credit and spoils could go to commanders like Hekmatyar and Rasul Sayyaf (the leader of another fundamentalist mujahidin party that, like Hekmatyar's, depended on outside support and was thus easily manipulated by ISI).

So, a few weeks before I visited Kandahar, ISI had sponsored Hekmatyar on a tour through the region, providing him with a Pakistani army escort right up to the Afghan border. Following the tour, which both NIFA and Khalis's Hizb-i-Islami condemned, ISI began delivering Stingers and radar-guided mortars to whatever forces in Kandahar Hekmatyar could muster, as well as to Sayyaf's mujahidin, who were considerably stronger in Kandahar than Hekmatyar's fighters. In order to get the Americans to turn a blind eye to this risky policy, ISI had to show results in the field, such as claiming that Kandahar airport was under control.

The awful truth seemed to be that the only sources of information the United States had about the fighting in Kandahar, and anywhere else in Afghanistan during the later stage of the war, were their own satellite photographs and what ISI chose to tell them. (Before the mujahidin cut the road links between the major cities, officials at the American consulate in Kabul were at least able to debrief visa applicants who had recently traveled to the capital from Kandahar and Herat. And for much of the war, the American embassy in Islamabad had a cordial relationship with Peshawar-based journalists who frequently went inside and, in the time-honored tradition of foreign correspondents, subsequently swapped information with diplomats. But by the late 1980s, the diplomats had decided that the "Peshawar gang" were a bunch of loonies who lacked any credibility.)

*

My visit to the Kandahar area crystallized my thoughts about America's role in Afghanistan.

From a distance, this was the war in which Washington got things right for a change. Up close, it was more a case of Washington finally getting lucky. The conventional wisdom in the capital through most of the war held that the CIA played it smart by letting the locals — in this case, the Pakistanis — run the fighting. Up close, however, one got a very different impression.

The Washington wisdom, again, was that Afghanistan proved that supporting guerrilla proxies in a superpower turf battle will pay off when there is bipartisan support in Congress for it. But up close, what was clear to me, to everyone on the Northwest Frontier, and especially to Abdul Haq, was this: had the mujahidin lacked the will to suffer as they did, even bipartisan support in Congress and the billions of dollars in weaponry placed in ISI's trust as a result would not have been enough to thwart the Soviet reach for this latest satellite state. The American intelligence community may in fact have performed little better in Afghanistan than in Lebanon or Nicaragua.

For American policy makers, there may be no reliably applicable lessons of the Afghan war except that you win some and you lose some.

The following day I departed Arghandab with Akbar, Haji Baba, and several of his men. We planned to head south, across the Herat–Kandahar stretch of the ring road, and then east into the southern suburbs of Kandahar.

After forty-five minutes of bumpy circumvolutions to avoid mines and destroyed vehicles, we approached a battered bridge on the ring road, under which a tributary of the Arghandab River flowed. At the foot of the bridge was a bombed-out hotel. It was hard to imagine, but in prewar times upper-class Afghans held wedding receptions by the hotel's swimming pool, and newlyweds spent their first amorous night in one of the rooms. The empty pool, with its peaceful view of the swampy river tributary, still appeared to be in good condition, but Soviet soldiers had occupied — and in the process trashed — the building. In their wake had come a unit of rugged Khalis mujahidin, who now sat with their guns and grenade launchers at poolside, brewing tea while keeping an eye on the bridge. They didn't seem to think much of the pool or the view.

As our Land Cruiser turned eastward onto the Herat–Kandahar highway to Kandahar, we saw the rusted carcasses of Soviet tanks lined up back to front for over a mile. There must have been close to a hundred of them. Each had a monumental, Rodinesque quality, bent and twisted into a separate archetype of destruction that made it easy to visualize the sheets of flame and the agony of the men as they died. Some of the tanks were burned almost completely black, others were brick-red. Severed cannons and turrets lay off to the side of the road. The desert was littered with many more tanks, transport trucks, and armored personnel carriers. I had visions of Egyptian-Israeli tank battles in the Sinai and World War II campaigns in North Africa. I thought of the opening scene of *Patton,* which depicted the wreckage of American armored vehicles destroyed by Rommel in Tunisia's Kasserine Pass. Other journalists had dubbed the Iran-Iraq war a replay of "World War I in the trenches"; I thought of the Kandahar front as "World War II in the desert." Except that the desert campaigns in World War II were reported to the outside world, while men died by the thousands on these central Asian battlefields with barely a word of coverage.

The mujahidin had created this wall of tanks, moving each one into place after it had been destroyed, in order to protect a large outpost behind the road from a Soviet ground attack. The guerrilla outpost was inside the gardens of an early-eighteenth-century tomb, where the Pathan tribal leader Mirwais Khan Hotaki lies buried. He fought many battles against the Safavid Persians in the decades preceding the rise of Ahmad Shah Durrani. Mirwais openly thought of the Persians as degenerate and effeminate; he was the first known Pathan leader to think of his race in the same heroic, masculine terms as did Kipling and other foreigners since. Miraculously, the blue faience dome of Mirwais's mausoleum, surrounded by poplar trees, was still in perfect condition behind the tanks — a badge of medieval glory amid the Kiplingesque turbans and bandoleers, and this World War II desert backdrop.

The driver turned off the paved highway a few miles west of Kandahar and headed southeast over a well-rutted track. Mortar and artillery fire became louder again, and for the first time I heard the rattle of light machine guns. The driver stopped and Akbar, Haji Baba, and I climbed to the top of a sandstone cliff to espy the city.

Everything I saw and thought at that moment summoned up antiquity. The capital of southern Afghanistan lay spread out in front of the same chain of mountains that I had seen at Arghandab a few hours earlier from the other side. The city was a vast quilt of ruins etched on the barren sand, like Palmyra in the Syrian desert. Kandahar in 1988 looked not all that much different from the cities Alexander himself had seen and founded: a Hellenistic archeological site with a regular army holed up in a fortified perimeter and guerrillas firing in from all sides. The only real landmarks were the KhAD prison on the western edge of the city and the medieval blue dome to the east, which according to Moslem folklore holds the remains of some of the Prophet Mohammed's clothing.

This was a historic moment: the Soviets still left in the city and at the airport were farther south than any of their other comrades had ever been, and their imminent departure would signal the first northward redrawing of the Kremlin's imperial map since the late seventeenth century. Kandahar airport, once called an American white elephant, had become the Russian Khe Sanh.

Haji Baba sighed. "We have already given God over a million martyrs. That is more than enough."

After only a few more minutes of driving we were in the cratered back streets of Mahalajat, the southern suburb adjacent to the main bazaar of Kandahar city, now reduced to rubble. Clusters of tall wooden poles affixed with ragged white *shaheedan* banners flared like porcupine quills out of the ground. On the cassette player inside the Land Cruiser blared the haunting, melodramatic voice of Ahmad Wali, an exiled Afghan singer.

Though Mahalajat was considered a mujahidin stronghold, once in the city the battle lines were haphazard, with Afghan regime posts only about two hundred yards away from our car in several directions. Small arms, light and heavy machine guns, and mortars and artillery pieces were all being fired simultaneously; after a few minutes I got used to the racket. Twice we had to cross an open field in sight of an enemy post. The driver swerved and accelerated, yet still we attracted fire. Then the Land Cruiser got stuck behind a tonga that was having difficulty negotiating an irrigation ditch. It was incredible: a tottering horse-drawn carriage with a veiled woman in the back seat holding a sack of groceries in the middle of a free-fire zone. The spotted white horse, decked out in red and purple pompoms as if out for a stroll in Central Park, was so emaciated that I could see the outline of its skeleton beneath the flesh. The horse served as an apt symbol for Afghanistan, I thought; almost dead, yet defiant to the last.

Our driver parked behind a fragment of stone wall. From there we made a dash to a small NIFA base near the point where Mahalajat merges with the heart of the city — an idyllic spot if you could ignore the bombs. The mujahidin kept a patch of daisies next to a carpeted terrace in the shade of a vine pergola. Here we stretched out and relaxed until tea and mint-flavored curds were served. A cage with a singing canary hung from the vines. Despite the nearby explosions of artillery and mortar shells, I dozed off for a few minutes.

Haji Baba shook me awake to greet a group of city elders, who had crossed over from the regime-held sector of Kandahar that morning so I could interview them. They all had long beards like Haji Baba's and resembled wise men in their white *shalwar kameezes* and white turbans draped over gold-threaded caps.

Local custom enabled the honored elders to cross safely back and forth between the two halves of the divided city. Women and children were similarly protected. In fact, the mujahidin regularly used boys of about ten years of age to carry messages in and out of the regime sector; that was how the old men knew to come to the NIFA post that morning. Only army-age men were stopped at checkpoints, to catch defectors from the government's desertion-ridden ranks.

The stories the elders told me would be familiar to anyone who knows what goes on in a besieged Third World city. There was no medicine, and the price of produce was exorbitant. Makeshift market stalls were shut for days at a stretch, and when open they were looted and ransacked by the regime's soldiers. These troops, claiming to be from the northern Afghan province of Jozjan, were actually mercenaries brought in from Soviet central Asia, who roamed the streets in unruly gangs, holding people up and breaking into the ruins of homes in search of young boys to do menial labor for them in their barracks. Though the Soviets constantly charged the Pakistanis with violations of the Geneva accords, they themselves were guilty of much more basic offenses, such as bombing populated areas from air bases inside the Soviet Union and putting Soviet troops in Afghan regime uniforms, as they evidently were doing in Kandahar.

The city elders I interviewed desperately wanted a negotiated settlement with the Communist governor of Kandahar, a disaffected Parchami named Nur-ul Haq Ulumi. That, of course, was what NIFA wanted too, so that the only Afghan city with a strong royalist base would fall first and serve as a springboard for King Zahir Shah's return. But since the fundamentalist parties, the Pakistanis, and the Americans did not back a settlement, Kandahar's inhabitants were doomed to go on suffering. (Had the Pakistanis and Americans supported NIFA's course of action, it is possible that Kandahar would have fallen to the mujahidin before the end of 1988, leading to mass army desertions in Kabul and the subsequent collapse of the Najib regime — making unnecessary the badly organized, bloody siege of Jalalabad that began in March 1989, in which large numbers of civilians were killed. Kandahar was bigger than Jalalabad, psychologically almost as vital to the regime, already destroyed, and much harder for the Communists to defend. But because the fundamentalists were stronger in Jalalabad, the Pakistani intelligence services controlling mujahidin arms supplies concentrated on that city.)

I had wanted to get as close to the city center as possible without running the risk of being stopped at a regime checkpoint. The youth who accompanied Akbar and me on this foray had lost a leg in a mine explosion, but he was as fast and agile as most people are with two. He led the way, checking for mines and enemy lookouts hidden behind sandbag emplacements, then waved when it was safe for us to follow.

We had to cross one of several open fields in sight of hostile machine gun nests, where, incredibly, a shepherd was grazing his sheep. Bullets sprayed the field a few seconds after we had crossed it: a sheep lay bleeding as I looked back. The shepherd cursed aloud, caressed the dying animal, and by tossing a few stones moved the flock on. The stones startled the sheep; the bullets hadn't.

"The bullets they are more used to," Akbar observed.

The scene was not what I expected on the basis of my visit

to Kandahar fifteen years earlier. I imagined an urban setting: streets, shops, and pavements, some in place, some destroyed. But as we moved northward from Mahalajat toward the Herat Gate area, where I had spent that miserable night in 1973, there was no sign of a true cityscape. The ashen monotony of an archeological site continued almost to the center of Kandahar. We ran along remnants of walled streets and arched portals with smashed networks of ceramic underground plumbing systems, and past weeds and wildflowers that grew in stony places where ground had been churned up. People had once lived in these ruins, I knew, but it seemed as if that must have been thousands of years ago. Only the bombs and bullets and that dead sheep kept me from believing I was a tourist visiting an ancient city.

This was not a military landscape of the past but of an eerie doomsday future. The twentieth century had come late to Afghanistan, but when it came, it came with a vengeance. The Soviets had sown so many mines, dropped so many bombs, and fired so many mortars and artillery shells over such a wide swath of territory that the effect of a nuclear strike had been achieved.

No city in North Vietnam was destroyed to the extent that Kandahar was. Whereas American air strikes on the North early in the Vietnam war were initially so restrictive that President Lyndon Johnson had personally to approve the targets in advance, the Soviets engaged in indiscriminate carpet bombing throughout their war. Whereas the American military tended to use attack helicopters against specific targets or to insert troops, the Soviets usually used those helicopters against mud brick villages. Whereas the Americans at least tried to carefully map their minefields, and deploy mines mainly along strategic routes like the Ho Chi Minh trail and around their base perimeters, the Soviets kept few maps and sowed millions of mines. The Soviets lost between 12,000 and 50,000 men in Afghanistan, considerably fewer than the 58,000 troops the Americans lost in Vietnam. Yet the number of Afghan civilians who were killed — estimated at over a million — probably exceeded civilian Vietnamese fatalities, even though North and South Vietnam had a combined population two and a half times larger than Afghanistan.

Another sign of the future was the absence of battle and its attendant drama: I saw only monotonous images of mass destruction. In *The Face of Battle*, the military historian John Keegan intimates that the totality of future wars will render battle itself obsolete. Battle implies limits, but in Kandahar and elsewhere in Afghanistan there was little ebb and flow to the killing. The Soviets carpet bombed Kandahar and the Panjshir Valley north of Kabul for months at a time. Mines killed about thirty Afghans, more or less, every day of the entire decade.

Kipling's vision only partially illuminated the true symbolism of the war in Afghanistan. Kipling could be an imperialist and a moralist at the same time precisely because he had little inkling of modern totalitarian ideologies like fascism and communism and the extremes to which they would take the imperialist impulse. Though Kipling's chivalrous world of manly honor had in Afghanistan vanquished the modern world of mechanized destruction, Afghanistan in the 1980s was still no Kiplingesque war — the glorious escapades of the likes of John Wellesley Gunston and Savik Shuster notwithstanding. These two were brave men and brave journalists. But, like me, they were living an illusion. Abdul Haq, and Haji Baba too, despite what we thought, were only in a small sense Kiplingesque Pathans. They represented some sort of primitive, vestigial lone warrior from the past but also of the future, when the only people willing and able to fight a superpower will be poverty-stricken peasant guerrillas who have no motive to surrender because they have no material possessions at risk.

Because the historical images, particularly in Kandahar, were so vivid and intimidating, the relatively few journalists

who went inside, like myself, were for the most part blind to
these revelations. We tended to look backward only — to
World War II, to Kipling, and to Alexander the Great.

We left Mahalajat and returned to Arghandab in time for
the night fireworks display. Red flares crossed the sky as if in
slow motion, followed by exploding artillery shells that caused
small brush fires to break out in the mined desert between
Kandahar's southern suburbs and the ring road. Again the
driver swerved and accelerated, and drove without headlights.
Then, still in artillery range, he stopped and the others got out
of the Land Cruiser to pray. With no water in sight, they
washed their hands and faces with the dust, just as I had seen
the fundamentalists do in Nangarhar.

Epilogue

~~~~~~~~~~

Something I Only Imagined

IT WAS THE WORST possible place to get a flat tire: in broad daylight on the undulating stretch of desert directly under the flight path between the Shindand and Kandahar air bases. Again the driver built a wobbly tower of rocks under the jack and was able to change the tire in just a few minutes. Nobody talked or worried about the driver under the car. Each of us knew what the other was thinking. I felt fear leave my gut as we climbed back into the Land Cruiser.

After fifteen minutes' more driving, the smooth, American-laid asphalt of the Kandahar–Kabul road appeared on the open desert. At the same moment that we saw a spiraling pillar of black smoke rise from a burning truck on the road to our left, we heard the whining *boom* of two helicopter gunships swinging sideways and upward, away from us in the southern sky. The driver speeded up and over the other side of the road and zigzagged into the Arghastan desert, heedless of mines. But the gunships were already winging their way home to Kandahar air base.

Our flat tire had saved us. Had we arrived at the road crossing a few minutes earlier than we did, our fate might have been the same as that of the burning truck and its driver.

The rain came down in sheets, driven by the wind against the ranks of lonely tents on the muddy hillside. The mud was like glue and splattered all over my army surplus jacket, inside which I shivered. It was February 1988. A few miles outside the Northwest Frontier town of Miram Shah, near the Afghan border, a few hundred Afghan men, women, and children had just stampeded over the border to escape the fighting in Paktia province. They were the newest of over five million Afghans in refugee camps in Pakistan and Iran — more than five times the number of Palestinians in refugee camps. Stranded on the freezing mud, the UN-supplied tents were all these Afghans possessed. The children had no *patous* (blankets); against the wind, rain, and low temperatures all they had to wear were cotton *shalwar kameezes*. Several of them coughed and shivered.

With two other journalists I drove into Miram Shah and, for the equivalent of a few dollars in Pakistani rupees, bought several dozen old sweaters and pairs of pants to distribute to the children. A UN group or some other relief organization would have gotten around to distributing warm clothes to the children eventually. But for the moment, no one else was even thinking about them.

Away from Pakistan and Afghanistan, I could barely speak about the war. When I told people where I had been, their blank expressions indicated I might as well have been on the moon. Of the few who were truly interested in what I had to say, the retort that often greeted me was: "Really? Well then, how come we read so little about it in the newspapers?" The conversation would shift abruptly to another subject. It was nothing they needed to think or concern themselves about. It was happening so far away, to a people unrelated to them or to anybody they knew. Most listened to me only out of politeness, as though the stories I had brought back from central Asia were just that — stories, something I had only imagined.

American conservatives claimed that the media deliberately avoided Afghanistan because of a double standard regarding the Soviets. It was worse than that. Afghanistan, which on the scale of human suffering vastly overshadowed any other military conflict of the 1980s, was, quite simply, almost unconsciously ignored.

ACKNOWLEDGMENTS

THE SEVEN-PARTY MUJAHIDIN ALLIANCE

CHRONOLOGY

BIBLIOGRAPHY

INDEX

Acknowledgments

John D. Panitza and Kenneth Tomlinson of *Reader's Digest* encouraged me to go to Afghanistan the first time and showed an interest in my project throughout, as did Cullen Murphy and William Whitworth of *The Atlantic*. Editors at *The New Republic* and the *Wall Street Journal* were also helpful. The book was written with the help of a grant from the John M. Olin Foundation and the Institute for Educational Affairs; I am especially grateful to Kimberly Ohnemus and Tom Skladony of those two organizations. My agent, Carl D. Brandt, made the selling of this book to a top publisher seem easy, something I had never thought possible. My editor, Michael C. Janeway, helped me to progress technically as a writer for the first time in years. Thanks are also due to Julia Carmel and Larry Cooper at Houghton Mifflin, and to Eric Haas at *The Atlantic*.

In chapter 5, a short quote from Abdul Haq is taken from an interview he once gave John Fullerton, whose 1983 book, *The Soviet Occupation of Afghanistan,* is the best of the early primers on the war. In chapter 6, much of the information on Quetta is taken from an article I wrote for the March 1988 issue of *The American Spectator.* Other, smaller sections of the book previously appeared in *The Atlantic, The New Republic,* and *Reader's Digest.*

In Greece, Alice Anne Demosthenos and Eleni Angelinos were great friends to my family during a difficult period, and their kind help allowed me many more hours of writing than I normally would have had.

In Peshawar, Anne Hurd and Kurt Lohbeck opened their home to me and arranged my first interviews with Abdul Haq and others. Massoud Akram, Dr. Mohammed Yaqub Barikzai, Wakhil Abdul Bedar, Mohammed Es Haq, Hassan Kakar, Farouk Adam Khan, and Mohammed Anwar Khan, among many others, helped me to understand the culture and politics of the Pathans. Azima Atmar and Isabelle Moussard tutored me on the subject of women in Afghan society, as did Anne Hurd.

Joe Gaal, Kathy Gannon, Steve Masty, and Tony O'Brien were the most delightful friends one could have in a place like Peshawar. Joe Gaal died in 1989. I will miss him. He was a talented, understated photographer whose willingness to risk his life provided the outside world with many telling photos of the Soviet occupation.

Helena Beattie, Tony Davis, Ed Girardet, Ed Gorman, John Gunston, Peter Jouvenal, Abdul Jabar Sabit, Rob Schultheis, Lisa Schiffren, Savik Shuster, Nancy deWolf Smith, and Brian Wilder are friends and colleagues whose help and good company I will cherish forever.

.

The Seven-Party Mujahidin Alliance

FUNDAMENTALISTS

Hizb-i-Islami (Party of Islam). A radical, anti-Western group led by Gulbuddin Hekmatyar, a former Kabul University engineering student. Despite his extremist politics and lack of grassroots support, Hekmatyar was favored by the Pakistani and American intelligence services, who provided him with more arms than any of the other parties.

Hizb-i-Islami (Party of Islam). A more moderate group than Hekmatyar's, led by Yunus Khalis, an Afghan cleric and former schoolteacher. Because of its tribal support among Pathans in the regions of Kabul, Jalalabad, Ghazni, and Kandahar, Khalis's group was among the most significant militarily, boasting respected commanders like Abdul Haq, Haq's brother Abdul Qadir, and Jallaluddin Haqqani. Because of his age and lack of interest in details, Khalis allowed the day-to-day operation of his party to be controlled by another of Haq's brothers, Din Mohammed.

Jamiat-i-Islami (Islamic Society). A militarily powerful party dominated by ethnic Tajiks and led by Burhanuddin Rabbani, an academic and theologian. Jamiat's power was concentrated in the northern half of Afghanistan, inhabited by Tajiks, Uzbeks, and other minorities. Two of the most famous resistance commanders fought for Jamiat: Ahmad Shah Massoud in the Panjshir Valley and Ismael Khan in Herat.

Itihad-i-Islami (Islamic Unity). Led by a former university professor, Rasul Sayyaf, this party, like Hekmatyar's, derived its strength from outside aid. In Sayyaf's case, the aid came mainly from Saudi Arabia and the Persian Gulf states.

MODERATES

Mahaz-i-Milli Islami (National Islamic Front of Afghanistan, or NIFA). Led by Pir Syed Ahmed Gailani, a hereditary Sufi saint, NIFA was a royalist party supporting the return of deposed King Zahir Shah. The party's strongest base of support was in the southern region of Kandahar. Its commander there was Haji Abdel Latif.

Jabha-i-Nijat-Milli (Afghan National Liberation Front). Like NIFA, a royalist party with a base of support in Kandahar. Despite the brave personal record of the party's leader, Sibghatullah Mojadidi, it had few troops in the field and consequently got the least aid from the Pakistanis and the Americans. Mojadidi was a compromise figure selected to lead the mujahidin government-in-exile in March 1989.

Harakat-i-Inqilab-i-Islami (Islamic Revolutionary Forces). Led by a cleric, Mohammed Nabi Mohammedi, Harakat was less a moderate party than a neither-nor group of urban intellectuals and village clerics under the same roof. Because it was loosely organized and had an opaque political personality, Harakat got little attention among Peshawar-based journalists, but nevertheless boasted a large number of fighters in Afghanistan.

Chronology

	1973
July 17	King Zahir Shah is overthrown in a nearly bloodless coup by his cousin and former prime minister, Mohammed Daoud. Daoud presides over an increasingly unstable regime that is friendly to the Soviet Union.

	1978
April 27	Afghan Communists belonging to the Khalq (Masses) faction stage a violent coup. Daoud is killed. Nur Mohammed Taraki and his deputy, Hafizullah Amin, head the new government.
June	As a result of purges and a brutal land reform program, the Afghan guerrilla movement is born in the countryside.

	1979
September 16	Amin takes power after having Taraki murdered. Government violence increases, further encouraging the guerrilla movement and an exodus of refugees to Pakistan and Iran.
December 21	The Soviet invasion of Afghanistan begins. The United States reports three Soviet divisions at the Soviet-Afghan border and 1,500 Soviet troops near Kabul.
December 27	Massive airlift of Soviet troops into Afghanistan is under way. Amin is killed. Babrak Karmal, a member of the Parcham (Banner) faction of the Afghan Communist party, is flown into Afghanistan by the Soviets to replace Amin.

1980

January

As the number of Soviet troops in Afghanistan reaches 100,000, President Jimmy Carter announces punitive measures and calls for resisting Soviet aggression.

1981

December

The number of Afghan refugees in Pakistan reaches 2.5 million.

1984

November

As Soviet carpet bombing of heavily populated farming villages in Afghanistan continues, U.S. aid to the guerrillas reaches $280 million annually.

1985

May 16

Seven Afghan guerrilla groups form a united political front based in Pakistan.

June 20

The government of Pakistan begins talks with the Afghan Communist regime in Geneva through UN intermediaries.

1986

May 4

Karmal is forced out by the Soviets. He is replaced by Najib, a fellow Parchami who has run KhAD, the Afghan secret police, since 1980. The first Stinger antiaircraft missiles, sent by the United States, begin arriving in Pakistan for use by the Afghan guerrillas.

1987

January 1

The Afghan Communist regime offers a cease-fire, which the guerrillas reject.

December

Soviet leader Mikhail Gorbachev indicates at a Washington summit meeting with President Ronald Reagan that his forces are prepared to leave Afghanistan within twelve months after a withdrawal agreement is signed.

1988

February

Gorbachev says Moscow is ready to withdraw from Afghanistan even without a guarantee that the Afghan Communist regime will remain in power. The Soviet leader then says that if talks at Geneva succeed, Soviet troops can start pulling out on May 15.

April 14

A withdrawal accord is signed in Geneva between the United States, the Soviet Union, the Afghan Communist regime, and the government of Pakistan.

May 15

Soviet troops begin withdrawing from Afghanistan.

August 15

The Soviets report that half their troops have left Afghanistan.

August 17

Pakistani President Zia ul-Haq and U.S. Ambassador to Pakistan Arnold Raphel are killed in an air crash. An investigation of the incident clearly indicates it was an act of sabotage. Suspicion is cast upon KhAD and the Soviet KGB.

November

Benazir Bhutto is elected prime minister of Pakistan. She retains Zia's former foreign minister and Zia's chief of intelligence.

1989

February 15

The Soviet Union completes its troop withdrawal from Afghanistan.

March

The Afghan guerrillas elect Sibghatullah Mojadidi, a moderate, as the head of their government-in-exile. The guerrillas fail to topple the eastern Afghan city of Jalalabad after a full-scale conventional assault.

May

Prime Minister Bhutto removes the Zia-appointed head of Pakistani intelligence, Lieutenant General Hamid Gul, from his post. Mrs. Bhutto begins to put her own stamp on Afghan war policy.

June

Prime Minister Bhutto meets President George Bush in Washington. The two leaders announce that they will pursue a two-track policy, arming the mujahidin and talking with the Soviets, in order to encourage the formation of a neutral, non-Communist Afghan government that will end the fighting.

Bibliography

Ahmed, Akbar S. *Millennium and Charisma Among Pathans.* Routledge & Kegan Paul, London, 1976.

Ajami, Fouad. *The Vanished Imam: Musa al Sadr and the Shia of Lebanon.* Cornell University Press, Ithaca, N.Y., 1986.

Babel, Isaac. *Collected Stories.* Translated and revised by Walter Morison, with an introduction by Lionel Trilling. Penguin Books, Middlesex, England, 1961.

Babur Padshah, Zahirud-din Muhammad. *Babur-nama.* Translated from Turki by Annette S. Beveridge. Sange Meel Publications, Lahore, Pakistan, 1987.

Barry, Michael. "Le Grand Jeu Afghan." *Politique Internationale,* Paris, Spring 1985.

Behr, Edward. *"Anyone Here Been Raped and Speaks English?" A Foreign Correspondent's Life Behind the Lines.* Viking Press, New York, 1978.

Biddulph, C. E. *The Poems of Khush Hal Khan Khatak.* Saeed Book Bank, Peshawar, Pakistan, 1890, reprinted 1983.

Bradsher, Henry S. *Afghanistan and the Soviet Union.* Duke University Press, Durham, North Carolina, 1983.

Byron, Robert. *The Road to Oxiana.* Macmillan, London, 1937.

Caroe, Olaf. *The Pathans.* Macmillan, London, 1958.

Cornell, Louis L. *Kipling in India.* St. Martin's Press, New York, 1966.

Dupree, Louis. *Afghanistan.* Princeton University Press, Princeton, N.J., 1973.

Elphinstone, Mountstuart. *An Account of the Kingdom of Caubul.* Vol. 1. Oxford University Press, Karachi, Pakistan, 1972.

Evans, Rowland, and Robert Novak. "Pakistan: Moscow's Terror Target." *Reader's Digest,* July 1988, pp. 124–28.

First Consolidated Report. Office of the United Nations Coordinator for Humanitarian and Economic Assistance Programs Relating to Afghanistan. Geneva, 1988.

Follett, Ken. *Lie Down with Lions.* William Morrow, New York, 1986.

Fullerton, John. *The Soviet Occupation of Afghanistan.* Far Eastern Economic Review, Hong Kong, 1983.

Girardet, Edward R. *Afghanistan: The Soviet War.* St. Martin's Press, New York, 1985.

Gunston, John. "A Quick Killing on the Road to Kabul." *You* (London magazine), October 30, 1988, pp. 96–100.

Hemingway, Ernest. *Men at War.* Crown Publishers, New York, 1955.

Hodson, Peregrine. *Under a Sickle Moon: A Journey Through Afghanistan.* Hutchinson, London, 1986.

Holy Quran. With English translation by Abdul Majid Daryabadi. Taj Company, Karachi, Pakistan, 1984.

Howarth, David. *The Greek Adventure: Lord Byron and Other Eccentrics in the War of Independence.* William Collins, London, 1976.

Keegan, John. *The Face of Battle.* Jonathan Cape, London, 1976.

———. *The Mask of Command.* Viking Penguin, New York, 1987.

Khan, Muhammad Hayat. *Afghanistan and Its Inhabitants.* Translated by Henry Priestly. Indian Public Opinion Press, Lahore, British India, 1874.

Kipling, Rudyard. *A Choice of Kipling's Verse.* Selected and with an Essay on Rudyard Kipling by T. S. Eliot. Faber and Faber, London, 1941.

———. *Kim.* Penguin Books, London, 1901, reprinted 1987.

The Koran. Translated with notes by N. J. Dawood. Penguin Books, Middlesex, England, 1975.

Lessing, Doris. *The Wind Blows Away Our Words.* Pan Books, London, 1987.

Levi, Peter. *The Light Garden of the Angel King.* William Collins, London, 1972.

Lindholm, Charles. *Generosity and Jealousy: The Swat Pukhtun of Northern Pakistan.* Columbia University Press, New York, 1982.

Mackenzie, Richard. "A Brutal Force Batters a Country." *Washington Times,* December 5, 1988.

Majrooh, Sayd B., and S. M. Y. Elmi. *The Sovietization of Afghanistan.* Printing Corporation of Frontier, Peshawar, Pakistan, 1986.

Manning, Olivia. *The Danger Tree.* Weidenfeld and Nicolson, London, 1977.

Moorhouse, Geoffrey. *To the Frontier.* Hodder and Stoughton, London, 1984.

Newby, Eric. *A Short Walk in the Hindu Kush.* Secker and Warburg, London, 1958.

Newell, Nancy Peabody, and Richard S. Newell. *The Struggle for Afghanistan.* Cornell University Press, Ithaca and London, 1981.

Orwell, George. *The Penguin Essays of George Orwell.* Essay on Rudyard Kipling. Penguin Books, Middlesex, England, 1984.

Pennell, T. L. *Among the Wild Tribes of the Afghan Frontier.* Seeley and Company, London, 1909.

Pinney, Thomas. *Kipling's India: Uncollected Sketches 1884–88.* Macmillan, London, 1986.

Reeves, Richard. *Passage to Peshawar.* Simon and Schuster, New York, 1984.

Revel, Jean-François. "The Awful Logic of Genocide." *National Review,* October 4, 1985, pp. 22–29.

Ridgway, R. T. I. *Pathans.* Saeed Book Bank, Peshawar, Pakistan, 1983.

Robinson, J. A. *Notes on Nomad Tribes of Eastern Afghanistan.* Nisa Traders, Quetta, Pakistan, 1934.

Roy, Olivier. *Islam and Resistance in Afghanistan.* Cambridge University Press, Cambridge, England, 1986.

Rushdie, Salman. *Shame.* Jonathan Cape, London, 1983.

Saberi, Helen. *Noshe Djan: Afghan Food and Cookery.* Prospect Books, London, 1986.

Santiago, José Roleo. *Pakistan: A Travel Survival Kit.* Lonely Planet Publications, South Yarra, Australia, 1987.

Schofield, Victoria. *Every Rock, Every Hill: A Plain Tale of the North-West Frontier and Afghanistan.* Buchan and Enright, London, 1984.

Schultheis, Rob. "Going Inside." *The Washington Post Magazine,* February 15, 1987, pp. 26–31.

Spain, James W. *The Way of the Pathans.* Robert Hale, London, 1962.

Swedish Committee for Afghanistan. *The Agricultural Survey of Afghanistan.* First draft. Peshawar, Pakistan, 1988.

Sweetman, Bill. *The Hamlyn Concise Guide to Soviet Military Aircraft.* Hamlyn Publishing Group, Middlesex, England, 1981.

Theroux, Paul. *The Great Railway Bazaar.* Houghton Mifflin, Boston, 1975.

United States Department of State. *Afghanistan: Eight Years of Soviet Occupation.* Washington, D.C., December 1987.

Van Dyk, Jere. *In Afghanistan.* Coward-McCann, New York, 1983.

Index

Abdal, 196
Abdalis (later Durranis), 192–93,
    195, 196, 203
Abdul Haq. *See* Haq, Abdul
Abdul Qadir. *See* Qadir, Abdul
Abdul Wakhil, 77
Achakzais, 203
Achin government post, 139
Adam Khel Afridis, 99
Afghan government. *See* Com-
    munists, Afghan
Afghan guerrillas. *See* Mujahidin
Afghanistan, 15
    British invasions of, 20, 43, 59,
      82, 147
    climate of, 122
    emaciated horse as symbol of,
      220
    family strength in, 153
    history of, 192–94, 197
    Islamic culture in, 107–10
    and Kipling, 224 (*see also* Kip-
      ling, Rudyard)
    politics and urbanization miss-
      ing from, 126
    U.S./West view of, 15, 170
Afghanistan conflict
    and media, 10–11, 11–12, 14–
      15, 128, 227 (*see also* Media)

mujahidin in, 3, 8, 16–17, 171
    (*see also* Mujahidin)
Taraki as cause of, 116
Afghanistan conflict, stages of,
    235–37 (Chronology)
Daoud coup, 147, 149–50,
    188–89, 194, 235
Communist coup(s) and guer-
    rilla resistance, 115–16, 152–
    53, 174, 179, 235
Soviet invasion, 116–17, 235–
    36 (*see also* Soviet invasion of
    Afghanistan)
Najib government, 161, 173–
    76, 236 (*see also* Najib)
Soviet withdrawal, 13–14, 214–
    15, 236–37 (*see also* Soviet
    withdrawal)
postwithdrawal situation
Communists, 167, 173–76,
    177
mujahidin, 17, 70, 137, 139,
    166–67, 172, 178, 222, 237
Afghanistan (Dupree), 185–86
Afghan Communists. *See* Com-
    munists, Afghan
Afghan National Liberation
    Front (Jabha-i-Nijat-Milli),
    191–92, 234

Afghanistan Relief Committee, 5
Afghans
  Britishers' view of, 19–20
  Pakistanis (Punjabis) as viewed
    by, 32–33
  Pathans, 21–22 (see also Pa-
    than)
  Tajiks, 37–38 (see also Tajik)
Afridis, 82–84, 94, 99–104
  met in Tirah fort, 97–98
Ahmad Khan, 192
Ahmad Shah Durrani, 195
Ahmadzai tribe, 147
Ahmedjan (nom de guerre), 30
Aide Médicale Internationale, 8
Akbar, Mohammed, 202, 207,
    209, 212, 217, 219, 222
Akhrimiyuk, Yevgeny Nikolai-
    vich, 159–60
Alexander the Great
  and Afghanistan locations, 81,
    82, 96, 209
  and Kandahar, 194, 219
  looking backward to, 225
  and Pathans, 21, 83
Ali, Farouk, 140–41, 142–43
Aman, Mohammed (father of
    Abdul Haq), 145–46
Amanullah (king of Afghani-
    stan), 213
American Club, 28–29, 36–37,
    66, 69, 164, 181
Amin, Hafizullah, 116, 117, 152,
    174
Amnesty International, 115,
    120
Amputation, 1, 7
  for frostbite, 138
  on Abdul Haq, 46–47
Arabs, 69, 126, 135, 136, 140
Arghandab, 209–17, 225
Arghastan desert, 205, 207, 226

"Arithmetic on the Frontier"
    (Kipling), 27, 55, 80
Armacost, Michael H., 3
Arsala, Hadayat, 147
Arsala Khan, Wasir, 147
Arsala Khel, 147
Ashnagur, 129–32, 133, 136
  and Abdul Qadir, 137, 139
Atrocities
  by Communists, 39, 68, 120
  and Pathans, 135

"Baba," 199
Babar Khan (pseudonym), 79
Babel, Isaac, 134–35
Babur (emperor of India), 81,
    82, 111, 119
Babur-nama, 81
Baghram air base photos, 58,
    59
"Ballad of East and West, The"
    (Kipling), 2, 20
Baluchistan, 197–98, 204–5
Bamboo Garden, 28, 164
Barikot, Kunar province, 6
Beards, and mujahidin, 51, 182
Bedar, Wakhil Abdul, 88–89
  vs. Akbar, 202
  and eating of dates, 111
  and Abdul Haq, 89–90
  as hillman, 112
  as interpreter, 90, 93–94, 96,
    113, 114, 119, 126, 127, 128,
    129
  and pace of march, 128
  prayers led by, 106, 118, 123
  and religion, 109
  smoking by, 98
Behr, Edward, 25
Beirut, and Kandahar, 187
Bhutto, Benazir, 34, 237

Bhutto, Zulfikar Ali, 34
Bloom Star Hotel, 198, 201
Bombing, aerial
    and capture of Kunduz/Jalala-
        bad, 166
    effects of in villages, 118–19,
        128–29
    from inside Soviet Union, 221
    of Kandahar, 187–88, 224
    of Panjshir Valley, 39, 57, 224
    running toward to escape, 75
    during Soviet withdrawal, 13
    of Spinghar command post,
        126
    as unlimited, 224
Booby traps, Soviet, 6
"Bouncing Betty" mine, 4
Bradsher, Henry S., 116
Britain, Afghanistan invaded by,
        20, 43, 59, 82, 147
Brydon, William, 82
Burhanuddin Rabbani, 168, 233
Bush, George, 237
Butterfly mine, 4–5, 22, 57, 122,
        127–28
Byron, Lord, 17, 53–54
    Childe Harold's Pilgrimage, 56
Byron, Robert, 19

Carless, Hugh, 140
Caroe, Sir Olaf, 19–20, 82–83,
        95, 193
Cassandra, Abdul Haq as, 178
Castro, Fidel, and Massoud, 39
Casualties from Afghanistan con-
        flict, 10–11, 18, 224
Central Asia
    appearance of plateaus of, 96
    vs. Indian subcontinent, 24,
        26, 32, 81
Central Intelligence Agency. *See*
    CIA

Chatwin, Bruce, 19
China, and Massoud, 39, 40
Churchill, Winston, on Afridis,
        94
CIA
    arms program of, 85
    counterfeiting operation of, 23
    and Hekmatyar, 170
    newspaper forgery blamed on,
        78
    and Pakistani role, 217
    and Paulin accusation, 1
    on Soviets' 1979 hopes, 171
Class divisions, and parties, 190
"Clientitis," 35
Coca-Cola, 43, 51, 103, 142,
        166
Cockburn, Alexander, 15
Communism
    East German mujahid fights,
        30
    Gunston fights, 54
    as ideology (Haq), 148, 192
    see also Soviet Union
Communists, Afghan
    atrocities by, 68, 120
    and capture of Spinboldak,
        203–4
    divisions among, 173–74
    killing prisoners by alleged,
        120
    political executions by, 115
    and Saur Revolution, 153
    siege mentality of, 131
    and Zahir Shah regime, 149,
        189
Contras, Nicaraguan, 171
Cordovez, Diego, 149, 175
Cornell, Louis L., 9
Cossacks, 134–35
Counterfeiting, by CIA, 23
Cultural Revolution, 116

Danger Tree, The (Manning),
    134
Daoud, Mohammed, 149–50,
    188–89
  Haq in coup attempts against,
    151
  and NIFA, 191
  and Pul-i-Charki prison, 152
Dari, 38, 74, 117
Darra, 30–31, 83, 85, 99
Dean's Hotel, 26, 27, 28, 36, 53,
    66, 71
Depopulation strategy, 2, 5
Dihbala, 131
Din Mohammed, 42, 67–68, 151
  in cabinet-in-exile, 167
  and Daoud coup, 149
  and Daoud government, 150
  and Abdul Haq, 66, 67–68, 70,
    151, 155, 156, 158
  and Jalalabad attack, 166
  and Khalis, 154
  and "land reform," 115–16
  and Shuster, 68, 73–74, 75, 78
  and Zahir Shah, 189
Diseases. *See* Illness
Dolls, mines disguised as, 5–6
Drug trade, Afridi *khans* in, 84.
    See also Hashish; Heroin
Dupree, Louis, 38, 185–86
Durand, Sir Mortimer, 105
Durand Line, 105, 138
Durrani empire, 147, 193–94
Dysentery, 8–9, 140, 141–42, 143

Eastern Europeans, 65, 66
Ellis, Molly, 94
Elphinstone, Mountstuart, 19
Eriksen, Hugo, 9
Eritreans, 47
Explosives

Abdul Haq's early use of, 150–
    51
  mujahidin use of, 130, 132,
    151, 162–63, 165

Face of Battle, The (Keegan), 2,
    18, 224
Follett, Ken, 40
Food. *See* Meals
Foreigners aiding mujahidin
  East German refugee (Ahmed-
    jan), 29–30
  Hungarian doctor, 46
  Lars Grahnstrom, 11
  Laurence Laumonier, 39
  London window cleaner as, 30,
    75
  and mercenaries, 30
  Simon Mardel, 8
  Frank Paulin, 1
  Savik Shuster, 64–66, 68, 71,
    75 (*see also* Shuster, Savik)
  Koshiro Tanaka, 29, 75
  see also Relief workers
Freedom, Pathan's price for, 143
Freud, Sigmund, 135
Fullerton, John, 181

Gaal, Joe, 4
Gailani, Ismael, 210–12, 213, 214
Gailani, Pir Syed Ahmed, 181–
    82, 183, 190, 191, 192, 202,
    233
Gardez–Kabul highway, 61
Geneva accords, 214–15, 221,
    237
German Humanitarian Service,
    30
Ghanzni, and Hizb-i-Islami, 42
Gholam Issa Khan, 113, 115,
    117, 118, 125

Godfather, The, and Abdul Haq,
  145
Gorbachev, Mikàil, 11, 236–37
Grahnstrom, Lars, 11
Great Railway Bazaar, The (Theroux), 86
Greek *klephts,* mujahidin compared with, 17
Green's Hotel, 27
Greetings between mujahidin,
  92
"Gucci muj," 181–84, 195, 205,
  210
Guerrilla leaders (world), 47–48
Guerrillas, Afghan. *See* Mujahidin
Guevara, Che, and Massoud, 39
Gujar (driver), 28
Gulabzoi, Sayed Mohammed,
  174–75
Gulbuddin Hekmatyar. *See* Hekmatyar, Gulbuddin
Gulf war, 119, 131, 201
Gun making, in Darra, 31
Gunston, John Wellesley, 52–55,
  65
  and Haq, 59–60, 64, 72, 145
  Haq to on Moslem fundamentalism, 167
  and Hekmatyar forces, 55–58
  on Hekmatyar in Kabul, 172
  on Kabul mission, 60–63
  and Kipling, 224
  and Massoud over Haq, 177
  Soviet pilot photographed by,
    57–58

Habibullah, 121, 122, 124–26,
  136
  and Abdul Qadir, 137, 139
  safe-arrival signal to, 129
  tent shared by, 210

Hail, mines exploded by, 13, 122
Haji Baba (Latif), 182–84, 188,
  213–14, 217, 219, 220, 224,
  233
Halim, Zabet, 155, 156, 159
Hamid Karzai, 195–96, 197
Hamid, Syed, 60–63
Hamidullah, Said, 130–31
Haq, Abdul, 41–42, 43–44, 61,
  73, 180
  as abandoned, 177, 179
  characteristics of
    alone, 72
    appearance, 211
    dependence on foreigners,
      73
    emotional compensation, 212
    and female journalists, 133
    instinctive attitudes, 212
    as Kiplingesque, 224
    as larger than life, 195
    and mention of women, 50, 51
  and Gunston, 59–60, 64, 72
  headquarters of, 144–45
  during holiday feast, 165–66
  interviews with, 78
  and ISI, 168–69, 178
  and journalists, 52
  and Khairullah, 63–64
  and Khalis, 87, 148, 151, 154–
    55, 156, 158
  and "land reform," 115–16
  life story of
    family of, 42, 147
    childhood, 145–47, 148
    early guerrilla activities, 150–
      52, 154, 157
    imprisonment, 152–54
    Kabul front commander,
      155–59, 161–65, 173, 176
    and kidnapping of General
      Akhrimiyuk, 159–60

Haq, Abdul *(Cont.)*
  mine wound of, 44–48, 72,
    165, 183
  and Din Mohammed, 67–68,
    151, 155, 156, 158
  name taken by, 151
  and Pathan history, 147–48
  and rural resistance base, 132
  and seven-party alliance, 167–
    68
  shrapnel wounds of, 158
  and Shuster, 64–65, 66, 71,
    73–75, 78
  trip "inside" arranged by, 137
  UN appearance by, 66–67, 70–
    71
  views of
    and communism as ideology,
      148, 192
    on Hekmatyar, 168, 172
    on Jalalabad assault, 166–67
    on U.S. policy, 171–72, 217
    on Wali Khan Kuki Khel, 100
    and Wakhil, 89–90
  war-end strategy of, 167, 172–
    73, 176–77, 178
Haq, Fazle, 55
Haqqani, Jallaluddin, 120, 154
Haq Ulumi, Nur-ul, 221–22
Harakat-i-Inqilab-i-Islami (Islamic Revolutionary Forces),
  234
Hashish, 31, 85, 98
Hekmatyar, Gulbuddin, 55, 68–
  69, 70, 168, 233
  arguments against and in de-
    fense of, 169–70
  assassination attempt on, 168
  and future of Afghanistan,
    170
  Haq contrasted with, 73
  Haq's opinion of, 168, 172

  as inside rarely, 87, 110
  and Mojadidi, 192
  public-relations machine of,
    172
  Abdul Qadir on, 137
  and U.S., 169–70, 178, 182,
    233
  and Zahir Shah, 189
  and Zia, 68, 69, 110, 168–69,
    182, 215–16
Helicopter gunships, Soviet, 16
  Abdul Haq tactics against, 159
  and Kandahar terrain, 9, 184
  lucky avoidance of, 226
  machine guns against, 121
  mines dropped by, 5
  Shuster group hounded by,
    75–76
  and Stinger missiles, 118, 126,
    127, 129
  and Vietnam war comparison,
    223
Herat, 192, 194
Herat–Kandahar–Kabul (ring)
  road, 207, 218
Heroin, 27, 28, 31, 84, 85, 198
Hindu Kush mountains, 38, 57
Hindus, Moslems compared
  with, 33
Hizb-i-Islami (Party of Islam) (of
  Yunus Khalis), 42–43, 88,
  233
  flag of, 205
  Habibullah in, 125
  and Hamid, 60
  and Abdul Haq, 155, 158
  and Hekmatyar faction, 55
  and Hekmatyar tour, 216
  killing of prisoners alleged of,
    120
  Landi Kotal headquarters of,
    86–87

Hizb-i-Islami *(Cont.)*
  in Nangarhar, 154
  vs. NIFA, 189–90, 191
  salary paid by, 90
  and Shuster, 75
Hizb-i-Islami (Party of Islam) (of
    Gulbuddin Hekmatyar), 55,
    110, 233
  base of, 110–11
  and Zia, 182
  see also Hekmatyar, Gulbuddin
Hodson, Peregrine, 12
Holy war. *See Jihad*
Hurd, Anne, 43

Illness
  and Afghanistan reporters, 8–
    9, 10
  cholera of Paulin, 1
  dysentery, 8–9, 140, 141–42,
    143
  prevalence of among Afghani-
    stan travelers, 140
Intelligence network of Abdul
    Haq, 156, 157–58
Intercontinental Hotel, 77
Inter-Services Intelligence
    Agency. *See* ISI
Iran and Iranians, 8, 108, 119–
    20, 126, 170, 182
Isby, David, 120
ISI (Inter-Services Intelligence
    Agency), Pakistan, 168–69,
    172, 177–78, 215–16
  and Jalalabad siege, 222
  and U.S., 171
Islamabad, American embassy in,
    169, 173, 216
Islamic culture, 107
  in Afghanistan, 107–10
  Khalis on Western understand-
    ing of, 149

Islamic revolution
  drug trade closed by, 27
  see also Moslem fundamental-
    ism
Islamic Revolutionary Forces
    (Harakat-i-Inqilab-i-Islami),
    234
Islamic Unity of Afghan Mujahi-
    din. *See* Seven-party mujahi-
    din alliance
Ismatullah Muslim, 203–4
Itihad-i-Islami (Islamic Unity),
    233

Jabha-i-Nijat-Milli (Afghan Na-
    tional Liberation Front),
    191–92, 234
Jabbar Khel, 147
Jalalabad, 121
  assault on, 139, 222
  Abdul Haq on capture of,
    166–67
  Abdul Haq network in, 157
  and Hizb-i-Islami, 42
  ISI for attack against, 169
  ISI/U.S. plans for capture of,
    178
  views on fall of, 137–38
Jalalabad plain, 131
Jallaluddin Haqqani, 120, 154
Jamiat-i-Islami (Islamic Society),
    42, 43, 44, 56, 88, 233
Jamrud Fort, 80
Jihad (holy war)
  Afghan as only true version of,
    131
  of mine victim, 7
Jihan-zeb, 90–91, 120
  and Afridis as enemy, 104
  Akbar contrasted with, 202
  apparent age of, 114

Jihan-zeb *(Cont.)*
  and Arabic language, 107
  as bodyguard, 96, 97, 119, 127
  and eating of dates, 111
  prayers of, 113, 123
  smoking by, 98
  and torn rucksack, 112, 118
  and water, 92
Journalists (worldwide)
  comfortable stories pursued
    by, 185, 201
  in search of noble savage, 135
Journalists covering Afghanistan,
    35–36
  Afghans as seen by, 19, 20–21
  and Babur's tomb, 82
  behavior of in Peshawar, 28
  and border guards, 84–85
  Darra visited by, 31
  in diplomat information swap,
    216
  female, 133
  and going "inside," 8–9, 25, 74
  and Haq, 52
  hardships endured by, 8–10,
    14, 25
  Hekmatyar and killing of, 55,
    170
  and help from mujahidin, 94
  and Hizb-i-Islami, 42, 88
  and Jalalabad, 167
  and *"jihad* trail," 91–92
  and life of mujahidin, 123–24
  and Massoud, 39, 40
  and mines, 3–4
  and mujahidin factions, 36–37
  Soviet threats against, 10
  and Soviet withdrawal, 13–14,
    165
  uselessness of money for, 10
  See also Media; War freaks
Jouvenal, Peter, 6

Kabul
  and Babur, 81
  bastardized culture of, 192
  and Durranis, 194
  Gunston's visit to, 59–63
  Haq's strategy for toppling of,
    172–73, 176–77, 178
  Hekmatyar raid into, 55–56
  and Hizb-i-Islami, 42
  ISI/U.S. plans for capture of,
    178
  Massoud for conquest of, 178
  Shuster's trip into, 75–78
Kabul airport, Haq rocket strikes
  on, 176
Kabul area, and Abdul Haq, 41,
    156, 159, 163–65, 178–79
Kabul–Jalalabad–Torcham high-
    way, 147, 121
Kandahar, 225
  and Afghan history, 192–94,
    196–97
  bombing of, 224
  combat in and destruction of,
    186–88, 199, 223, 224
  foray into, 222–24
  journey to, 202–3, 204–10,
    217–20
  name of, 194
  and NIFA/royalists, 188, 215–
    16, 222
  1973 visit to, 194–95, 222–23
  population decline in, 188
  report on from elders in, 221
  settlement desired for, 221–22
Kandahar airport, 185–86, 219–
    20
  reports on control over, 215–
    16
Kandahar area, 184–85
  Hekmatyar tour of, 216
  helicopter gunships in, 9

Kandahar area *(Cont.)*
  minefields in, 4
  and Quetta, 197, 198
  and Soviet withdrawal, 214
  as World War II in desert,
    218
Kandahar–Kabul road, 226
Karmal, Babrak, 117, 161, 189
Karzai, Abdulahad, 195
Karzai, Hamid, 195–96, 197
Keegan, John, 2, 18, 181, 224
Keshtmand, Sultan Ali, 161
KGB
  assassinations by, 72
  currency operation of, 23
  mujahidin leaders' policies to-
    ward, 99
  and Najib, 161
  and Nadar Khan, 102
  and Sharq, 175
  and Zia's death, 35, 237
KhAD (Khedamat-e Aetelaat-e
    Dawlat), 12, 34
  and Afridis, 83
  Kandahar prison of, 219
  Khyber Pass train bombed by,
    86
  mujahidin leaders' policies to-
    ward, 99
  mujahidin underground in,
    60, 63
  and Najib, 161, 173
  and Zia's death, 35, 237
Khairullah, 63–64
Khalis, Yunus, 42, 86–88, 149,
    168, 233
  and Akhrimiyuk killing, 160
  and Abdul Haq, 148, 151,
    154–55, 156, 158
  and Jalalabad attack, 166
  in Kandahar, 188
  and Nurzais, 204

  as Pathan symbol, 191
  politics of as useful, 192
  U.S. diplomats on, 170
  and Wakhil, 89
  war aims of, 191
  and Wardak, 183
  and Zahir Shah, 189
  see also Hizb-i-Islami
Khalq (Masses) faction, 117, 150,
    174
Khalq-Parcham infighting, 173,
    175, 176, 177
Khan, Ajab, 94
Khan, Gholam Issa, 113, 115,
    117, 118, 125
Khan, Ismael, 161, 233
Khan, Wazir Arsala, 147
Khatak, Khushal Khan, 22, 136,
    141
Khedamat-e Aetelaat-e Dawlat.
    See KhAD
Khel, Malik Nadar Khan Zakha,
    100–103
Khel, Malik Wali Khan Kuki, 99–
    100
Khe Sanh, Kandahar airport as,
    220
Khost, siege of, 181
Khyber Pass, 26, 80–82
  and Afridis, 82–84
  heroin laboratories near, 27
  Pakistani checkpoints in, 84–
    85
Kidnappings, 94, 102
Kipling, Rudyard, 24, 224, 225
  on Afghanistan, 15
  "Arithmetic on the Frontier,"
    27, 55, 80
  "The Ballad of East and West,"
    2, 20
  and Gunston, 55
  Kim, 24, 25, 112

Kipling, Rudyard *(Cont.)*
"The Man Who Would Be
King," 9
and Pathans, 135, 219
Klephts, Greek, and mujahidin,
17
Koh-i-noor diamond, 193
Kolangar, 61, 62
Koran
and authoritarianism, 107, 124
mujahidin recital from, 106
reading from, 124
Kot Valley, 13, 127, 128–29
Kuchi tribe, 125
Kuki Khel Afridis, 99
Kunduz, capture/loss of, 166,
179

Laghman province, 56
Landi Kotal, 85
Nadar Khan fort in, 101, 103
and watermelons, 142
Land mines. *See* Mines
Land reform, Taraki program
for, 115–16
Latif, Haji Abdel (Haji Baba),
182–84, 188, 213–14, 217,
219, 220, 224, 233
Laumonier, Laurence, 39
Lawrence, T. E., 107
Lear, Edward, 86
Lenin, and antiwar phrase, 77
Levi, Peter, 125, 194
Lie Down with Lions (Follett), 40
*Light Garden of the Angel King,
The* (Levi), 125
Lindalos, Jim, 170
Lindholm, Charles, 72–73
Local militias, pro-Communist,
and Hekmatyar command-
ers, 170

Logar province, 61
Lohbeck, Kurt, 10
Lurang, 90, 91
and Afridis as enemy, 104
Akbar contrasted with, 202
apparent age of, 114
and Arabic language, 107
as bodyguard, 96, 97, 127
and eating of dates, 111
prayers of, 113, 123
smoking by, 98
and water, 92

McGurn, William, 17
Mackenzie, Richard, 9
Mahalajat, 220, 223, 225
Mahaz-i-Milli Islami (National Is-
lamic Front of Afghanistan).
See NIFA
Mahmoud, Atta, 199, 200
Mahmoud, "Engineer," 137–38,
157, 167
Malaria, return of after coup,
128
Malik Nadar Khan Zakha Khel,
100–3
Malik Wali Khan Kuki Khel, 99–
100
Manning, Olivia, 134
"Man Who Would Be King,
The" (Kipling), 9
Mardel, Simon, 8
Masjid Mosque, 82
Massoud, Ahmad Shah, 38–41,
42, 161, 233
alliance formed by, 70
and Gunston, 57, 58
and ISI, 178
and Kabul capture, 177
and keeping fast, 59
and media on Qarga attack,
164

Massoud, Ahmad Shah (*Cont.*)
  name recognition of, 172
  and Rabbani, 168
  and rural resistance base, 132
  see also Jamiat-i-Islami
Meals, 8
  at Afridi fort, 98
  at camps, 90, 131, 210–11, 220
  from farmer, 129
  with Abdul Haq, 166
  in Kandahari village, 207–8
  and military-camp stocks, 88
  in Nangarhar village, 118
  for Qadir, 139
  on trail, 124
Médecin du Monde, 46
Médecins sans Frontières (Doctors Without Borders), 170
Media, Soviet, 121, 172
Media coverage, 10–12, 14–15, 128, 227
  and Kandahar, 185, 188
  mujahidin as subjects for, 18–19, 110
  and Qarga attack, 164
  and Soviet withdrawal, 13, 14, 214
  see also Journalists
Mercenaries, 27, 30
Mercy Fund, 43
Mine(s), 2–6
  in Afghan village, 118
  Akhrimiyuk's WWII wound from, 160
  avoiding of by Haq group, 162
  "Bouncing Betty," 4
  butterfly, 4–5, 22, 57, 122, 127–28
  death toll from, 224
  game with, 22
  Abdul Haq wounded by, 45–46

Jihan-zeb wounded by, 90
  around Kandahar, 186, 208
  to mutilate not kill, 2, 5
  number of, 3
  pressure-pad, 46
  on trail, 111
  victims of, 1, 6–8, 111
Minefields
  clearing of, 13, 162
  and Vietnam war comparison, 223
Mirwais Khan Hotaki, 218–19
Mirwas Maidan square, 76–77, 152
Moghul dynasty, 81, 192
Mohammed, Din. *See* Din Mohammed
Mohammed Akbar, 202, 207, 209, 212, 217, 219, 222
Mohammed Aman (father of Abdul Haq), 145–46
Mohammedi, Mohammed Nabil, 234
Mojadidi, Sibghatullah, 191–92, 234
Mojadidi, Zia, 199–200, 214
Mongols, and Afghanistan, 15, 41
Moslem fundamentalism
  vs. Afghan self-assurance, 108
  and Afridi drug business, 84
  and Haq, 73, 167
  and Hizb-i-Islami, 42
Moslem fundamentalists of Afghanistan
  and Daoud regime, 150
  vs. Iran or Lebanon, 126
  mujahidin as, 17, 109–10
  and NIFA, 190
  in seven-party alliance, 168
  and Zahir Shah, 189

Moslems
  eyes of, 8, 47
  vs. Hindus, 33
  mujahidin as, 17, 19, 109, 133
  politicized/urbanized proletar-
    iat among, 126
  women oppressed among, 49
Mujahidin, 3, 8, 16–17
  bravery of explained, 119
  equipment of, 16, 122
  exotic appearance of, 15
  factions among, 36–37, 69, 87
    (see also Seven-party mujahi-
    din alliance)
  foreigners' view of, 19, 20–21
  as future warriors against
    superpowers, 224–25
  government-in-exile of, 167,
    234, 237
  Greek klephts compared with,
    17
  greetings between, 92
  ISI role toward, 168, 222
  and journalists, 36
  life of, 123–24
  and media, 18–19, 110
  and mercenaries, 30
  and mines, 2–6 (see also Mine)
  mountain goats compared to,
    112–13
  Pathans as, 21 (see also Pathan)
  raids by, 44–45, 55–56, 75–78,
    131–32, 162–65
  social attitudes of, 51, 72–73
  Soviet media on, 121
  against Taraki regime, 154
  terrorism rejected by, 18
  toughness of, 16
  treatment of prisoners by, 120
  and 20th-century warfare, 18
  uncompromising will of, 120–
    21

  and U.S./Pakistan mistakes,
    171
  and U.S. support, 217
  and women, 133–34
Mujahidin, foreigners with. See
    Foreigners aiding mujahidin
My Lai, and Soviet massacres,
    120

Nadar Khan Zakha Khel, Malik,
    100–103
Nadir Khan Nurzai, 204
Nadir Shah the Great, 192–93
Najib, 161, 173–74
  and bomb attack, 165
  Gulabzoi lobbies against, 174–
    75
  and Kuki Khel people, 100
  Nadar Khan on, 102–3
  as "Najibullah," 161
  and Wakhil on Afridi, 94
  Zahir Shah compared with,
    189
Names, among Pathans, 42
Nangarhar province, 88, 119,
    125
  and Abdul Haq, 148, 154, 155
  malaria in, 128
  refugees met in, 13
  watermelons in, 141–42
Naswar, 98–99, 137
National Islamic Front of Af-
    ghanistan. See NIFA
"National liberation," as mean-
    ingless for mujahidin, 17
Newby, Eric, 140
New Lourdes Hotel, 198, 201
Niazi, Commander, 58
Nicaraguan contras, 171
NIFA (National Islamic Front of
    Afghanistan, Mahaz-i-Milli

NIFA *(Cont.)*
    Islami), 180–84, 188, 190–
      91, 233
    camp of, 205
    flag of, 205
    headquarters of, 201–2
    and Hekmatyar tour, 216
    and Kandahar settlement, 222
Niquet, Thierry, 170
Noble savage
    Cossacks as, 134–35
    and "Gucci muj," 205
Noriega mines, 6
Northwest Frontier, 31–32
    and Durand Line, 105
    and establishment media, 36
    fact and fiction on, 144
    Tirah Valley, 94
    and women, 50
Nuclear strike, Soviet bombard-
    ment with effect of, 223
Nur-ul Haq Ulumi, 221–22
Nurzai, Nadir Khan, 204
Nurzais, 203, 204

O'Brien, Tony, 3, 124

Paghman, Abdul Haq forces in,
    155, 158, 159, 164
Pagie Louch, 184
Pakistan
    Haq and Bhutto, 33–35
    ISI of, 168–69, 171, 172, 177–
      78, 215–16, 222
    Islam in, 108, 109
    and Kandahar settlement, 222
    and mujahidin clinics, 6
    opposition to Afghan refugees
      or resistance in, 69, 85
    and Hekmatyar, 233
    Northwest Frontier, 31–32

    as U.S. main concern, 170–71
    see also Zia ul-Haq, Mohammed
Pakistani cities
    Communist-inspired bombing
      in, 5
    Darra, 30–31, 83, 85, 99
    Peshawar, 1, 8, 14, 25–29 (*see
      also* Peshawar)
    Quetta, 1, 7, 197, 198, 200,
      201–2
    terrorism in, 12–13, 34–35
Pakol (hat), 24, 88, 123, 130, 207
Panjshir Valley, 38
    bombing of, 39, 57, 224
    Gunston sent to, 56–57
    Massoud in, 39, 40, 161
    and media coverage, 12
    mines dropped in, 5
    and Soviet counterinsurgency,
      186
    Soviets ejected from, 177
Panjwai, 215
Parcham (Banner) faction, 117,
    149–50, 174
    Khalq infighting with, 173,
      175, 176, 177
Pathan(s), 21–22
    and Achakzais/Nurzais tribal-
      ism, 203–4
    Afridi branch of, 82–84, 94,
      97–98, 99–104
    Ahmadzai branch of, 147
    atrocities impossible for, 135
    and dependents, 89
    endurance as weapon for, 143
    gun making by, 31
    and Gunston, 59
    and Abdul Haq, 41, 64, 72,
      73
    and Hebrews, 21–22, 197
    Hekmatyar as, 69
    as hillmen, 112

Pathan(s) *(Cont.)*
  and Hizb-i-Islami, 42
  inner-city guerrillas contrasted
    with, 152
  Khalis and Gailani as symbols
    of, 191
  Kuchi branch of, 125
  and Massoud cease-fire, 40–41
  Mirwais as leader of, 219
  as mujahidin, 21 *(see also* Muja-
    hidin)
  multiple siblings among, 130
  native costume of, 24
  Pakistanis (Punjabis) as viewed
    by, 32–33
  political life of, 136
  Abdul Qadir as, 138
  and Tajiks, 37–38, 41
  Westerners' view of, 35, 135–
    36
  and women, 33, 49–51, 133–
    34
  Zia as honorary member of, 35
Pathans, The (Caroe), 82–83, 193
Patou (Pathan blanket), 79, 90,
    121–22, 227
Paulin, Frank, 1
Pearl Continental Hotel, 36, 51
People's Democratic Party of Af-
    ghanistan (PDPA), 174
Pérez de Cuéllar, Javier, 66, 70
Persian Gulf
  Gulf war, 119, 131, 201
  Soviets close to, 186
Persian Gulf states, and Islamic
    Unity, 233
Peshawar, 1–2, 8, 14, 25–29
  atmosphere and heat of, 26,
    80
  departure from, 23–24
  factionalism expressed in, 36–
    38

and going "inside," 74
  individuals found in, 29–30
  as Pathan city, 141
Peter the Great, 186
Photographs
  at Baghram air base, 58, 59
  of dead Soviet pilot, 57–58
  of Soviets stopping truck, 62–
    63
  villager forbids of self, 114
Poetry, of Pathans, 136, 141
Popalzai tribe, 195, 196–97
Prayers, by mujahidin, 106–7,
    109, 118, 123, 124, 207, 225
Press. *See* Journalists; Media
Pressure-pad mines, 46
Pukhtu, 21, 106–7
Pukhtunwali, 21, 41, 136
Pul-i-Charki prison, 65, 115, 116,
    152
Punjabis, 32–33
Pushtuns, 21. *See also* Pathans

Qadir, Abdul, 42, 68, 88, 136–
    40, 151
  on Afridi leaders, 100, 103
  and Daoud coup, 149
  and Abdul Haq, 151, 155, 158
  and Jalalabad, 167
  and "land reform," 115–16
  sexual attitude of, 133
  and Wakhil, 90
Qarga region, Abdul Haq opera-
    tions in, 44, 163–65
Quetta, 197, 198
  hospital/clinic in, 1, 7, 200
  NIFA villa in, 201–2

Rabbani, Burhanuddin, 168, 233
Rahman, Abdur, 105
Raids by mujahidin, 44–45, 55–
    56, 75–78, 131–32, 162–65

Ramadan, 59, 190
Randal, Jonathan, 24
Raphel, Arnold, 46, 237
Rasul Sayyaf, 168, 216, 233
Reagan, Ronald, and Reagan ad-
    ministration, 43, 67, 118,
    158, 169, 171
Rebel leaders, 47–48
Redmon, Charles, 3
Red Star, forgeries of, 77
Refugees from Afghanistan, 11,
    27, 227
  in Baluchistan, 198
  Atta Mahmoud, 199
  Zia Mojadidi, 199–200
  Pakistan opposition to, 69
  return of group of, 13
  U.S. debriefing of, 216
  wounded in hospital, 200
  and Zia ul-Haq vs. Bhutto, 33–
    34
Relief workers
  Afghans as seen by, 19, 20–21
  and Babur's tomb, 82
  Darra visited by, 31
  and going "inside," 8
  Hekmatyar and killing of, 170
  and Hizb-i-Islami, 43
  and Massoud, 39–40
  and mines, 13
  and mujahidin factions, 36–37
  in search of noble savage, 135
  Stinger benefits noticed by,
    129
  see also War freaks
Religion
  in Afghanistan vs. other Mos-
    lem countries, 107–10
  Hindu vs. Moslem, 33
  see also Moslem fundamental-
    ism; Moslems; Prayers
Reporters. See Journalists

Ridgway, R. T. I., 21
Rizvi, Zia, 14
Road to Oxiana, The (Byron), 19
Rosenthal, A. M., 176
Rupert, James, 187
Rushdie, Salman, 34

Sabotage operation by mujahi-
    din. See Raids by mujahidin
Safed Koh (White Mountain). See
    Spinghar
Saleh (Abdul Haq alias), 151
Samar Khel, 121
Sarandoy, 174
Sareena Hotel, 201
Sarobi dam and power station,
    Haq attacks on, 162–63, 165
Satellite imaging, 215
Saudi Arabia
  and Hekmatyar, 110
  and Islamic Unity, 233
Saur Revolution, 153
Sayyaf, Rasul, 168, 216, 233
Schultheis, Rob, 57, 58
Seven-party mujahidin alliance,
    167–68, 233–34
  fundamentalists vs. nonfunda-
    mentalists in, 190
  moderates vs. radicals in, 191
  see also specific parties
Seven Pillars of Wisdom (Law-
    rence), 107
Sex, and Pathans/mujahidin, 72,
    133–34, 140. See also Women
Shagai Fort, 84
Shaheedan (martyrs), 119, 190,
    206
Shaheedan banners, 5, 119, 220
Shah Jahan (emperor of India),
    82
Shah Shuja-ul-Mulk (king of Af-
    ghanistan), 19, 189

Shalwar kameez, 24, 60, 121–22, 123, 145, 227

Shame (Rushdie), 34

Shapiro, Lee, 170

Sharq, Hassan, 175–76

Shevardnadze, Edvard, 175

Shinwar district, 42, 88, 136

Short Walk in the Hindu Kush, A (Newby), 140

Shuster, Savik, 64–66, 68, 71, 75
  and Haq, 64–65, 71, 73–75, 78
  and Haq UN appearance, 66–67, 70–71
  Kabul trip by, 75–78
  and Kipling, 224

Sibghatullah Mojadidi, 191–92, 234

Sickness. *See* Illness

Singh, Hari, 80

Smirnov, Vitaly, 10

Smuggling, 27, 83, 85
  in Cockburn's view, 15
  by Din Mohammed, 158

Soldier of Fortune magazine, 35

Soviet invasion of Afghanistan
  atrocities in, 39, 120
  casualties in, 10–11, 18, 224
  CIA prediction on, 171
  and Communist coup, 116–17
  first months of, 156–57
  and Kandahar airport, 186
  in Kuchi area, 125
  1985 as bloodiest year of, 11
  and siege mentality, 131
  tactics in, 15–16 (*see also* Bombing, aerial; Helicopter gunships, Soviet withdrawal; Mine)
  and U.S. in Vietnam, 223–24
  see also Afghanistan conflict

Soviet Union
  advisers on torture from, 153

and Afghan Communist in-fighting (1988), 174–75

Afghan government aided by, 177

Afghans' feelings toward, 108

journalists threatened by, 10

moderate parties talk to, 191

and Taraki, 115

troops of in Afghan uniforms, 221

and Zahir Shah reign, 189

Soviet withdrawal, 236–37
  and Afghan Communist con-flicts, 173–74
  bombing during, 13
  "clinging to helicopters," 13, 178
  and Haq intelligence network, 60
  and Kandahar area, 214–15
  media attention to, 13, 14, 165, 214
  mujahidin effort after, 17
  and mujahidin leadership, 70
  U.S. objectives after, 170–71, 178

Spain, James W., 33, 136

Spinboldak, capture of, 203–4

Spinghar (White Mountain, Safed Koh), 111–12, 122, 126, 127, 128–29

Stinger missiles, 43, 118, 126, 127, 129, 171, 216

Sufi Qadirrya sect, 181

Tajik(s), 37–38
  Hamid as, 60, 61
  Haq's accountant as, 145
  and Jamiat-i-Islami, 42, 43, 44 (*see also* Jamiat-i-Islami)
  Massoud as, 38, 40

Tamurlane, 81
Tanai, Shahnawaz, 175
Tanaka, Koshiro, 29
Taraki, Nur Mohammed, 115,
    117, 174
  Haq in prison with, 152
  students required to honor, 89
  villager's condemnation of, 114
Taraki regime, 115–16
  executions and torture by,
    152–53
  guerrillas forced underground
    by, 123
  and Karzai, 195
  and Kuchi tribe, 125
Television, 10. *See also* Media
Terrorism
  and mujahidin, 18, 172
  in Pakistan, 12–13, 34, 35
Thatcher, Margaret, 43, 67, 73,
    158, 169
Theroux, Paul, 86
Thesiger, Wilfred, 140
"Third World," as meaningless
    for mujahidin, 17
Thirst. *See* Water
Thornton, Charles, 9, 186–87,
    201
Tibet, destruction of, and Af-
    ghan land reform, 116
Tirah Bazaar, Valley of, 93–99,
    142
Tito, Massoud compared to, 39
Tolstoy, Leo, on Cossacks, 134–
    35
Torcham border post, 85, 120
Torture, by Communists, 152–53
Toynbee, Arnold, on climate,
    122
Travel, Afghanistan journalism
    as, 132
Tribalism, 38, 41, 99, 203

and Hizb-i-Islami, 42
and Spinboldak battle, 203–4
Trilling, Lionel, 134
Tsagolov, Kim, 175

Under a Sickle Moon (Hodson), 12
United Nations, Haq appearance
    at, 66–67, 70–71
Urbanization, 126, 133–34
U.S. government
  aid from, 122, 168, 171, 177
  Abdul Haq dismissed by, 179
  Abdul Haq on policy of, 171–
    72
  and Abdul Haq wound treat-
    ment, 46–47, 71
  Afghanistan role of, 217
  and Hekmatyar, 169–70, 178,
    182, 233
  information sources of, 215,
    216
  and Kandahar settlement, 222
  and moderate vs. radical muja-
    hidin parties, 191
  and NIFA, 182
  Pakistan as prime interest of,
    170–71
  see also CIA; Reagan, Ronald,
    and Reagan administration

Valley of Tirah Bazaar, 93–99,
    142
Vietnam war
  Afghanistan invasion com-
    pared with, 15, 186, 223–24
  Bouncing Betty mine in, 4
  "clinging to helicopters" com-
    parison with, 13, 178
  Khe Sanh, 220
Voinovich, Vladimir, 77

WAD Ministry of State Security, 12. *See also* KhAD
Wakhil. *See* Bedar, Wakhil Abdul
Wakhil, Abdul, 77
Wali, Ahmad, 220
Wali Khan Kuki Khel, Malik, 99–100
Walker, Bertie, 55
Wardak, Amin, 182–83
Wardak, Rahim, 180–81, 190, 211
Wardak, Ruhani, 183
Wardak province, 183
War freaks, 35
  and Kandahar destruction, 210
  and Northwest Frontier, 32
  on "free elections," 34
  on Haq, 33, 35
  on Punjabis, 33
  see also Journalists; Relief workers
Water
  Afghans rarely request, 13
  and dysentery, 141–42
  need of on trail, 91, 92, 112
  promise of, 109
  from Tirah pool, 96
Watermelons, 141–42
Way of the Pathans, The (Spain), 33, 136
Wilson, Charlie, 137
Women
  Afghan denigration of, 107–8

in cities of Afghanistan, 51
and Haq, 72
and Pathans, 33, 49–51, 133–34
as safe among mujahidin, 133
World War II, looking backward to, 225

Yar Mohammed, 123, 124
Yunus Khalis. *See* Khalis, Yunus

Zakha Khel Afridis, 100, 101, 103
Zahir Shah (king of Afghanistan), 149, 188–89
  deposing of, 147, 149, 189, 194
  Haji Latif memory of, 213
  and Kandahar, 216, 222
  and NIFA, 188, 201, 216, 233
Zia ul-Haq, Mohammed, 33–35
  death of, 35, 168–69, 182, 237
  and Hekmatyar, 68, 69, 110, 168–69, 182, 215–16
  hypocrisy of, 191
  and ISI, 168–69, 171
  and Islam, 109
  and Nadar Khan, 102
  and Pakistan policy, 171
  posters of, 206
  and Western journalists, 85
  and Charlie Wilson, 137
Zia Mojadidi, 199–200, 214

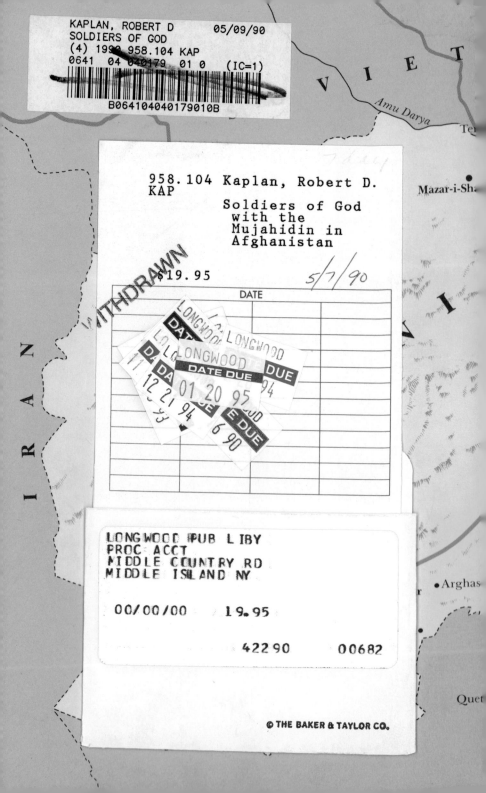